MW01446358

The Luwians of Western Anatolia

The Luwians of Western Anatolia

Their neighbours and predecessors

Fred C. Woudhuizen

Archaeopress Archaeology

ARCHAEOPRESS PUBLISHING LTD
Summertown Pavilion
18-24 Middle Way
Summertown
Oxford OX2 7LG

www.archaeopress.com

ISBN 978 1 78491 827 9
ISBN 978 1 78491 828 6 (e-Pdf)

Cover illustration: 'Tarkondemos' seal (Pope 1999: 139, Fig. 86)

Printed in England by Holywell Press, Oxford

This book is available direct from Archaeopress or from our website www.archaeopress.com

Contents

List of Figures iii
List of Tables iv
Preface 1
1. The Homeland of the Luwians 5
2. Geography of Western Anatolia 19
3. Origin of the Luwian Hieroglyphic Script 36
  3.1 Introduction 36
  3.2 Catalogue of the Middle Bronze Age Luwian Hieroglyphic Inscriptions 37
  3.3 Middle Bronze Age Luwian Hieroglyphic Signary 39
  3.4 In Search of the Cradle of the Luwian Hieroglyphic Script 41
  3.5 Overview of Luwian Hieroglyphic Inscriptions from, or Attributable to, Assuwa/Arzawa/Mira-Kuwaliya, Seḫa-Appawiya, and Ḫapalla 46
  Addendum 51
4. Luwian Hieroglyphic Evidence on the Great Kingdom of Assuwa 55
  4.1 Introduction 55
  4.2 Two Assuwian Royal Seals 56
  4.3 An Assuwian Royal Seal from Thebes 59
  4.4 On the Reading of the Luwian Hieroglyphic Legends of the Schimmel Rhyton 66
5. Western Anatolia under Hittite Rule 74
  5.1 Introduction 74
  5.2 The Sealing of Prince Masḫuiluwas 79
  5.3 The Stone Inscription of *tuḫkanti* Urḫitesup 80
  5.4 The Seal and Rock Relief of Tarku(ndimu)was 80
  5.5 The Stone Inscription of Prince Masḫuittas 83
  5.6 The Luwian Hieroglyphic Stele from Afyon 83
6. Western Anatolia in the Final Stage of Bronze Age 88
  6.1 Introduction 88
  6.2 The Rediscovered Luwian Hieroglyphic Inscriptions from Western Anatolia in Transliteration and Translation 91
7. Amenhotep III: Historical Background to his Aegean Policy 107
  7.1 Introduction 107
  7.2 KUB 26.91 & the Tawagalawas-letter 108
  7.3 The Phaistos Disc 111
  7.4 The Madduwattas-text 114
  7.5 Conclusion 115
8. The Arzwan Language 117
  8.1 Cuneiform Luwian 117
  8.2 Luwian Hieroglyphic 121
9. The Language of the Trojans 123
  9.1 Introduction 123
  9.2 The Relevant Late Bronze Age Data 124
  9.3 The Relevant Homeric Data 128

List of Figures

Fig. 1. Distribution of Luwian place-names in *-ss-* and *-nd-*.......... 12
Fig. 2. Seal of Tarku(n)timuwas from Malia.......... 15
Fig. 3. Cylinder seal from Klavdia.......... 17
Fig. 4. Cylinder seal impression from Kourion.......... 17
Fig. 5. Map of western Anatolia.......... 32
Fig. 6. Geography of the Hittite empire.......... 33
Fig. 7. Distribution of Middle Bronze Age Luwian hieroglyphic seals and sealings.......... 42
Fig. 8. Sealing Tell-Atchana-Alalaḫ no. 154.......... 43
Fig. 9. Erlenmeyers' seal.......... 43
Fig. 10. Seal Hogarth no. 154.......... 44
Fig. 11. Seal of king Piyamakuruntas of Assuwiya.......... 51
Fig. 12. Stamp seal from Beycesultan.......... 51
Fig. 13. The Luwian hieroglyphic titular expression of the Indilima seal compared to its closest cognate on seal # 271 from Malia.......... 53
Fig. 14. Stamp side of stamp-cylinder seals Louvre AO 20.138 (a) and Aydin (b).......... 57
Fig. 15. Impression of the cylinder side of stamp-cylinder seal Louvre AO 20.138.......... 59
Fig. 16. Cyprian cylinder seal from Thebes.......... 61
Fig. 17. Luwian hieroglyphic cylinder seal from Thebes.......... 62
Fig. 18. Drawing of the scene on the Schimmel rhyton.......... 67
Fig. 19. Baltimore seal.......... 69
Fig. 20. Luwian hieroglyphic legend no. 1 with comparison from the Baltimore seal.......... 70
Fig. 21. Thus far enigmatic sign from the Luwian hieroglyphic legends with suggested equivalent of later date, LH 430 *sa*.......... 70
Fig. 22. Luwian hieroglyphic legend no. 2 with comparison from Südburg § 3.......... 71
Fig. 23. Rock inscription of great prince *Kupaā*.......... 78
Fig. 24. Sealing of prince Masḫuiluwas.......... 79
Fig. 25. Stone inscription Beyköy 1.......... 81
Fig. 26. Seal of 'Tarkondemos'.......... 81
Fig. 27. Rock relief at Karabel.......... 82
Fig. 28. Stele from Afyon.......... 84
Fig. 29. Beyköy 2.......... 102-103
Fig. 30. Edremit.......... 104
Fig. 31. Yazılıtaş.......... 105
Fig. 32. Beyköy 3-4 (A-B), Şahankaya (C), Dağardı 1 (D), Dağardı 2 (E-G).......... 106
Fig. 33. Throne-name of Amenhotep III.......... 107
Fig. 34. Cursive variant of the throne-name of Amenhotep III.......... 107
Fig. 35. Scarab of queen Tiyi.......... 108

List of Tables

Table I. Place-names in *-ss-* and *-nd-* from Late Bronze Age Hittite cuneiform and Luwian hieroglyphic texts 6
Table II. Place-names in *-ss-* and *-nth-* or names related to such place-names from the Late Bronze Age Linear B texts 8
Table III. Place-names in *-ss-* and *-nd-* from Anatolia as recorded for sources from the Classical period 9-10
Table IV. Place-names in *-ss-* and *-nth-* from Greece as recorded for sources from the Classical period 12
Table V. Identification of place-names from cuneiform Hittite and Luwian hieroglyphic with a bearing on western Anatolia. 22-25
Table VI. Overview of the dating criteria for Middle Bronze Age Luwian hieroglyphic seals or sealings. 41
Table VII. Analysis of the legends of the Erlenmeyers' seal and seal Hogarth no. 154 from Henri Frankfort's First Syrian Group 44
Table VIII. Overview of Proto-Indo-European roots in Middle Bronze Age Luwian hieroglyphic. 54
Table IX. Synchronisms between the dynasties of Ḫattusa, Arzawa, and Seḫa 86-87
Table X. Grammatical sketch of the cuneiform Luwian evidence on the Arzawan language. 121
Table XI. Grammatical sketch of the Luwian hieroglyphic evidence on the Arzawan language. 122
Table XII. Overview of western Anatolian hydronyms and toponyms of Indo-European nature. 133
Table XIII: Overview of literary evidence for Pelasgians in western Anatolia according to Lochner-Hüttenbach's *Die Pelasger* of 1960. 140
Table XIV. Names based on a Proto-Indo-European root associated in the Greek sources with Pelasgians. 141

Preface

Just recently, in spring of 2016, Eberhard Zangger wrote a stimulating book on the Luwian civilization. He aptly calls this the missing link in the history of the Aegean Bronze Age. As it happens, namely, there are 340 major archaeological sites in western Anatolia, 'very few of which have been excavated on a large scale—and virtually none of these were published in a western language.' (Zangger 2016: 14).

It will take at least a century to excavate at least some of the tells in western Anatolia, if not longer. So the prospects for this 'missing link' to become as profoundly prospected archaeologically as the Aegean in the west and central Anatolia and the Levant in the east are rather grim on the short term.

This state of affairs, however, should not discourage us from studying the culture of the Luwians of western Anatolia during the Bronze Age and collecting the relevant data presently at hand. In fact, this is precisely what Zangger aimed to do in his book and aims to put on a more solid basis with his foundation *Luwian Studies* (see esp. its website).

The interest in the Luwians as an object of study next to and apart from the Hittites is already growing for some time. A pioneer in this respect is Jacques Freu with his monograph entitled *Luwiya* of 1980. However, Luwian studies becomes of age, so to say, with *The Luwians*, edited by Craig Melchert, of 2003 and the publication of the papers to the conference in Reading on *Luwian Identities*, edited by Alice Mouton, Ian Rutherford, and Ilya Yakubovich, in 2013.

The habitat of the Luwians is not confined to western Anatolia, but included the later Hittite provinces of Tarḫuntassa (Konya basin), Kizzuwatna (Cilician plain), and the island of Cyprus in the east. In the west, it extended to the Aegean islands, up to and including Crete, and regions in southern Greece. In the present book, however, after an introductory chapter on the extent of the homeland, I will focus on the Luwians of western Anatolia because the reconstruction of their Bronze Age history up to this moment is a *desideratum*.

In my opinion, especially with the help of data from epigraphy and linguistics, the history of western Anatolia during the Bronze Age can be reconstructed in its bare outlines. Of fundamental importance to such an endeavor is the reconstruction of its geography. We cannot reach the stage of historical reconstruction before we know where the various places and countries named in cuneiform Hittite and Luwian hieroglyphic texts are situated. Therefore I first address the question of the geography of western Anatolia before I set out to discuss the relevant Luwian hieroglyphic and cuneiform Hittite texts.

Since I finalised the first draft of this book in July 2016, our knowledge of the geography of especially northwestern Anatolia has improved dramatically. It so happens, namely, that in the meantime Eberhard Zangger acquired the files on the so-called 'Beyköy

Text' from the inheritance of James Mellaart (Zangger 2017: 309). In these files there were, next to the translation of the cuneiform Beyköy Text, drawings of Luwian hieroglyphic inscriptions discovered at Beyköy and some other sites in northwestern Anatolia between 1854 and 1878. One of these Luwian hieroglyphic inscriptions, Beyköy 2, actually is, with its 50 phrases, the longest Late Bronze Age text known to date and as such highly informative on the Arzawan language (Zangger & Woudhuizen 2018). Among the remaining Luwian hieroglyphic texts, the one from Edremit, which only entails 4 phrases, records numerous toponyms from the Troad, whereas those from Yazılıtaş and Dağardı consist almost exclusively of place-names from the realm of Seḫa. Owing to this discovery, then, the formerly almost blank region of northwestern Anatolia can be filled in with toponyms primarily known from Greek sources.

The joy about this sensational find is somewhat hampered, however, since the foremost specialist in Luwian hieroglyphic, David Hawkins, considers it forged. Hawkins' successor Mark Weeden informed me on September 29, 2017 in personal communication, that Beyköy 2 as well as the smaller fragments are merely the product of the lively imagination of James Mellaart, who falsified them apparently out of resentment of his critics and in order to give a surge to his otherwise ruined career. Weeden presented me with the copies of these inscriptions as they were in David Hawkins' possession since 1989. The proposed scenario, however, is highly unlikely if we realise that Mellaart was not a specialist in Luwian hieroglyphic and, in view of the attempts at interpretation of the inscriptions also present in his files, had only limited understanding of their contents. I believe that no one, not even Hawkins himself, could falsify a Luwian hieroglyphic text of the length of Beyköy 2.

The desire to declare Beyköy 2 a forgery may rest in the fact that the inscription does not fit in the framework of Hawkins' readings. These were introduced in 1973 and are currently generally applied in the field of Luwian hieroglyphics. Since 1931 and until Hawkins' introduction of the new reading, the sign LH 376 was interpreted as expressing the value *i*, – one of only three vowels in Luwian. Hawkins then proposed that it should be read as the expression of the value *zi* – and every scholar in the small field of Luwian studies followed him. I, for one, challenged this interpretation, arguing that sign LH 376 is indeed polyphonic and thus can be used as expressing both the values *i* and *zi* (Woudhuizen 2004c: 11). There are indeed 24 cases certified by bilingual evidence for the *zi*-reading, but also 18 cases, also with bilingual evidence, for the *i*-reading (latest count, cf. Woudhuizen 2011: 92-97). Thus, a 'readjusted old reading' of sign LH 376 would be called for.

As it happens, in Beyköy 2, sign LH 376 is used twice for the expression of the value *i*, in the name of a great king of Mira, *ma-sa-ḫù+i-ti* (§§ 1, 5), corresponding to Hittite cuneiform *Masḫuittas*, and the place-name *i-ku-wa-na* (§ 50), corresponding to Hittite cuneiform *Ikkuwaniya* 'Konya'. Only once is sign LH 376 in Beyköy 2 used for the expression of the value *zi*, in the country name *mi-zi+r(i)* (§ 28), corresponding to Hittite cuneiform *Mizri* 'Egypt'.

It is inconceivable that Mellaart based his forgery in the 1980s on a theory about the reading of Luwian hieroglyphic that would appear over twenty years later! Far more likely, Beyköy 2 and the other texts are indeed genuine. In that case, they provide us with further evidence that the new reading and current paradigm in the study of Luwian hieroglyphics is flawed and needs to be adjusted.

What is more, Hawkins proposal to read sign LH 376 exclusively as the expression of the value *zi* reduced the number of available vowels from three to only two. He therefore suggested that sign LH 209 should now be read as the expression of the value *i*. The Beyköy 2 inscription, however, contains the Luwian word for 'sea', of which we know from Hittite cuneiform texts, that is *aruna*. It is spelled correctly in the document, but when transcribed using Hawkins' system, it would read †*iruna* – which is evidently incorrect.

The study of cuneiform Luwian is also of relevance, as the so-called songs from Istanuwa presumably bear direct testimony of the language of Ḫapalla, one of the Arzawa lands. The town of Istanuwa, namely, is directly associated with Saḫiriya or the Sangarios river, and therefore likely to be situated within the bend of this river. Now, within this bend the Arzawa land Ḫapalla happens to be situated. Accordingly, it may reasonably be inferred that the songs of Istanuwa are conducted in the Arzawan language.

For our understanding of the history of the Luwians of western Anatolia, even in its bare outlines as aimed at here, it is also helpful to distinguish their neighbours. An unknown fraction of the inhabitants of the Troad in northwest Anatolia was presumably of a stock different from the Luwians. They spoke another language, closely related to Thracian and Phrygian. Furthermore, the Luwians of western Anatolia were in contact with the Hittites of the central Anatolian plateau in the east and with the Mycenaean Greeks in the west.

Finally, it should be realised that the Luwians, like most other Indo-European peoples, were not indigenous in their Anatolian habitat but entered this at some point in the Bronze Age. Accordingly, they were preceded by earlier inhabitants of the region, called a substrate population. From the relevant hydronymic and toponymic evidence, then, it can positively be deduced, at least in my opinion, that among the substrate populations of western Anatolia there were speakers of an Old Indo-European tongue well-known in the Classical sources by the ethnonym Pelasgians.

It is to be hoped that this book will serve as a worthy tool in the development of Luwian studies into a discipline in its own right and in the ongoing process to turn the civilization of the Luwians of western Anatolia from a 'missing link' into a 'link' between cultures of the Hittites in the east and the Mycenaean Greeks in the west.

Fred C. Woudhuizen
Heiloo, October 2017

1. The Homeland of the Luwians

In the late 1950s and early 1960s, Emmanuel Laroche studied the place-names in *-ss-* and *-nd-* as recorded in the Hittite Late Bronze Age sources. In these studies he came to the conclusion that the given elements are of an Indo-European nature (Laroche 1961: 91; Laroche 1957: 7). What the distinguished French scholar actually meant with this verdict is that the toponymic elements *-ss-* and *-nd-* are a typical feature of the Indo-European languages of Anatolia (= IE Anatolian), viz. Hittite and Luwian. However, if we put examples of the place-names in question which can be localised on the map, it so happens that the Hittite core land within the bend of the Marassantiya or Halys river—apart from the case of Zippalanda—forms no integral part of the distribution zone.[1] By means of deduction, then, it may safely be concluded that the place-names in *-ss-* and *-nd-* are typically Luwian.

In Table I below an overview is presented of place-names in *-ss-* and *-nd-* from Hittite cuneiform and Luwian hieroglyphic sources which can be localised. From this overview it can be deduced that these types of place-names are attested for the regions of Arzawa and Lukka in western Anatolia, of the Lower Land, Tarḫuntassa, and Kizzuwatna in the adjacent part of southern Anatolia, up to that of Karkamis along the upper Euphrates in the east. In this manner, then, we get a fairly accurate idea of the confines of the homeland of the Luwians (see Table I).

The inclusion of the region of Karkamis in the distribution zone of place-names in *-ss-* and *-nd-* is based on the localization of *Urussa* and *Terussa* along the Euphrates to the north of Karkamis by Jacques Freu (1980: 178 [map]). Now, it is well known that Karkamis is included into the Hittite empire by Suppiluliumas I (1350-1322 BC) and from this time onwards produced inscriptions, more in specific seal legends, in the Luwian hieroglyphic script. However, already during the Middle Bronze Age the region of Karkamis was under the sway of a king with an IE Anatolian name, *Aplaḫandas*, who in turn was in contact with functionaries using the Luwian hieroglyphic script at the time (Özguç 1980: 82; Fig. III-17). As it seems, therefore, the region of Karkamis may well have been an integral part of the Luwian homeland from the very beginning, even though, if so, it evidently forms its easternly limit.

Outside the distribution zone of place-names in *-ss-* and *-nd-* are the regions of Troy in the northwest corner of Anatolia and Ḫapalla within the bend of the Saḫiriya or Sangarios river. Both these regions were counted by Muwatallis II (1295-1271 BC) among the four Arzawa lands, Mira-Kuwaliya, Seḫa-Appawiya, Ḫapalla, and Wilusa (Alaksandus-treaty § 17, see Latacz 2010: 165).

---

[1] Note that in Kaskan territory along the southern Pontic littoral there are some place-names in *-ss-*, but the only ones in *-nd-*, *Wistawanda* and *Ḫinariwanda* (von Schuler 1965: 102-103), are in *-wanda*, presumably, as we will see below, a separate category featuring a reflex of Luwian *wanta-* 'mountain' and attributable to Luwian population groups resettled by the Hittites in former Kaskan territory devastated by their incessant wars against the latter.

region	-ss-	-nd-
Lesbos	*Wanata*$_6$*sa*	
Arzawa	*Ḫuwalus(iy)a*	*Puranda*
		Arinnanda
	Mutamutassa	*Millawanda*
	Ḫursanassa	*Iyalanda*
		Waliwanda
Lukka	*Kuwalapassa*	*Luwa*^{n}*ta*
		Wiyanawanda
Lower Land	*Tiwatassa* (Mt.)	*Lalanda*
	Parnassa	
	Nenassa	
Tarḫuntassa	*Pitassa*	*Naḫḫanta*
	Ḫantassa	*Ḫuwatnawanda* (Mt.)
	Ḫadduassa	*Kuwarsuwanta*
	Walistassa	*Arlanda* (Mt.)
	Paraiyassa	*Sinuwanda*
	Gurtanassa	*Ḫassuwanta*
	Watassa	*Ḫarḫasuwanta*
		Sarnanta
		Ḫassuwanta
		Mattarwanta
		Talwisuwanta
		Iyasanta
Kizzuwatna		*Paduwanda*
		Wiyanawanda
Karkamis	*Urussa*	
	Terussa/Tarwaza	

Table I. Place-names in *-ss-* and *-nd-* from Late Bronze Age Hittite cuneiform and Luwian hieroglyphic texts (in the main based on del Monte & Tischler 1978, Otten 1988, and del Monte 1992).[1]

[1] I include *Ḫuwalus(iy)a* in this overview because it corresponds to Classical *Kolossai*. *Luwa*^{n}*ta* (= Classical *Loanda*) and *Tarwaza* are only attested for Luwian hieroglyphic texts, Yalburt (§ 9) and the Ankara silver bowl (§ 2), see Woudhuizen 2015a: 15 and 17; on the silver bowl, see now Woudhuizen 2017b.

But, as I will argue in later on (see chapter 9), the language of the population of the region of Troy to all probability in the main falls outside the scope of the Luwian language group. As opposed to this, the region of Ḫapalla (< Luwian *ḫapa-* 'river') in the river land of the Sakarya and Porsuk most likely of origin formed an integral part of the Luwian homeland. In any case, in this region the town of Istanuwa is situated and the songs of Istanuwa as preserved in cuneiform Luwian texts of early date bear the testimony of a Luwian dialect distinct from Kizzuwatna Luwian (Yakubovich 2010: 22) which in my opinion (see chapter 8) is most adequately to be defined as the language of Arzawa—i.e. the language of the Arzawa lands with the exception of Wilusa. It seems likely, therefore, that the place-names in *-ss-* and *-nd-* are obliterated here by the incursion of Thracian and Phrygian population groups which started as early as 15th century BC. Note in this connection that according to Homeros (*Iliad* 3, 184-187) Phrygian troops headed by Otreus and Mygdon were already mustered along the banks of the Sangarios when Priamos was still able to fight himself, which means about a generation before the Trojan War of *c.* 1280 BC (Woudhuizen 2012a: 267).

However this may be, the Luwian nature of place-names in *-ss-* and *-nd-* can be further substantiated by linguistic evidence. First of all, the morpheme *-ss-* is no doubt related to adjectival *-s(s)-* which is a distinctive feature of all the extant Luwian dialects. To this comes that the roots of the place-names sometimes are patently Luwian, like in case of *Wiyanawanda* (< Luwian *wiyana-* 'wine'), *Tiwatassa* (< Luwian *Tiwata-* 'sun-god'), *Tarḫuntassa* (< Luwian *Tarḫunt-* 'storm-god'), *Pitassa* (< Luwian *pata-* 'plain'), *Parnassa* (< Luwian *parna-* 'house'), *Nenassa* (< Luwian *nana-* 'brother'), and *Terussa* (< Luwian *taru-* 'wood'). Finally, the toponyms characterised by the final element *wanda-* may well be distinct from the ones in *-nd-*, in any case this particular element is a reflex of Luwian *wanta-* 'mountain'.

The distribution of place-names in *-ss-* and *-nd-* is not confined to western and southern Anatolia, but also includes Greece. As rightly pointed out by Laroche in his aforesaid studies, the Greek toponymic morphemes *-ss-* and *-nth-* (= Greek reflex of Anatolian *-nd-* or *-nt-*) are of Indo-European nature, but not Greek. In effect, this means that the place-names in question are to be attributed to a population group which inhabited Greece before the formation of the Greek ethnos took place. What is even more, this particular pre-Greek population group can positively be identified as Luwian. It follows from this line of reasoning that the Aegean with the islands (including Crete) and the Greek mainland of origin formed an integral part of the homeland of the Luwians.

The latter conclusion can be substantiated already by the Late Bronze Age sources. It so happens, namely, that place-names in *-ss-* and *-nth-*, or names or indications related to such place-names, feature in the Linear B texts from Knossos, Thebes, and Pylos dated between *c.* 1350 BC and *c.* 1200 BC as *termini ante quo*. An overview of the Linear B evidence is presented in Table II.

Now, this Linear B evidence has a bearing on southern and central Greece, including the islands of Euboia to the east and Zakynthos to the west. Of particular interest, however, is the fact that it also includes the island of Crete.

region	-ss-	-nth-
Hellespont		*pe-ri-te-u* 'Perinthian'
Troas	*ru-na-so* 'Lyrnessos'	*si-mi-te-u* 'Sminthian'
Euboia		*a-ma-ru-to* 'Amarynthos'
Argolis		*ti-ri-to* '*Tirynthos'
Ionian islands		*za-ku-si-ja* 'Zakynthian'
Messenia	*ku-pa-ri-so* 'Kyparissia'	*o-ru-ma-to* 'Erymanthos'
Crete	*a-mi-ni-so* 'Amnisos'	*da-pu$_2$-ri-to-jo* 'of the Labyrinth'
	ko-no-so 'Knossos'	*ku-ta-to* '*Gurtanthos'
	tu-ri-so 'Tylissos'	*ra-su-to* '*Lasynthos'

Table II. Place-names in -*ss*- and -*nth*- or names related to such place-names from the Late Bronze Age Linear B texts (based on Ventris & Chadwick 1973: glossary, s.v.).

Here, namely, the Luwian nature of the place-names in -*ss*- and -*nth*- receives additional confirmation from the fact that the root sometimes is of a Luwian or IE Anatolian nature as well, as in case of *Tylissos* (< Hittite *tuliya*- 'assembly') and *Labyrinthos* (< Lydian *labrus* 'double-axe'). Finally, it deserves our attention in this connection that the relevant Linear B evidence also indicates Mycenaean Greek contacts with the region of the Hellespont (*Perinthos*) and the Troad (*Sminthē*, *Lyrnēssos*). In the latter instance, it should be noted that the place-names in question according to Homeros (*Iliad* 20, 92-96; 21, 86) are situated in the land of the *Leleges*, a Luwian population group (see further below) inhabiting the southern Troad also addressed by the poet as *Kilikes* or Cilicians (*Iliad* 6, 397; 415; cf. Strabo, *Geography* 13, 1, 7). That Luwian influence indeed radiated to the north-Aegean as early as in the Late Bronze Age is further emphasised by Linear B *i-mi-ri-jo* 'Imbrian' (KN Db 1186)—the name of the island *Imbros* being related to cuneiform Luwian *immara/i*- 'open country, wilderness' and likewise showing a reflex of Proto-Indo-European (= PIE) $*\hat{g}^{h}im$- 'winter, snow' characterised by the typical Luwian loss of the intial voiced velar *[ĝ].

After the Bronze Age, the typical Luwian place-names in -*ss*- and -*nd*- remained a productive factor in the toponymy of Anatolia as illustrated in our list of these place-names from the Classical period of Table III below. For the sake of emphasis, in this table the examples with a Late Bronze Age forerunner are rendered in bold type and those with a parallel in Greece in italic. In this manner on the one hand continuity from the Bronze to the Iron Age is visualised, whereas on the other hand the Aegean nature of this class of toponyms receives proper attention. The list is not a comprehensive one but only serves illustrative purposes and focuses on those examples of which the location is secured so that they can be put on the map (= our Fig. 1). Note that in the Classical period the eastern extremity of the distribution zone, the region of Karkamis, is no longer represented.

region	*-ss-*	*-nd-*
Troas	*Assos*	***Sminthē*** **(*si-mi-te-u*)**
	Lyrnēssos **(*ru-na-so*)**	
Mysia	*Larissa*	Kalandos
Lydia	Attanassos	Mormonda
	Korēssos	Salinda
	Mykalēssos	***Puranda***
	Myessos	Diginda
		Ariandos
		Silandos
		Blaundos
		Isindos
W. Phrygia	Prymnessos	Trokonda
	Kidyessos	***Lalanda/Lalandos***
	Ḫuwalusiya/Kolossai	
Caria	Iassos	***Iyalanda/Alinda***
	Mylasa	***Millawanda/Milete***
	Kasossos	*Labraunda*
	Alossos	***Waliwanda/Alabanda***
	Hali*karnassos*	Karyanda
	Bybassos	Kyllandos
	Hygassos	
Lycia	Telmēssos	Kalynda
	Karmylēssos	***Luwa^{n}ta/Loanda***
	Termēssos	Aloanda
	Habēssos	Kadyanda
	Tyberissos	***Wiyanawanda/Oinoanda***
	Tragalassos	Isinda
	Idebessos	Arykanda
	Akalissos	
Pisidia	*Termēssos*	Isinda
	Ariassos	Sibidunda
	Alassos	Perminunda
	Tymbrianassos	
	Mylasa	
Pamphylia	Kolybrassos	Aspendos

region	-ss-	-nd-
Lycaonia		Sinethandos
		Laranda
Cilicia	Marassa	Selindos
	Adrassos	Mysanda
	Koropissos	Kyinda
	Kindyassos	Myriandos
Cappadocia	***Parnassa/Parnassos***	Rodandos
	Nenassa/Nanassos	Dasmenda
	Aliassos	Tzamandos
		Paduwanda/Paduandos
		Wiyanawanda/Oiniandos

Table III. Place-names in *-ss-* and *-nd-* from Anatolia as recorded for sources from the Classical period (italic: paralleled for Greece; italic and bold: already attested in the Late Bronze Age sources; in the main based on Zgusta 1984).

A list of place-names in *-ss-* and *-nth-* from Greece as recorded for the Classical sources is presented in Table IV below. It deserves our attention that in this list the island of Cyprus is included. Further, it is remarkable that the island of Rhodes consistently shows *-nd-* and therefore in this sense actually belongs to the Anatolian sphere of influence. Conversely, the north-Aegean region, including *Sminthē* in the Troad from the previous list, consistently shows *-nth-* and therefore in its entirety should be grouped with the Greek side of the evidence.

region	-ss-	-nth-
Cyprus	Tamassos	Melanthos
	Lemessos	Arabanda
	Amamassos	
	Tegessos	
Rhodes	Ialysos	Keskindos
		Kamyndos
		Erindos
		Lindos
Crete	*Karnēsso*polis	***Labyrinthos*** (***da-pu$_2$-ri-to-jo***)
	Knossos (***ko-no-so***)	Berekynthos
	Amnisos (***a-mi-ni-so***)	*Pyranthos*

region	*-ss-*	*-nth-*
	***Tylissos* (*tu-ri-so*)**	****Gurtanthos* (*ku-ta-to*)**
	Poikilassos	****Lasynthos* (*ra-su-to*)**
	Pyrgiotissa	Syrinthos
	Rhytiassos	Priansos (< *Prianthos)
Cyclades	Marpēssa	Lebinthos
	Korēssos	Prepesinthos
	Bolissos	
	Kaukasa	
	Greece	
Laconia	Kardamylessos	
Argolis	*Larissa*	****Tirynthos* (*ti-ri-to*)**
		Saminthos
		Korinthos
Arcadia		Erymanthos
Ionian islands		***Zakynthos* (*za-ku-si-ja*)**
Messenia	***Kyparissia* (*ku-pa-ri-so*)**	
Attica	Kephissos	Probalinthos
	Ilissos	Trikorynthos
Euboia		Koskynthos
		***Amarynthos* (*a-ma-ru-to*)**
		Kērinthos
Boiotia	*Mykalēssos*	
	Teumēssos	
	Termēssos	
	Kerēssos	
	Permēssos	
Phokis	*Assos*	
	Ambrossos	
	Parnassos	
	Kyparissos	
Locris	Amphissa	
Aetolia	Taphiassos	Arakynthos
Thessaly	*Larissa*	
Macedonia	Turissa	
Chalcidicè	Thyssos	Olynthos

region	-ss-	-nth-
	Assa	Akanthos
Samothrace		Zērynthos
Hellespont	Kabassos	Bisanthē
	Marpēssos/Myrmissos	***Perinthos* (*pe-ri-te-u*)**
Lesbos	Antissa	

Table IV. Place-names in -*ss*- and -*nth*- from Greece as recorded for sources from the Classical period (italic: paralleled for Anatolia; italic and bold: already attested in the Late Bronze Age sources; based on Kretschmer 1970, Blegen & Haley 1928, and Nilsson 1972).

Fig. 1. Distribution of Luwian place-names in -*ss*- and -*nd*-.

Also with respect to the place-names in *-ss-* and *-nd-* or *-nth-* as recorded for sources from the Classical period their Luwian nature can be substantiated by the evidence from the roots. Thus *Trokonda* is based on the name of the Luwian storm-god *Tarḫunt-*, again, whereas *Halikarnassos* and *Karnēssopolis* show a reflex of Luwian *ḫarnas-* 'fortress'. In both these instances the Luwian laryngeal [ḫ] has been subject to fortition and is expressed by a velar, [k]—a development typical for the west-Luwian dialects Lycian, Carian, and Lydian. Of special interest is the attestation of *Parnassos*, the Greek equivalent of Anatolian *Parnassa* (< Luwian *parna-* 'house'), for Phokis in central Greece, as this was used by Leonard Palmer (1965: 30; 343-348) as a show case to prove his theory that there were Luwians among the pre-Greek population groups of Greece.

We have already seen reason to agree with Palmer in his basic tenet: the place-names in *-ss-* and *-nth-* are indeed evidence of the presence of Luwians among the population groups inhabiting Greece before the formation of the Greek ethnos. However, the matter is a little bit more complicated. In order to understand the complexities we first of all need to distinguish Greece proper from the Cyclades, Crete, Rhodes, and Cyprus as we did in our Table IV.

Now, a paradox is formed by the prolific nature of place-names in *-ss-* and *-nth-* attested for Greece proper on the one hand and the relatively speaking rarity of evidence for Luwians in this particular region as provided by the literary sources on the other hand. In the main, namely, the literary sources on the pre-Greek population groups of Greece bear testimony of Thracians and Phrygians, who in turn are stated to be preceded by Pelasgians (Woudhuizen 2013c).

Pre-Greek population groups featuring in literary tradition which come into consideration as being of Luwian nature are the *Leleges* and *Tyrrhenians*. The first mentioned population group is attested for Boiotia, the Megarid, Argolid, Laconia, and Messenia (Strabo, *Geography* 9, 2, 3 [Boiotia]; Pausanias, *Guide to Greece* 4, 1, 1 [Laconia]; 36, 1 [Messenia]; 1, 39, 5; 40, 5; 44, 3-5 [Megarid]). Now, according to Herodotos (*Histories* 1, 171) Leleges is just another name for the Carians, who in the reign of the Cretan king Minos lived on the Aegean islands, no doubt predominantly the Cyclades. Against the backdrop of this information, the evidence for Carians in the Argolid provided by Strabo (*Geography* 8, 6, 15) and for their heros eponym *Kar* as a mythical king of the Megarid reported by Pausanias (*Guide to Greece* 1, 39, 5; 1, 44, 9) no doubt has a bearing on the same branch of west-Luwian population groups. As we have noted in the above, the Leleges are also mentioned by Homeros (*Iliad* 20, 92-96; 21, 86), who situates them precisely in the region of the Troad characterised by place-names in *-ss-* (*Lyrnēssos*) and *-nth-* (*Sminthē*) and variously adresses them as *Kilikes* (*Iliad* 6, 397; 415; cf. Strabo, *Geography* 13, 1, 7). In line with the information of Herodotos the Leleges or Carians no doubt inhabited the Cyclades during the Late Bronze Age and moved to southwest Anatolia only during the time of the period of the upheavals of the Sea Peoples at the start of the Early Iron Age.[2] However this may be, just like the Carians, the Leleges are

[2] Note, however, that Homeros (*Iliad* 2, 867-869) in his enumeration of the Trojan allies already situates the Carians in the region of Miletos and Mycale on the Anatolian continent. However, this is likely to be considered an anachronism as Miletos is safely in the hands of the Mycenaean Greeks at the time of the Trojan War, c. 1280 BC.

reported for various regions in southwest Anatolia, like Tralles in Lydia (Plutarchos, *Greek Questions* 46), the region of Miletos in Caria itself (Strabo, *Geography* 7, 7, 2), and even as far southeast as Pisidia (Strabo, *Geography* 12, 7, 3). Note in this connection that Caria is most densely dotted with the place-names in *-ss-* and *-nd-* as recorded for the Classical sources (see Fig. 1).

As we noted in the above, the second pre-Greek population group which comes into consideration as being of Luwian nature are the Tyrrhenians. According to Thucydides (*Peloponnesian War* 4, 109) this population group once inhabited the region of Athens. If we realise that Herodotos (*Histories* 6, 137-140) probably confuses the Tyrrhenians with another pre-Greek population group, the Pelasgians, it may safely be deduced that it were the Athenian Tyrrhenians who subsequently settled in the north-Aegean region, especially the island of Lemnos, and no doubt were responsible for the place-names in *-ss-* (*Thyssos*, *Assa*, *Kabassos*, *Marpēssos*) and *-nth-* (*Olynthos*, *Akanthos*, *Zērynthos*, *Bisanthē*, *Perinthos*) here. At any rate, the Luwian nature of this pre-Greek population group is underlined by the fact that, as we will see in the next chapter, their name is a derivative of the Arzawan place-name *Dura* or Lydian *Tyrrha*.

Although the Luwians in mainland Greece may not have been the most numerous among the pre-Greek population groups, there is reason to believe that they may have been particularly influential in religion. Thus the mystery cult of the Demeter was disseminated to various regions of Greece, like for instance Andania in Messenia, by the *Lykomidai* of the Attic deme Phlya (Pausanias, *Guide to Greece* 4, 1, 5-9). An important role in this process is attributed to the founding father of the Lykomidai, *Lykos*, son of Pandion. Even if the claim by Herodotos (*Histories* I, 173) and Pausanias (*Guide to Greece* 1, 19, 4) that the Lycians were named after Lykos is incorrect, it cannot be denied that the ethnic *Lukka* and the personal name *Lykos* are based on one and the same root. Against the backdrop of the religious zeal of the pre-Greek Luwian population groups it should not really come as a surprise that according to Herodotos (*Histories* 8, 135) at the sanctuary of Akraiphia in Boiotia Carian persisted as a kind of church Latin until well into historical times.

In order to substantiate the assumption, based on the presence of place-names in *-ss-* and *-nth-*, that there are Luwians among the pre-Greek population groups of mainland Greece we only have Greek literary tradition to rely on. This situation changes dramtically as soon as we turn to the islands Crete and Cyprus. Here, namely, we can back up our claim by hard evidence from linguistics in the form of a direct testimony of the Luwian language in the local scripts.

For starters, the relevant literary data. According to Herodotos (*Histories* 1, 173) the Lycians originally inhabited the island of Crete, and, because of a quarrel between Minos and his brother Sarpedon went over with the latter to Lycia in southwest Asia Minor. As Minos embodies the period of the Minoan thalassocracy (*c.* 1550-1450 BC), this emigration of the Lycians is to be situated in the early phase of the Late Bronze Age. Further evidence for the presence of Lycians in Crete is provided by toponymy. Thus, the place-names *Lyktos* (Linear B *ru-ki-to*) and *Lykastos* (Homeros, *Iliad* 2, 647) are both based on the same root as the ethnic *Lukka*.

More importantly, however, is the fact that the Cretans were already literate from the beginning of the Middle Bronze Age, *c.* 2000 BC, onwards. First there is the so-called Cretan hieroglyphic script, which class of writing was continued in use for about 650 years up till *c.* 1350 BC. Its repertory consists for 75% of signs with an identical or closely related counterpart in the Luwian hieroglyphic script and for the remaing 25% of signs with an equivalent in the Egyptian hieroglyphic script. Now, the Luwian hieroglyphic mother-script indeed contains some signs originating from Egyptian hieroglyphic, like the winged sun-disc (LH 190) and the *ankh*-sign (LH 369), but not to such a substantial extent. In this sense, then, Cretan hieroglyphic is to be identified as Luwianizing rather than as being identical with Luwian hieroglyphic. Yet the similarities are far-reaching and can be demonstrated by, for example, the seal from Malia illustrated in our Fig. 2, which presumably dates from the first half of the 18th century BC. This contains on side 1 the goat-head sign LH 101 *TARKU*, on side 2 a non-predatory bird that looks like if it is dead but definitely corresponds to the non-predatory bird in Luwian hieroglyphic LH 128 expressing the value ti_5, and on side 3 the ox-head LH 105 *UWA* with four vertical strokes on top of its head, LH 391 *m*, for the conversion of *UWA* into *m+UWA* (numbering of the Luwian hieroglyphic signs according to Laroche 1960). In sum, we thus arrive at the typical Luwian personal name *Tarku(n)timuwas*, well known in its Greek form *Tarkondemos* as used in connection with the famous bilingual seal of the king of Mira, *Tarku(ndimu)was*, who reigned in the late 13th century BC. Now, what primarily concerns us here is that the writing of *m+UWA* is typically Luwian and paralleled for LH 107 depicting an ox-head with four strokes on its cheek. Only in Luwian, namely, PIE *g^wow- 'ox' develops into *uwa-* by the regular loss of the voiced velar *[g]—a phenomenon, in view of the personal names *Wa-wa-lá* and *Wa-wa-li* (< Luwian *wawa-/uwa-* 'ox', cf. Yakubovich 2010: 212-213), already attested for the Kültepe-Kanesh texts (*c.* 1920-1750 BC). No other Indo-European speaking people, therefore, could have arrived at such a ligature!

Fig. 2. Seal of Tarku(n)timuwas from Malia (Detournay, Poursat & Vandenabeele 1980: 160, Fig. 231).

As a matter of fact, the longer Cretan hieroglyphic texts, among which features most prominently the discus of Phaistos, are conducted in the Minoan Luwian language.

At a later stage, near the end of Middle Minoan II, *c.* 1700 BC, the Linear A script was developed under the influence of the likewise linearised Byblos script. As Byblos maintained close contacts with Egypt before these were interrupted by the invasions into the Levant and the Egyptian delta of gangs of charioteers from *c.* 1730 BC onwards, the local script developed after the loss of these regular contacts consists for a substantial part of linearised variants of Egyptian hieroglyphic signs. The same verdict applies to the related Cretan Linear A, which, however, apart from signs with a counterpart in the Byblos script, also includes linearised variants of signs from the Cretan hieroglyphic which in turn to a large extent originate from Luwian hieroglyphic. Also in this case, therefore, the verdict applies that Linear A is related to the Byblos script, but not identical. As a matter of fact, Lycian scribes can be shown to have played a key role in the development of Linear A (Woudhuizen 2014b). In any case, two Linear A inscriptions are demonstrably conducted in the Minoan Luwian language, and one of these, on an idol found at Monte Morrone along the Adriatic coast of Italy and presumably dating to Middle Minoan IIIA (*c.* 1700-1650 BC), is indeed inscribed by a Lycian scribe. Just like Cretan hieroglyphic, Linear A remained in use up to the Late Minoan IIIA1/2 transitional period, *c.* 1350 BC.

However, Linear A was not only used for inscriptions conducted in the Minoan Luwian language. In fact, most of the Linear A texts of some length happen to bear the testimony of Minoan Semitic which is most closely related to the northwest Semitic dialect (Byblian and Ugaritic). But the situation is even more complex as three inscriptions are conducted in Minoan Pelasgian. For the details, please consult my *Documents in Minoan Luwian, Semitc, and Pelasgian* of 2016 (= Woudhuizen 2016). What primarily concerns us here is that the roots of the place-names *ku-ta-to* or **Gurtanthos* and *Pyrgiotissa* show reflexes of PIE *$g^h ord^h$- 'city, town' and *$b^h \mathring{r} \hat{g}^h(i)$- 'high', respectively, in which the voiced velars *[g^h] and *[ĝ], contrary to the procedure in Luwian, are preserved. In line with this observation, the place-names in question can only be attributed to another Indo-European language spoken on Crete during the Bronze Age, which in effect boils down to Minoan Pelasgian. As we will see later on (see Chapter 10) a similar verdict applies to related southwest Anatolian toponyms like *Ḫursanassa* or *Gurtanassa*, *Parḫa* (= Classical *Pergē*), and *Párahámа* (= Classical *Pergamos*). Note, finally, that Cretan *Priansos* (< **Prianthos*) and western Anatolian *Pariyana* (= Classical *Priēnē*) bear the testimony of the expected Luwian reflex of PIE *$b^h \mathring{r} \hat{g}^h(i)$- 'high' characterised by the for Luwian regular loss of the voiced velar *[ĝ].

Notwithstanding the fact that the evidence for place-names in *-ss-* and *-nth-* is from Classical sources only, the island of Cyprus can be shown to be an integral part of the Luwian homeland on the basis of direct evidence for the Luwian language. The first object to be discussed in this connection is a cylinder seal from Klavdia dating from the Middle Bronze Age, or, to be more specific, presumably from the early 18th century BC. It is inscribed with a legend in the local variant of the Luwian hieroglyphic script, featuring the porcipine sign as a substitute for the wild boar sign (LH 529). In sum, the legend reads as follows: ***aper*$_2$-*sà*** *TAPAR-sà sà-ti*$_5$*-TAPAR* 'Eburosos, governor (of) Santitaparas' (see Fig. 3). This cylinder seal probably served as the owner's entry-ticket into the trade with the Near East, especially in metals, in which Cyprus under the name of Alasiya already took part during the era of Hammurabi of Babylon (1792-1750 BC). However this may be, the involvement in the international metal trade of the owner of the seal is certified in the case of a cylinder seal from Kourion, dated to *c.* 1550-1400 BC and decorated with a scene of a man carrying ingots of Buchholz type 1 on his shoulders. The name of this owner is written in Luwian hieroglyphic, again, and reads *tú-tà-MUWA* 'Teutamuwas' (see Fig. 4).

Sometime during the 16th or 15th century BC, the Cretan Linear script radiated to Cyprus and this caused the development of the local Cyprian Linear C. The most important documents in this class of writing, cylinder seals from Amathus (K-AD 389) and Enkomi (Inv. Nr. 19.10) and a tablet from Ugarit (RS 20.25), all date from the reign of Suppiluliumas II (1205-1190 BC). This Hittite king started his reign by providing the Hittite conquest of Alasiya by his father Tudḫaliyas IV (1239-1209 BC) with a firm footing. One of the pillars of his policy vis-à-vis Alasiya was that maritime trade in the region had to be painstakingly recorded. And this economic registration was for convenience sake conducted in the local Linear C script and the local Luwian vernacular.

Fig. 3. Cylinder seal from Klavdia (Kenna 1972: Fig. 79, 3a).

Fig. 4. Cylinder seal impression from Kourion (Knapp 2008: 157, Fig. 26a).

Now, it is during the first decade of the 12th century BC that in Enkomi, the capital of Alasiya, the Linear C script became subject to a development of simplification and at the same time towards a more cuneiform-like ductus, which resulted in the so-called Linear D. In this particular class of writing, then, incoming letters of international correspondence, like the one reasonably well-preserved on the front side of tablet Enkomi Inv. Nr. 1687, were transposed. The aforesaid letter deals with maritime raiders who in the previous period had been trading partners, like Akamas of Ilion. Just like the economic records, these letters also are conducted in the local Luwian vernacular. For the details, please consult my update on the topic entitled *The Language of Linear C and Linear D from Cyprus* of 2017 (= Woudhuizen 2017a).

In contrast to the situation on Crete, where the indigenous languages of the Bronze Age were discontinued, the local Luwian dialect persisted in Cyprus into the Classical period, as evidenced by the bilingual Eteo-Cyprian inscription from Amathus (Masson 1983: no. 196, see Woudhuizen 2018: 227-232).

2. Geography of Western Anatolia

The reconstruction of the geography of western Anatolia during the Hittite empire period has been a hotly disputed subject, with widely differing views being ventilated in the course of time. It is true that the identification of place-names like *Millawanda* and *Apasa* with Classical *Miletos* and *Ephesos*, respectively, goes back to the days of Bedrich Hrozný (1929)[1] and John Garstang & Oliver Gurney (1959), but nonetheless Susanne Heinhold-Krahmer wrote her in-depth study of the western country, and later province, Arzawa (1977) without attempting to draw it on a map.

A major step forwards in the reconstruction of the geography of western Anatolia, producing unimpeachable identifications, was achieved by Heinrich Otten with the publication in 1988 of a treaty between great king Tudḫaliyas IV (1239-1209 BC) and his vassal king Kuruntas of Tarḫuntassa on a bronze tablet from Boğazköy-Ḫattusa. In this treaty the boundaries of the province of Tarḫuntassa are meticulously described. This description of the border begins with *Pitassa* in the northwest, then runs clockwise along the northern and eastern confines up to the sea. Hereafter, it continues with the region of the city of *Parḫa* along the river *Kastaraya* along the southwestern confines in order finish with *Walma*.[2] As the description of the border herewith has reached full circle, Walma is situated to the west or southwest of Pitassa. Here already we have a fixed point, as the capital of the province Walma is likely identified with Classical *Holmoi*. Most fundamental for our purposes, however, is that *Parḫa* along the river *Kastaraya* is convincingly identified by Otten as Classical *Pergē* along the *Kestros* in Pamphylia.[3] It is added as a side remark that the great king is planning a military campaign against Parḫa and that, after it has been conquered, it will become part of the province of Tarḫuntassa.[4]

A second milestone in the reconstruction of the geography of western Anatolia, and the first one provided by Luwian hieroglyphic sources, we owe to the merit of Massimo Poetto. In his publication of the Yalburt inscription, in 1993, he was able to establish on the basis of the correspondence of the place-names *Pinatí*, *Awarna*, *Talwa*, and *Patar* to epichoric Lycian *Pinale*, *Arñna*, *Tlawa*, and *Pttara*, that this text deals with a military campaign by Tudḫaliyas IV in the valley of the Xanthos river in the western part of Lycia.[5] As explicitly indicated in the epilogue of the text, 'in these lands the great kings of Ḫatti, my fathers (and) grandfathers, no one has marched' (Yalburt, § 42), which in effect means that this region of western Anatolia is conquered by the Hittites for the first time. As I have argued in my own contribution to the interpretation of the Yalburt text, this also commemorates an earlier part of the same military campaign in the river land of *Luwata* and *Kwalatarna*, which for the correspondence of these names

1 See del Monte & Tischler 1978, s.v.
2 Otten 1988: I § 3, 18-§ 5.
3 Otten 1988: 37 (= commentary to VIII, 61).
4 Otten 1988: VIII, 62-64.
5 Poetto 1993: 78-81.

to Classical *Loanda* and epichoric Lycian *Xbide* (= Classical *Kaunos*), respectively, has a bearing on the valley of the Indus river situated immediately to the west of the Xanthos valley.[6] It is made very clear by the expression *apa muwaḫa* 'I *re*conquered' (Yalburt, § 12) that this latter region of western Anatolia, in contrast to that of the valley of the Xanthos river, already formed an integral part of the Hittite empire. (Note that from a geographical point of view the given sequence of affairs is fully understandable, as the mountainous terrain of the Xanthos valley is much more difficult to penetrate than that of the Indus river.)

A third major advance in the reconstruction of the geography of western Anatolia, and the second one based on Luwian hieroglyphic sources, comes from a recent article of John David Hawkins. In this article Hawkins brilliantly demonstrated that one of the well-known rock reliefs at Karabel, in the hinterland of Smyrna, is the product of a vassal king of the land of *Mira*[7]—together with Kuwaliya in fact the successor-state of the aforementioned Arzawa after its defeat by Mursilis II (1322-1295 BC) in the years 3-4 of his reign.[8] As Hawkins himself quickly grasped, an immediate consequence of these stunning new readings is that the land of Mira (and before it that of Arzawa) stretches from the Anatolian plateau to the coast of the Aegean, and hence that the long standing identification of its capital *Apasa* with Classical *Ephesos* is virtually confirmed.[9]

A contribution to the reconstruction of the geography of western Anatolia of my own, and the third one based on Luwian hieroglyphic, is the identification of Beycesultan[10] with the ancient town of *Mira*.[11] This was merely the, so to say, spin-off of my reading of the legend of the stamp seal from Beycesultan, dated to *c.* 2000 BC and hence providing the earliest evidence of Luwian hieroglyphic in particular and an Indo-European tongue more in general. It so happens that this legend starts with the sequence *mi+ra* 'Mira', from which, with a view to the find spot of the seal, it reasonably follows that Beycesultan is to be identified as *Mira*.[12] Now, as the capital of the country *Arzawa*, before its conquest by the Hittite great king Mursilis II in his 3rd and 4th year (1319-1318 BC), happens to be *Apasa* 'Ephesos', situated along the Aegean coast, it may safely be deduced that the reorganization of this realm in the aftermath of its conquest involved a shift of its capital from the Aegean in the far west to a location closer to the confines of the Hittite empire, *i.c.* inland Beycesultan alias *Mira*. As it seems, then, the name of the country was changed after the new capital from *Arzawa* to *Mira*, which none the less

6 Woudhuizen 1995: 58-59; Woudhuizen 1994-5 [1996]: 173-174; Woudhuizen 2004a: 27-28; for the Yalburt text, see most recently Woudhuizen 2015a: 16-20.

7 Hawkins 1998b: 4-8 (Karabel A). The name of the vassal king, which is also known from bullae from Boğazköy-Ḫattusa, reads, with the goat's head sign LH 101 TARKU instead of the donkey-head LH 100 TARKASNA, *Tarkuwa-*. The inscription gives his genealogy up to the third degree, of which only the name of the father is readable as (with the bird sign LH 131-133) ARA+*li*—possibly a shorthand writing of *Alantallis*, mentioned as a witness to the treaty between Tudḫaliyas IV and Kuruntas of Tarḫuntassa, see Hawkins 1998b: 17-18. If so, the son Tarkuwas may have been a contemporary of Suppiluliumas II (1205-1190 BC).

8 Hawkins 1998b: 10; 15 (with reference to Heinhold-Krahmer 1977).

9 Hawkins 1998b: 23.

10 For the exact location of Beycesultan, see Lloyd & Mellaart 1962: 7; 70, Map I.

11 Cf. Garstang & Gurney 1959: Map; Cornelius 1973: 38 'dem Lande Miraa, das sich großenteils mit Karien deckt', cf. Karte [1]: Vorderasien um 1300 v. Chr., where Mira is located along the upper *Maiandros* in the region of the present-day Emir.

12 Woudhuizen 2011: 464-467; Woudhuizen 2012b.

preserved its extension towards the Aegean coast, of which fact, as conclusively shown by John David Hawkins in 1998 (= Hawkins 1998b), the Luwian hieroglyphic inscriptions of the late 13th century BC king of Mira, *Tarkuwas* (< **Tarku(ndimu)was*), at the rock site of Karabel, northeast of present-day İzmir, bear testimony (see Fig. 27).

It is of interest to note in this connection that the region of Beycesultan borders on the Hittite provinces *Walma* to the east and *Kuwaliya* to the northeast. Here we have two more fixed points, as the capital of Walma corresponds to Classical *Holmoi*,[13] and Kuwaliya is mentioned in lenited form *Ḫwálià* in the Luwian hieroglyphic text of a stele from present-day Afyon so that, as a fourth Luwian hieroglyphic contribution, the latter site may reasonably be identified as its center.[14]

Now, working from the fixed points *Mira* = Beycesultan and *Apasa* = Ephesos, it is possible to reconstruct the confines of the former country of *Arzawa* in particular and the geography of western Anatolia more in general. In so doing, it first of all is of importance to give our credits to the French specialist in Hittite history Jacques Freu for the following 4 identifications with a bearing on the confines of the country in question, namely:[15]

(1) *Ḫuwalusiya* = Classical *Kolossai* or present-day Honaz (first suggested by Friedrich Cornelius in 1973 [page 208]) along the Classical *Lykos*, a tributary of the *Maiandros* corresponding to the present-day Emir or Küçük Menderes and likely referred to in Hittite texts as the *Astarpa*;

(2) *Dura* = Classical *Tyrrha* or present-day Tire(h) along the *Kaystros* or present-day Küçük Menderes (first suggested by Emile Forrer in 1929);

(3) *Kurupiya* = Classical Mt. *Koruphē*, southwest of present-day İzmir; and

(4) *Ḫalluwa* = Classical *Koloē*, northwest of *Sardis* or present-day Sart (first suggested by Emile Forrer in 1929).[16]

In addition to this, we have to acknowledge that it is largely to the merits of the expert Luwian hieroglyphic epigraphist John David Hawkins that we are in the position to identify, alongside *Millawanda* with *Miletos* and *Apasa* with *Ephesos* (since Garstang & Gurney 1959: Map):[17]

(5) *Puranda* with present-day Bademgediği, southwest of Classical Mt. *Koruphē*;[18] and

(6) *Arinnanda* with Classical Mt. *Mycalē* or present-day Samsun Dağ.

[13] Bryce 2010: 444, note 14.
[14] Woudhuizen 2013a: 9-12; see section 5.6 below.
[15] Freu 2008b: 110; cf. del Monte & Tischler 1978, s.v.
[16] Note that Freu's form †*Ḫawalusiya*, with [a] instead of [u] in the first syllable, is probably due to a printing error.
[17] Hawkins 2002: 97-98; 95-96; cf. Hawkins 1998b.
[18] Cf. Meriç 2003; Yasur-Landau 2010: 157.

Furthermore, we owe the following identification concerning the geography of western Anatolia to the merit of Alexander Herda (2013: 456):

(7) *Pariyana* with Classical *Priēnē*.

Finally, for the place-names in the province of Assuwa (discussed below) I am indebted to Michael Bányai (*forthc.*), whereas those from Seḫa and the Troad have come to light thanks to the recent rediscovery of Luwian hieroglyphic inscriptions from these regions (see discussion in chapter 6 below).

Together with the identifications featuring in Gander 2010, this leads to the following list of identifications of place-names from cuneiform Hittite and Luwian hieroglyphic concerning western Anatolia (see Table V):

	Hittite/Luwian	Lycian	Greek	
I.	*Tarḫuntassa*		Κιλικία	'Cilicia Aspera'
II.	—		Παμφυλία	Antalya province
a.	*Kastaraya*		Κεστρος	Aksu
1.	*Parḫa, Páraḫá*		Πέργη	Perge
III.	*Lukka, Luka*	*Trm̃mis-*	Λυκία	'Lycia'
2.	*Kuwalapassa*		Κόλβασα	'Kolbasa'
3.	*Zumarri*	*Zẽmure*	Λίμυρα	'Limyra'
4.	*Ḫinduwa*	*Xãkbi*	Κάνδυβα	'Kandyba'
b.	*Siyanta*		Ξάνθος	Eşen Çay/Koca Çayı
5.	*Wiyanawanda*		Ὀινόανδα	'Oinoanda'
6.	*Talawa, Talwa*	*Tlawa*	Τλῶς	'Tlōs'
7.	*Pina, Pinatí*	*Pinale*	Πίναρα	'Pinara'
8.	*Awarna*	*Arñna*	Ἄρνα, Ξάνθος	'Xanthos'
9.	*Patar*	*Pttara*	Πάταρα	'Patara'
IV.	*ḫapir utna*			Indus valley
c.	—		Ἰνδός	Indus river
10.	*Luwata*		Λοανδα	'Loanda'
11.	*Kwalatarna*	*Xbide*	Καῦνος	'Kaunos'

	Hittite/Luwian	Lycian	Greek	
V.	*Arzawa/Mira*		Λυδία + Καρία	'Lydia (south)' + 'Caria'
d.	—		Μαίανδρος	Büyük Menderes
f.	*Astarpa*		Λύκος	Emir/Küçük Menderes
12.	*Mira* (town)		—	Beycesultan
13.	*Ḫuwalusiya*		Κολοσσαί	Honaz
14.	*Sallapa*		≈ Σάλβακος	'Salbacus Mons'
15.	*Wallarimma*		Ὑλλάριμα	'Hyllarima'
16.	*Waliwanda*		Ἀλάβανδα	'Alabanda'
e.	—		Μαρσύας	Çine
17.	*Iyalanda*		Ἄλινδα	'Alinda'
18.	*Atriya*		Ἰδριάς	Stratonicea/ Eskihisar
19.	*Utima*		Ἴδυμα	'Idyma'
20.	*Mutamutassa*		Μύλασα	'Mylasa'
21.	*Millawanda, Milawata*		Μίλητος	Miletus
22.	*Ḫursanassa*		Ἁλικαρνασ(σ)ός	Bodrum
23.	*Attarim(m)a, Tìtarma*		(unspecified location in Caria)	

	Hittite/Luwian	Lydian	Greek	
24.	*Pariyana*		Πριήνη	'Priene'
25.	*Arinnanda*		Μυκάλη	Samsun Dağ
26.	*Apasa*	*Ibśi-*	Ἔφεσος	Efes
g.	—		Κάϋστρος	Küçük Menderes
27.	*Dura*		Τύρρα	Tire(h)
28.	*Puranda*		—	Bademgediği
29.	*Kurupiya*		Κορυφή	Mt. near İzmir
30.	*[Sa]murna*		Σμύρνα	İzmir
VI.	*Kuwaliya, Ḫwálià*		—	region of Afyon
VII.	*Assuwa*		Ἀσία	'Lydia (north)'
h.	*Warmala*		Ἑρμός	Gediz
31.	*Sallauwassi*		Σαλόη	'Saloe'
32.	*Zipasla*		Σίπυλος	'Sipylos'

Hittite/Luwian		Lydian	Greek	
33.	*Assaratta, Asaruti*	*Śard-/Śfard*	Σάρδεις	'Sardis'
34.	*Ḫalluwa*	*Kulu-*	Κολόη	(N-W of Sart)[19]
VIII.	*Seḫa*		Τευθρανία	'Teuthrania'
i.	*Seḫa, Asaḫa*		Καϊκός	Bakırçay
35.	*Pita$_6$nasa*		Πιτάνη	'Pitane'
36.	*Tiwatatar(a)*		Θυάτειρα	'Thyateira'
37.	*Ta$_6$ta$_6$rnasa*		Ἀταρνεύς	'At(t)arneus'
38.	*Párahámа*		Πέργαμος	'Pergamon'
39.	*Lazpa, Lasapa*		Λέσβος	'Lesbos'
40.	*Ātarmuta$_6$*		Ἀδραμύττιον	Edremit
41.	*Lalakasa*		Λέλεγες	'Leleges'
IX.	*Appawiya*		—	'Abbaitis'
j.	—		Μέκεστος	'Makestos'
42.	*Masatur(i)wanata$_6$sa*		—	Dağardı
X.	*Atapali*		—	—
	—		—	Beyköy
XI.	*Ḫapalla, Ḫápala*		—	(Sangarios basin)
k.	*Saḫiriya*		Σαγγάριος	Sakarya
l.	—		Τεμβρις	Porsuk
XII.	*Wilusiya*		Ἴλιον	'Ilion'
(39.	*Lazpa, Lasapa*		Λέσβος	'Lesbos')
43.	*Wanta$_6$sa*		Ἄντισσα	'Antissa'
44.	*Ummitumina*		Μήθυμνα	'Methymna'
45.	*Mutilina*		Μιτυλήνη	'Mitylene'
46.	*[Ā]par(a)*		Ἴμβρος	'Imbros'
47.	*Lamina*		Λῆμνος	'Lemnos'
48.	*Ta$_6$nata$_6$*		Τένεδος	'Tenedos'
m.	—		Σκάμανδρος	'Skamandros'
49.	*Taruisa*		Τροία	Hisarlık
50.	*Āta$_6$pawasa*		Ἄβυδος	'Abydos'

[19] Note that *Ḫalluwa* ≠ *Ḫallawa*, see Garstang & Gurney 1959: 106; *Ḫallawa* = *Ḫalwan*, a variant writing of *Ḫarman* (Karkamis A15b, § 9), corresponding to cuneiform *Ḫalman* (Woudhuizen 2011: 196, note 18), bearing reference to *Ḫalpa* or Aleppo.

	Hittite/Luwian	Greek	
51.	*Ārsapa*	Ἀρίσβη	'Arisbe'
52.	*Parukita*$_6$	Περκώτη	'Perkote'
53.	*Pitu[?]*	Πιτύεια	'Pityeia'
54.	*Apasasawa*	Ἀπαισός	'Apaisos'
55.	*Parmu*$^?$*sa*	Πάριον	'Parion'
56.	*Kárkalasa*	Γάργαρα	'Gargara'
(40.	*Ātarmuta*$_6$	Ἀδραμύττιον	Edremit)
(41.	*Lalakasa*	Λέλεγες	'Leleges')
XIII.	Masa	Μυσία	'Mysia'
(j.	—	Μέκεστος	'Makestos')

Table V. Identification of place-names from cuneiform Hittite and Luwian hieroglyphic with a bearing on western Anatolia.[20]

Note that in the map of western Anatolia as presented below I have followed the opinion of G. Droysen in his atlas of 1886 in the location of *Ḫalluwa* at his *Coloë* and *Dura* at his *Tyrrha*,[21] whereas, in contradistinction, I adhered to William Calder & George Bean in their atlas of 1958 in the location of *Kurupiya* at their *Coruphe Mons* and, like Max Gander, Onofrio Carruba, and Wolf-Dietrich Niemeier, of *Sallapa* in the neighbourhood of their *Salbace Mons*.[22] Obviously, the exact location of these four sites is contested, as I stressed in my remarks to the various Atlasses in the bibliography.

But the existence of, for example, a *Koloē* in the neighbourhood of the later Lydian capital *Sardis* is assured by its mention in epichoric Lydian texts (Lyd. no. 1, lines 6-8: *Artimuś Ibśimsis Artimu(ś)-k Kulumsis ... vt*$_1$*bapẽnt* 'the Ephesian Artemis and the Koloan Artemis (...) will destroy';[23] Lyd. no 2, lines 10-13: *Artimui*$_1$ *Ibśimi*$_1$*ai*$_1$ *Kulumi*$_1$*a(i*$_1$*)-k ... vt*$_1$*bupid*

[20] Sources: del Monte & Tischler 1978 supplemented by del Monte 1992 (Hittite/Luwian); Melchert 2004 (Lycian); Gusmani 1964 (Lydian); Pauly-Wissowa Realencyclopädie and Zgusta 1984 (Greek); Brosnahan 1990 and Wikipedia (present-day).

[21] Note that *Tyrrha* was an important site in, if not actually the capital of, Lydia during the reign of Gyges in the 1st half of the 7th century BC (Zgusta 1984: 645, § 1387-4; cf. Pauly-Wissowa Realencyclopädie, s.v.). As we have seen in the previous chapter, it presents us with the basic root from which the ethnic *Tyrrhenoi* as attested for Attica is derived.

[22] For the localization of *Sallapa* in the neighbourhood of Mt. *Salbacus*, see Gander 2010: 193 'Einer neuerer Vorschlag bringt Sallapa mit dem Salbacus Mons nahe Laodikeia am Lykos in Verbindung', with reference to Carruba 1996, 28 and Niemeier 2008: 320; cf. Niemeier 2007b: 80 'In Sallapa, das wahrscheinlich östlich des Salbacus Mons im Gebiet des späteren Laodikeia zu lokalisieren ist'.

[23] Cf. Greek Ἄρτεμις Κολοηνή as reported by Strabo, *Geography* 13, 4, 5.

'the Artemisses of the Ephesisans and of the Koloans (...) will destroy').[24] Similarly, the Luwian *Kurupiya* and Greek *Koruphē* are both based on the PIE root *k̂erh$_1$- 'head, horn',[25] entirely appropriate for a promontory or headland.

In similar vein, just like in the case of *Millawanda*, which also shows a destruction layer at the end of level V or what was formerly known as the second building period at the transition from Late Helladic IIIA2 to Late Helladic IIIB1 attributed to the military campaign by Mursilis II (1322-1295 BC) in his 3rd and 4th year,[26] the identification of Bademgediği with *Puranda* can be supported by archaeological evidence in the form of an hiatus between levels III (with Late Helladic IIIA2 sherd) and II, explained in terms of its destruction by Mursilis II in the aforesaid campaign.[27]

As acknowledged in the above, we owe the location of Assuwa in the valley of the Hermos river to Michael Bányai. As he points out, the region of Assuwa is associated with the place-name *Assaratta* or *Sardis* and with the river name *Warmala*. Now, *Warmala* confronts us with a reflex of PIE *g^{wh}erm- 'warm',[28] characterised by the for Luwian regular loss of the initial voiced labiovelar [g^{wh}]. Furthermore, it can easily be shown to be the forerunner of Greek *Hermos* if we realise that [h] originates from [w] in like manner as in *Holmoi* < *Walma* and *Halmos* < *Walmus*. Note, however, that the name of the region Assuwa, though originally linked up with the Hermos river, may in the course of time have been used as a blanket term for western Anatolia in its entirety, as is the case with the Assuwian League (see chapter below).

One of the main points of disagreement with respect to the reconstruction of the geography of the western province by between Freu on the one hand and Hawkins and Starke on the other hand concerns the land of *Seḫa*. According to Freu this is situated in the valley of the Maiandros, south of Mira, whereas Hawkins and Starke locate it in the Kaikos valley north of Mira and south of Wilusa, corresponding to Classical *Teuthrania*. Freu argues from the fact that Seḫa is associated with *Appawiya*, and that the latter, in emended form *Aba[wiya]*, is directly associated with the toponyms *Iyalanda* and *Atriya*, corresponding with Classical *Alinda* and *Idrias* in Caria.[29] The northern location of Seḫa as suggested by Hawkins and Starke, however, is now ascertained owing to the rediscovery of the Luwian hieroglyphic inscriptions from Yazılıtaş and Dağardı. In these inscriptions (see discussion in chapter 6), namely, towns and regions belonging to the land of *Asaha* or *Seḫa* are enumerated, among which feature *Lasapa* 'Lesbos', *Ātarmuta*$_6$ 'Adramyttion', *Ta*$_6$*ta*$_6$*rnasa* 'At(t)tarneus', ^{WANTI}*Lalakasa* '(the town of) mount Leleges' (Yazılıtaş), *Páraháma* 'Pergamon', *Tiwatatar(a)* 'Thyateira', and *Pita*$_6$*nasa* 'Pitane' (Dağardı). There can be no doubt, therefore, about the location of Seḫa in the Kaikos

[24] Woudhuizen 2005a: 139; 143; cf. Gusmani 1964: 250-251.
[25] Cf. Mallory & Adams 2007: 137.
[26] Niemeier 1998a: 33; 38-40; Niemeier 1998b: 150-151; Niemeier 2007a: 14; 18; cf. Freu 2008a: 28; Woudhuizen in van Binsbergen & Woudhuizen 2011: 249, note 605
[27] Meriç 2003: 80; 97.
[28] Mallory & Adams 2007: 344-345.
[29] Freu 2008b: 112-113. Note that the location of *Seḫa* in the valley of the *Maiandros* was already proposed by Laroche 1966: map between pages 272 and 273, and Freu in his *Luwiya* of 1980: 286-289 (a pdf-version of this work was kindly made available to me by Max Gander).

valley. As a consequence, Masa can not be located here as sometimes assumed, but must—as the only possible alternative—be situated in the region of the lower Makestos to the east of Wilusa. Note that the inclusion of Lesbos in the domain of Seḫa tallies with the fact that in the Manapatarḫundas-letter *ṣāripūtu*-men or purple-dyers (as per Singer 2011: 425-458) from *Lazpa* 'Lesbos', which were abducted by Piyamaradus, partly fell under the authority of the vassal king of Seḫa after which the aforesaid letter is named. Note, however, that the remaining part of these abducted purple-dyers fell according to the same letter directly under the authority of the Hittite great king, Muwatallis II (1295-1271 BC); we appear to be dealing here with groups of specialised workers who had migrated from their specific regions of origin in Anatolia to the island of *Lazpa* 'Lesbos' in order to earn their daily living.

Further controversy is raging about the identification of Hittite *Wilusa* with Homeric *Ilios* (< **Wilios*) and whether this is indeed the Hittite name for the settlement at Hisarlık in the Troad. With regard to this issue, Susanne Heinhold-Krahmer remained skeptical in her discussion of 2003, in which she moreover gave an overview (on p. 167) of the divergencies between the reconstructions of the geography of western Anatolia as proposed by Starke 1997 and Hawkins 1998b. Even more critical about this topic is Freu 1998, who on the basis of the evidence provided by the Milawata-letter from the reign of Tudḫaliyas IV, argued that Wilusa must be situated in the neighbourhood of Millawanda or Classical Miletos. In the letter in question it is recorded that the ruler of Wilusa at the time, called Walmus, was forced to take refuge at the court of the ruler of Milawata, i.e. a shorthand writing variant of Millawanda. Yet another piece of evidence is formed by the mention of Wilusa in a letter by a Hittite great king presumably to be identified with Suppiluliumas II (1205-1190 BC) to a certain Masḫuittas who is addressed as a great king and therefore likely to be identified as the ruler of Mira at the time (KBo XVIII 18, see Hagenbuchner 1989, 2: 317). On the basis of these data, then, Freu draws the conclusion that Wilusa must be situated at the mouth of the Kaystros river, which in turn forces him to identify *Apasa* not with Classical *Ephesos*, but alternatively with *Habesos* in Lycia—a highly unlikely inference. In my view, however, the Milawata-letter is not addressed to Tarkuwas, the king of Mira during the reign of Tudḫaliyas IV, but to the son of Atpas, the governor of Millawanda at the time of the Tawagalawas-letter from the reign of Muwatallis II. In any case, the latter was a vassal of the great king of Aḫḫiyawa or Mycenaean Greece, and therefore disloyal to the Hittite king, whereas in the time of his successor and son the political situation had changed dramatically and Millawanda had returned to the Hittite fold. Now, owing to the discovery of the Luwian hieroglyphic inscriptions at Latmos, we know that the region of Miletos was ruled during the latest stage of the Hittite empire by a great prince with a *Kupanta*-name characteristic of the royal house of Mira—which country name in its turn is even mentioned in one of the Latmos inscriptions. Accordingly, it may safely be assumed that Miletos fell under the authority of the ruler of Mira in an advanced stage of the reign of Suppiluliumas II, and, as the title great prince strongly suggests subordination to a great king, the king of Mira may well have reached this preeminent status at the time—as evidenced, as we have just noted, for Masḫuittas. The same verdict may well apply to the latter's predecessor, Tarkuwas,[30] as well, who in that case obviously was the overlord of all Arzawa lands in western Anatolia, including its most northerly representative Wilusa in the Troad, which he apparently ruled through the medium of his great prince at Miletos. The alternative location of Wilusa in the neighbourhood of Beycesultan or even its identification with the latter site as proposed by Vangelis Pantazis (2009: 305) on the basis of the similarly sounding *Ilouza* as recorded for a polis and a bishopric in this region in Christian texts from the 5th century AD onwards, in which suggestion he is followed by Frank Kolb (2010: 100-102; 98-99, Taf. Abb. 3) and, most recently, Heinhold-Krahmer (2013: 72), is definitely ruled out by the identification of the ancient name of Beycesultan as Mira on the basis of the reading of the stamp seal from this site as referred to in the above.[31]

In the light of the fact that the toponym *Tarwisa* is mentioned only once in Hittite sources, viz. the annals of Tudḫaliyas II (1425-1390 BC), its identification with Classical Greek *Troia* or *Troiē* necessarily remains hypothetical. But it should be noted that the threefold equasion *Wilusa* = *(W)ilios*, *Tarwisa* = *Troia* or *Troiē* and *Alaksandus* = *Alexandros* provides impressive cumulative evidence as to its validity. Note that in my map as presented below as Fig. 5 I have taken Wilusiya as the name of the region and Tarwisa as that of the town, which is convenient but arbitrary as both occur as toponyms. Yet, it might be pointed out in this connection that *Wilusiya* alongside *Wilusa* is a formation of the same type as *Arzawiya* alongside *Arzawa* and *Assuwiya* alongside *Assuwa*, which definitely are names of countries and not of towns.

The location of Wilusa in the Troad is now definitely assured by the rediscovery of the Luwian hieroglyphic inscription from Edremit (see discussion in chapter 6). In this text the regions and place-names belonging to the realm of Muksas, great prince of Mira and Wilusa (i.e. the ruler of Wilusa on behalf of great king Kupantakuruntas III of Mira), are enumerated. This enumeration runs clockwise and starts with the islands *[Lasa]pa* 'Lesbos' (including its main towns *Wanata*$_6$*sa* 'Antissa', *Ummitumina* 'Methymna', and *Mutilina* 'Mitylene'), *[Ā]par(a)* 'Imbros', *Lamina* 'Lemnos', and *Ta*$_6$*nata*$_6$ 'Tenedos' in the west, continues with the place-names *Āta*$_6$*pawasa* 'Abydos', *Ārsapa* 'Arisbe', *Parukita*$_6$ 'Perkote', *Pitu[?]* 'Pityeia', and *Parmu*$^?$*sa* 'Parion' in the northeast, in order to end with *Kárkalasa* 'Gargara', *Ātarmuta*$_6$ 'Adramyttion', and ^{WANTI}*Lalakasa* '(the town of) mount Leleges' in the south. The overlap with the realm of Seḫa (Lesbos, Adramyttion, and mount Leleges) as recorded by the inscription from Yazılıtaş can easily be explained by the fact that the latter inscription is dedicated by the son of Kupantakuruntas III,

[30] Note that the title of great king attributed to Tarkuwas of Mira by Recai Tekoğlu in his presentation of the Luwian hieroglyphic inscription on a fragmentarily preserved stele from Torbalı as published in Fahri Işık, Mahir Atıcı & Recai Tekoğlu 2011: 22-25, is convincingly argued by Oreshko 2013: 373-386 to be based on a flawed reading of this text.

[31] One of the arguments put forward by Pantazis is that from the Manapatarḫundas-letter, § 3, lines 3-4: '[Kassus] came (here) and brought the troops of Ḫatti. [And when] they went back to attack Wilusa' (cf. Beckman e.a. 2011: 141), it may be inferred that Wilusa lies in between Ḫatti and Seḫa. It should be noted in this connection, however, that the Hittite general Kassus to all probability went with only a detachment of his army from his military headquarters to the residence of the loyal vassal king of Seḫa, Manapatarḫundas, added the forces of the latter to his detachment and subsequently went back to his military headquarters in order to launch an attack on (the enemy besieging!) Wilusa at the time with his entire army. Pantazis' misunderstanding of these phrases results from their *brevitas*.

Walwamuwas, and therefore dates from a later period as the Edremit inscription. At this point in time the realm of Seḫa may have been expanded at the expense of the Troad as its king Walwamuwas had risen to the status of great king.

Next, I would argue that *Karkisa*, the Bronze Age forerunner of Classical *Karia* which also occurs in variant form *Karkiya*, is likely to be located on the islands in the Aegean known as the Cyclades. Greek literary tradition is affirmative in this connection on the point that the Carians, which in the Classical period inhabited southwest Asia Minor, originated from the islands in the Aegean. It is only disputed when they moved from the islands to their later habitat on the continent: according to Thucydides, *Peloponnesian War* I, 4 they were driven from the Cyclades in the times of Minos, who embodies the period of the Minoan thalassocracy (*c.* 1550-1450 BC),[32] whereas Herodotos, *Histories* I, 171 on the other hand maintains that they served Minos while living on the islands and, by means of deduction, moved to southwest Asia Minor sometime after the period of the Minoan thalassocracy—which probably means in the time of the upheavals of the Sea Peoples. Further supporting evidence may be provided by Hittite sources. In the Tawagalawas-letter from the reign of Muwatallis II it is reported about the Hittite renegade and troublemaker Piyamaradus that, during his stay in the Aḫḫiyawan or Mycenaean Anatolian bridgehead *Millawanda* 'Miletos' he said: ŠÀ ^{KUR}*Ma-a-ša-wa-kán* ^{KUR}*Kar-ki-ya pár-ra-an-[da] pa-a-i-mi* 'I will cross over to the land of Masa or the land of Karkiya' (Taw § 11, lines 53-54, see Beckman e.a. 2011: 114-115). As we have seen, Masa probably lies on the continent, namely in the region of the lower Makestos, which means that it can most easily be reached from Millawanda by ship, so this is no argument for Karkiya lying on the Cyclades. But in another text, the Manapatarḫundas-treaty from the reign of Mursilis II, we come across the same combination of preverb and verb in the following phrase: *nu-kán* A.NA LÚ^{MEŠ} ^{URU}*Kar-ki-ša pár-ra-a[n-da pa-it x]* 'Und [du gingst] zu den Leuten von Karkiša [hinüber]' (Man-treaty § 1, line 7, see Friedrich 1930: 4-5). Here it is used for the flight by Manapatarḫundas from his homeland Seḫa to Karkisa, and *paranda pāi-* most likely also expresses the meaning 'overseas' (cf. Latacz 2010: 180-181 with 159 'hinüber gehen' = 'in Übersee'). It is true that Muwatallis II in his campaign in western Anatolia just prior to the showdown with Egypt at Kadesh (1274 BC) recruited auxiliaries from Dardania (= Troy), Masa (= Mysia), Arzawa (≈ Lydia), Lukka (= Lycia), and Karkisa (Bryce 2010: 235), but the last mentioned contingent may have been called to service through the intermediacy of the vassal king of Seḫa, so that we do not have to assume Muwatallis II personally embarking on a ship to arrange this matter—though it is perfectly possible that he sent a messenger by ship in order to do so.

Finally, *Ḫapalla*, the name of which consists of an adjectival derivative in *-(a)lla* of the word *ḫapa-* 'river', is grouped with the Arzawa lands Mira-Kuwaliya, Seḫa-Appawiya, and Wilusa in the Alaksandus-treaty from the reign of Muwatallis II.[33] In addition, we know that it was successively ruled by the kings Tarkasnallis during the reign of Mursilis II,[34] and Uraḫattusas during the reign of Muwatallis II.[35] Now, this land may reasonably be

[32] Cf. Thucydides, *Peloponnesian War* I, 8 with reference to Carian graves on Delos.

[33] Latacz 2010: 162, § 4; 165, § 17.

[34] Bryce 2010: 214.

[35] Latacz 2010: 165, § 17.

located in the river land formed by the Classical Sangarios or Hittite Saḫiriya (= present-day Sakarya) and its tributary, the present-day Porsuk or Classical Tembris, if we realise that the Ḫulana river is associated with the land Kassiya, named after mount Kassu (= present-day Ilgaz Dağları), in texts with reference to a campaign by Suppiluliumas I during the reign of his predecessor Tudḫaliyas III (1370-1350 BC),[36] and to the territory assigned to the control of Ḫattusilis III during the reign of his brother Muwatallis II when the latter had moved the capital to Tarḫuntassa.[37] From this association, namely, it may be inferred that the Ḫulana river is to be identified with the present-day Kirmir, also a tributary to the Sangarios, but to the east of it and the source of which is very close to that of the Daḫara running south of mount Kassu. In any case it seems clear that the river land in which the Porsuk takes a central position was situated outside of the confines of Ḫatti-land proper. The location of Ḫapalla as proposed here coincides with that by Starke (1997: 449, Abb. 1), which, however, in the text itself lacks any further argumentation, but Hawkins (2002: 98) informs us that according to Starke the land of Ḫapalla was reached by the Hittites by means of *Lalanda* corresponding to Classical *Lalandos*. Now, Lalandos in its turn is located in the region of Classical Amorion to the northeast of present-day Afyon and just south of the upper course of the Sangarios,[38] and may reasonably be argued to belong, if not to the nearby Kuwaliya (= Afyon region), to the Hittite Lower Land.

It seems very well possible that, with shifting borders through the course of time, *Ḫuwalusiya* and *Sallapa* near or along the *Astarpa* river at one time belonged to *Arzawa*, as argued here, and at another time fell directly under Hittite command. In any case, *Wiyanawanda*, corresponding to Classical *Oinoanda*, which lies at the upper course of the *Xanthos* river or Hittite *Siyanta*, is reported to be a border town of the country *Mira*, so that the latter, at least at the time from which the text in question originates, bordered in the south on *Lukka* or *Lycia*, beyond the region of *Sallapa* and *Ḫuwalusiya*.[39] In the coastal region *Millawanda* no doubt of origin also belonged to *Arzawa* or *Mira*, but it was subsequently lost. Indeed, from the Middle Bronze Age up to an advanced stage in the Late Bronze Age (*c.* 1450 BC) *Millawanda* or *Miletos* belonged to the Minoan sphere of influence, and after this time, up to an advanced stage in the reign of the Hittite great king Tudḫaliyas IV, it constituted a foothold of *Aḫḫiyawa* or the Mycenaean Greeks in Asia Minor (Niemeier 2007a: 18).

According to the evidence of the Milawata-letter as I understand it the Hittite great king Tudḫaliyas IV handed over hostages from *Pina* and *Awarna* to the father of the recipient of the letter, presumably the governor of *Millawanda*, who himself failed to fulfill his promise to hand over hostages from *Atriya* and *Utima* in return, and not *vice versa* (Woudhuizen 2005a: 115). The rationale behind this all is self-evident: Tudḫaliyas IV had just conquered the Xanthos valley in Lycia, as recorded in the Yalburt text, so that handing over hostages from locations in this region (*Pinara* and *Tlōs*) did not harm him much politically, whereas *Atriya* and *Utima* in accordance with their identification

[36] Bryce 2010: 149.
[37] Bryce 2010: 232.
[38] Pauly-Wissowa Realencyclopädie, s.v. and cf. the map in Zgusta 1984: no. 67.
[39] Bryce 2010: 475, note 47.

with *Idrias* and *Idyma* may reasonably be argued to be border towns of Millawanda (so also Freu 2010: 135), so that the political costs for the ruler of Millawanda were also minimal (though still more painful than Tudḫaliyas IV's 'cigar from another man's box').

The identification of Atriya and Utima as border towns of Millawanda may receive further emphasis from the fact that in the Yalburt text the conquest of the Xanthos valley, which Tudḫaliyas IV proudly proclaims to be an accomplishment which his forefathers did not achieve, is preceded by a campaign in the valley of the Indus river. In this latter region, which is specified as being *re*conquered and therefore must be assumed to be already an integral part of the Hittite empire, are situated the places *Luwata* (note that the preceding *ḫwaḫwa* is not part of this toponym, but an indefinite form of the relative also present in Köylütolu § 7: *ḫwā ḫwā tìtarma*^{UMINA} 'whatever (belongs to) Attarim(m)ma') and *Kwalatarna*,[40] which can positively be identified with Classical *Loanda* and Lycian *Xbide* 'Kaunos' (see Woudhuizen 2004a: 27-31). If we realise, then, that Classical Kaunos borders on Classical Idyma, it necessarily follows that already early in the reign of Tudḫaliyas IV the Hittite empire effectively shared a border with the territory of Millawanda in this southern corner of western Asia Minor.

The route description in the Tawagalawas-letter is, within the frame of the current identifications, highly plausible. The Hittite king first heads for *Sallapa*, the military head quarters for campaigns in the west likely to be situated in the region of Laodikeia near *Salbacus Mons*. Then he goes to *Waliwanda* or *Alabanda* along the lower Marsyas river, and subsequently penetrates into enemy territory by marching on *Iyalanda*, situated west of the Marsyas river if identical with *Alinda*. Next, the Hittite king addresses centers of resistance along the upper *Marsyas*, southeast of *Iyalanda*, namely *Atriya* or *Idrias*, situated at Classical Stratonikeia, the fortress of which he does not succeed in destroying, and *Aba[wiya]*, a region which, concerning the fact that its name is based on PIE **h*$_2$*eb*$^{(h)}$- 'river' (Woudhuizen 2016a: 66),[41] is likely named after the river it is associated with (cf. Freu 2008a: 113). No doubt, his intentions were to prevent an attack in his back when proceeding to Millawanda. After this interlude, then, the Hittite king goes on to *Millawanda* or *Miletos* along the Aegean coast.

Now, if we are right in our reconstruction of the geography of western Anatolia as set out in the above, Trevor R. Bryce, in his recent contribution to the *Oxford Handbook of Ancient Anatolia*, is entirely mistaken in his statement that 'Wiluša (in form of Wilušiya) is the only 'Arzawa land' to appear in a list of twenty-two countries forming what is commonly known as the Aššuwian Confederacy'.[42] Firstly, the leader of the Assuwian

---

[40] Note that this place-name, against the backdrop of the lenition [k] > [ḫ], is analyzable as a compound of Luwian *ku(wa)lana-* 'army' with *tarna-* 'camp'; for the second element, cf. the Lydian TN *Tarnē* and Lycian *tere-* or *τere-*.

[41] For other 'Old Indo-European' or 'proto-Celtic' toponyms in the region, cf. *Parḫa*, which is a lenited (*[ĝ^h] > [ḫ]) variant of Hittite *parku-* 'high' < PIE *b*^{h}*r̥ĝ*^{h}*(i)-*, *Ḫursanassa*, which is a lenited ([g^h] > [ḫ]) and assibilated ([t] > [s]) variant of *Gurtanassa* < PIE **g*^{h}*ord*^{h}- as recorded for the province of Tarḫuntassa, and *Seḫa* < PIE **seik*^{w}- also by means of lenition of *[k] into [ḫ] (see Whatmough 1963: 68 in connection with the Celtic river name *Sequana* 'Seine'). See further Chapter 10.

[42] Bryce 2011: 366.

Fig. 5. Map of western Anatolia (see Table V; design Clio Stronk).

Fig. 6. Geography of the Hittite empire (design Eberhard Zangger).

League, *Piyamakuruntas*,[43] bears a name typical of the royal house of Arzawa as it is paralleled for a son of its king Uḫḫazitis during the reigns of the Hittite great kings Suppiuliumas I (1350-1322 BC) and his son and successor, Mursilis II.[44] To this comes that in the enumeration of the towns and places which were involved in the Assuwian League,[45] which starts with *[L]uqqa* or *Lycia* in the south and ends with *Wilusiya* or *Ilion* and *Taruisa* or *Troia* in the north, feature at least four place-names which we have shown in the above to belong to the realm of *Arzawa*, namely: *Dura* = *Tyrrha*, *Ḫalluwa* = *Koloē*, *Ḫuwalusiya* = *Kolossai*, and *Kurupiya* = Mt. *Koruphē*. In line with our analysis of the name of the leader of the Assuwian League, *Arzawa* can therefore positively be identified as the *core region* of the coalition in question instead of being absent!

Considering the fact that the Assuwian League encompasses the entire region of western Anatolia, from *Lukka* in the south to *Wilusiya* and *Taruisa* in the north, it strikingly recalls the catalogue of the Trojan forces as enumerated in Homeros' *Iliad* II, 816-877, which conversely starts with the Trojans and ends with the Lycians. But, the Trojan War can be dated to *c.* 1280 BC,[46] and therefore belongs to an entirely different historical period as the Assuwian League, which first turns up in form of *'Isy* in the Egyptian records from the years 34 and 38-39 of the reign pharaoh Tuthmosis III (1479-1425 BC), so 1445 BC and 1441-1440 BC in terms of absolute chronology,[47] and was defeated by the Hittite great king Tudḫaliyas II (1425-1390 BC)[48] presumably in beginning of his reign.[49] It deserves our attention in this connection that the rise of the Assuwian League coincides with the fall of the Minoan maritime empire after the for northeastern Crete disastrous Santorini-eruption, now positively datable to the end of Late Minoan IB, which means *c.* 1450 BC in absolute chronological terms.[50] At any rate, against the backdrop of the fact that the name Assuwa is probably related with the 'Asian field' (Homeros, *Iliad* II, 461: Ἀσίῳ ἐν λειμῶνι) in the neighbourhood of Ephesos, it should not really surprise us that the king of Assuwa is associated with *gursawara* 'islands' in the Aegean (KUB 26.91) and even with *Kftiw* 'Crete' (in the poetic stele of Tuthmosis III, see Vercoutter 1956: 87).

In form of *á-su-wi(-ya)* the name of the coalition is recorded for various seals. In the first place, it is secondarily inscribed on the stamp side of cylinder seal Louvre AO 20.138, catalogued by Clelia Mora (1987) as her number 1.3 of group Ia, which originally presumably belonged to a Luwian great king ruling in western Anatolia sometime during the Middle Bronze Age. Furthermore, it turns up at the stamp side of a cylinder seal from Aydin (Louvre AO 1180), catalogued by Mora 1987 as her number 1.2 of group Ia.[51] Finally, if it may be assumed that the sign *370 *su* at the front side of the seal belongs to the legend at its back, the geographic name *á-su-wi(-ya)* also features on the

[43] Bryce 2010: 126.
[44] Bryce 2010: 194.
[45] Garstang & Gurney 1959: 121-122; Bryce 2010: 124-125.
[46] Woudhuizen in van Binsbergen & Woudhuizen 2011: 249-250.
[47] Woudhuizen 2004b: 115; Woudhuizen in van Binsbergen & Woudhuizen 2011: 247-248.
[48] For the distinction between Tudḫaliyas I and Tudḫaliyas II, and the datings of these great kings, see Freu 2007: 211.
[49] Woudhuizen in van Binsbergen & Woudhuizen 2011: 326, note ad p. 248.
[50] Woudhuizen 2016: 126-132.
[51] Woudhuizen 2006-7; Woudhuizen 2011: 83. See chapter 4 below.

seal of a certain king *Kuruntas* as discovered in Alacahöyük within the Halys bend (i.e. in the nuclear zone of the Hittite empire).[52] As I have argued in my book on Luwian hieroglyphic of 2011, the name of the royal owner of the seal, *Kuruntas*, is probably a shorthand version of *Piyamakuruntas*, and we are actually dealing here with the seal of the leader of the Assuwian League as recorded in the annals of the Hittite great king Tudḫaliyas II.[53] No doubt, the find spot of the seal can be explained by the fact that this king had a diplomatic and/or commercial representative or seal-bearer stationed in the Hittite heartland or, more simply, because, after his defeat, the king and his entire entourage with 600 charioteers and 10,000 men infantry had been transported to Ḫatti-land.[54]

In any case, one thing is clear: in the period of the Assuwian League the regional name *Assuwa* was used as a blanket term for a short-lived coalition of forces headed by the royal house of *Arzawa*—an observation which happens to coincide with the fact that its name is probably related to the Homeric *Asios leimōn* 'Asian field' in the neighbourhood of capital of *Arzawa*, viz. *Apasa* 'Ephesos' (see above). Whatever the specifics, the name did clinch to the region in the minds of the Greeks, as shown by the ethnic *a-si-wi-jo* (m) in the Knossos tablets (KN Df 1469), dated *c.* 1350 BC, and *a-si-wi-ja* (f) as well as *a-si-wi-jo* (m) in various tablets from Pylos and Mycenae, dating from the destruction level of *c.* 1200 BC,[55] and the name of the country and later continent *Asia* in Classical Greek and Roman sources.

[52] Mora 1987: XIIb, 1.1. See our Fig. 11.
[53] Woudhuizen 2011: 88.
[54] Bryce 2010: 124-126.
[55] Ventris & Chadwick 1973: glossary, s.v.

3. Origin of the Luwian Hieroglyphic Script[1]

3.1 Introduction

In connection with the origin of the Luwian hieroglyphic (= LH) script, it has been suggested by Clelia Mora (1991: 20, note 21; 1994) and, in a somewhat less pertinent manner, by Isabella Klock-Fontanille (2007: 8) that the earliest hieroglyphic inscription bearing testimony of signs expressing syllabic values is that of *sà-tà-tu-ḫa-pa* on a sealing from Maşat-höyük, which renders the name of the consort of Tudḫaliyas III (1370-1350 BC). However, this view, which most recently found support from the side of Ilya Yakubovich (2010: 285-99), who explicitly situates the formation of the Luwian hieroglyphic script in the mixed Hittite-Luwian milieu at Boğazköy-Ḫattusa at the time, is in reality eccentric. John David Hawkins in his corpus (2000: 3) adheres to the old view of Emmanuel Laroche and others that the seal of Isputaḫsus, king of Kizzuwatna and contemporary of the Hittite king Telipinus (1525-1500 BC), provides the earliest evidence of the script. To this comes that already before the appearance of the corpus, Jutta Börker-Klähn (1995) had pointed to the Old Kingdom sealing of Ḫattusilis I (1650-1620 BC), in which the latter's name is rendered in abbreviation by a ligature of the signs LH 196 *ḫá* and LH 278 *li*, which therefore patently render a syllabic value at this early time. Some years earlier, again, Rainer Michael Boehmer and Hans Gustav Güterbock (1987: 38-40; Abb. 26a) even went as far as to consider the Indilima seal, attributed to Tarsos and dating to the same period as Tell Atchana-Alalaḫ VII (1720-1650 BC), as the earliest attestation of the script. In this sealing we do not only come across the Luwian hieroglyphic signs LH 369 ***vita*** and LH 370 ASU, which are often discarded as mere symbols, but also the titular expression (written in ligature to be read from bottom to top) LH 398 + LH 14 *ta?*+PÁRANA 'tabarnas' *written out phonetically*.[2] Most recently the tendency to attribute an earlier date to the formation of the Luwian hieroglyphic script seems to be reinforced by the publication of an inscribed vessel from Kültepe-Kanesh by John David Hawkins (2011),[3] which firmly dates to the period of *c.* 1920-1750 BC, but of which it is still considered questionable by the author whether the signs in question indeed represent equivalents from the Luwian hieroglyphic repertory.

What everybody seems to have missed so far is that Luwian hieroglyphic legends can also be traced for, amongst others, the stamp seal from Beycesultan, dating from the Early Bronze Age (= EBA) III/Middle Bronze Age (= MBA) transitional period, *c.* 2000 BC (Woudhuizen 2011: 464-467; Woudhuizen 2012b; cf. Mora 1987: XIIb 3.3), for the stamp seal in the form of a foot discovered by a farmer in the region of Nevşehir, which owing to its form is dateable to the first quarter of the 2nd millennium BC (Erdem 1969: 114-115;

[1] An earlier draft of this section was presented as a paper at the IXth international congress of Hittitology, held at Çorum in 2014, and will appear in its proceedings.
[2] Note that sign LH 398 is a variant of the horizontal stroke for the number '10' (LH 397) of which the value *ta?* acrophonically derives from PIE **dék̂m̥t-*, represented during the Early Iron Age by *tinata/i-* or *tiniti-* 'tithe' (Çiftlik § 13; Sultanhan § 28; Boybeypınarı § 3, see Woudhuizen 2015a).
[3] My thanks are due to Willemijn Waal for kindly drawing my attention to this publication.

Taf. IVb; cf. Mora 1987: XIIb 3.9),[4] for the stamp-cylinder seal Louvre 20.138, originating from the region of the later kingdom of Arzawa and (if we disregard for a moment its later reuse) also datable to the period of Tell Atchana-Alalaḫ VII (Woudhuizen 2006-7), as well as for seals from Henri Frankfort's First Syrian Group, dating *c.* 2000-1700 BC (Woudhuizen 2005b). All these latter examples date from the period *before* the founding of the Hittite Old Kingdom, which means in the Middle Bronze Age,[5] and in this manner exclude the possibility of the formation of the Luwian hieroglyphic script in the mixed Hittite-Luwian milieu at the Hittite capital Boğazköy-Ḫattusa as envisaged, as we have noted in the above, by Yakubovich and others.

3.2 Catalogue of the Middle Bronze Age Luwian Hieroglyphic Inscriptions

	object class
A. **EBA III/MBA transitional period (c. 2000 BC)**	
1. stamp seal Beycesultan[6]	seal
mi+ra ḪAPA *i -ḫa* UMINA *1000* ^{mm}	
'Mira: (with respect to) the river and this town (overseer of) 1000 men'	
B. **Kültepe-Kanesh phases II-Ib (c. 1920-1750 BC)**	
2. grafitto Kültepe-Kanesh[7]	vase
ta_4*-sá-lí* 'Tasalis'	
3. Kültepe-Kanesh no. 2[8]	sealing
ti_5-ti_5*-sà-ú-na* '(MN)'	
4. Kültepe-Kanesh no. 73[9]	sealing
TAPAR*-sà* MUWA-WALWA 'governor Muwawalwas'	

[4] My thanks are due, again, to Willemijn Waal for kindly drawing my attention to this seal.
[5] The situation concerning the beginning of the Late Bronze Age in the Near East and Anatolia is variously judged in the relevant literature, with dates varying as widely as between *c.* 1750 BC to *c.* 1600 BC. In this chapter I favor the opinion that the Late Bronze Age period starts after the period of Tell Atchana-Alalaḫ VII (1720-1650 BC), with the ascent of Ḫattusilis I (1650-1620 BC) to the Hittite throne, i.e. from *c.* 1650 BC onwards. As such, the reign of Labarnas I (1670-1650 BC), the predecessor of Ḫattusilis I and founder of the dynasty, strictly speaking still belongs to the Middle Bronze Age.
[6] Mora 1987: XIIb 3.3; Woudhuizen 2012b with refs. to which should be added Güterbock in Mellaart & Murray 1995: 119, who, given its early dating, is skeptical about the presence of Luwian hieroglyphic signs on this seal, and the photograph (Pl. XIII(a)) and highly impressionistic drawing (Fig. O.12) in this work.
[7] Hawkins 2011.
[8] Garelli & Collon 1975: 30; Pl. 48.
[9] Matouš & Matoušová-Rajmová 1984.

5. Kültepe-Kanesh, Walters Art Gallery 48.1464[10] sealing

ARA-WALWA PIA ***vita*** 'Arawalwas, given life'

6. stamp seal Nevşehir[11] seal

ARMA-na-ti-à 'Armantis'

7. Acemhöyük III-17[12] sealing

ÁMU MUWA-WALWA 'I (am) Muwawalwas'

8. Konya no. 4[13] seal

ARA-TARKU PIA 'Aratarkus has given'

9. Konya no. 5[14] seal

sol suus *TARKU-TAPAR* 'his majesty Tarkutaparas'

10. Klavdia[15] seal

aper$_2$*-sà TAPAR-sà sà-ti*$_5$*-TAPAR* 'Eburosos, governor (of) Santitaparas'

11. Gaza[16] seal

TAPAR-sà 'governor'

12. Erlenmeyers' seal[17] seal

ú-na-ra-á TARKU-ara-MUWA-á TAPAR-sà PIA

'Tarkunaramuwas, governor (of) Unaras, has given'

13. Hogarth no. 154[18] seal

á+tì-ná TAPAR-sà TARKU-ti$_5$*-mu-wa*$_8$ *PIA-á*

---

[10] Canby 1975. Surfaced on the market in Kayseri, but no doubt actually originating from Kültepe-Kanesh where it may reasonably be argued to have come to light in the course of illegal diggings. However this may be, it seems most likely to be attributed to phase Ib (so Canby), see Woudhuizen 2011: 76.

[11] Mora 1987: XIIb 3.9.

[12] Özgüç 1980: 82.

[13] Alp 1968: 115; Taf. 11, 21.

[14] Alp 1968: 116; Taf. 11, 22.

[15] Kenna 1972: Fig. 79, 3a.

[16] Flinders Petrie 1933: 4; Pl. III, 37. As observed by Flinders Petrie 1933: 4 the hare sign on top of the cartouche 'blundered from that of Amenemhat II or Senusert III' replaces the expression *sꜣ Rꜣ* 'son (of) Re' and may therefore reasonably be assumed to be part of a titular expression—viz. the one expressed by hare with antelope, the latter sign being added to the left of the hare.

[17] Erlenmeyer & Erlenmeyer 1965: 2-3, Abb. 5.

[18] Hogarth 1920: 34; Pl. VI. According to Hogarth 1920: 34 bought at Beirut.

'Athena(ios), governor (of) Tarkundimuwas, has given'

C. Tell Atchana-Alalaḫ VII (c. 1720-1650 BC)

14. Tell Atchana-Alalaḫ no. 154[19] sealing
TARKU-WALWA TAPAR<-na> á-mu-sà-mi$_4$
'Tarkuwalwas, governor of Ammusama'

15. Eskiyapar[20] sealing
kà-su USA *ḫa*$_4$*-mu-ra* 'year-lord Ḫamuras'

16. Tarsos, Indilima seal[21] seal
ta?+ PÁRANA ***vita*** *ASU* 'governor, life (and) health'

17. Aydin, Louvre AO 20.138: cylinder side[22] seal
ÁMU TARKU-KURUNT 'I (am) Tarku(ku)runtas'

18. Tyszkiewicz seal[23] seal
(pseudo-hieroglyphs) **148-ZITI* '(MN)'

3.3 Middle Bronze Age Luwian Hieroglyphic Signary

1.	LH 14	*PÁRANA*
2.	LH 15	***domina***; *mi*$_4$
3.	LH 19	*ÁMU*, *á*
4.	LH 35	***navis***, *na*
5.	LH 56	*KATA*, *kà*
6.	LH 60	*TIWA*, *ti*; *PATA*
7.	LH 66	*PIA*, *pi*; *ár*
8.	LH 97	*WALWA*, *wal*, *ú*

[19] Colon 1975: 84-85.
[20] Mora 1990: IIb 2.9.
[21] Boehmer & Güterbock 1987: 40, Abb. 26a. Seal acquired in Cilicia, but attributable to the capital Tarsos on account of the fact that the owner in the cuneiform legend stages himself as a servant of the goddess *Isḫara*, of whom a cult centre is reported for the nearby mount *Isḫara*, see Haider 2006. On the origin of this seal, see now addendum below.
[22] Mora 1987: Ia 1.3; Woudhuizen 2006-7: 129. Seal of unknown origin, but likely to have surfaced on the market in Aydin as its stamp side is inscribed with the legend *á-su-wi* 'Assuwiya' in like manner as another seal from Aydin, Louvre AO 1180 (= Mora 1987: Ia 1.2), see Woudhuizen 2006-7: 125. But note that the inscription on the stamp side is secondarily added no doubt during the latter half of the 15th century BC.
[23] Boehmer & Güterbock 1987: 38, Abb. 24.

9.	LH 100	TARKASNA, *ta*$_4$
10.	LH 101	TARKU
11.	LH 102-3	KURUNT, KARUWANT, *kar*; RU(WA)NT, *rú*; INARA
12.	LH 104	SÁSA, *sà*
13.	LH 107	MUWA (*m*+UWA), *mu*
14.	LH 111	ḪAWA, *ḫa*$_4$
15.	LH 115	TAPAR, *tà*
16.	LH 125	*lí*
17.	LH 128	**tintapu-*, *ti*$_5$; ZINZAPU, *zì*; *i*$_5$
18.	LH 130-3	ARA, *ar*, *ra*
19.	LH 134	*ara*
20.	LH 138	*wa*$_8$
21.	LH 148	**148*
22.	LH 172	(+)*tì*
23.	LH 174	*sá*
24.	LH 190	***sol suus***
25.	LH 193	ARMA
26.	LH 199	TARḪUNT; TÉSUP; *ḫà*[24]
27.	LH 212	ḪAPA; NAḪAR, *ná*
28.	LH 215	LULIA; *ḫa*
29.	LH 225	UMINA, *um*
30.	LH 312	ZITI, *zí*
31.	LH 336	USA; *i*$_4$
32.	LH 369	***vita***; WÀSU, *was*, *wa*$_{12}$
33.	LH 370	ASU, *[as]*, *su*
34.	LH 376	*i*; *zi* (LBA: also *za*)
35.	LH 383, 2	*[+ti]*, *+r*, *+ra*, *+ri*
36.	LH 386, 1	^{m} (LBA)
37.	LH 391	*m*, *má*, *mi*
38.	LH 397-8	**déḱm̥t-*, *ta?*
39.	LH 400	'1000'
40.	LH 450	*à*
41.	LH 529	***aper***$_2$

[24] Alp 1968: 214, nos. 191-192.

3.4 In Search of the Cradle of the Luwian Hieroglyphic Script

From a chronological point of view it is of relevance to note that the titular expression *taparsa-* typical of the Kültepe-Kanesh phases II and Ib is replaced by *taparna-* in the subsequent period of Tell Atchana-Alalaḫ VII. Similarly, the wish- or transaction-formula PIA ***vita***, formed after the example of Egyptian *dỉ ʿnḫ* 'given life', is a typical feature of the Kültepe-Kanesh periods II and Ib, whereas it is replaced during the period of Tell Atchana-Alalaḫ VII by a 'more modern' variant of the wish-formula, ***vita*** ASU (see Table VI).

date	title	greeting formula
Kültepe-Kanesh c. 1920-1750 BC	*TAPAR-sà* *Labarša*	PIA(*-á*) ***vita***
Tell Atchana-Alalaḫ VII c. 1720-1650 BC	*tá?-* PÁRANA *Labarnaš*	***vita*** & ASU

Table VI. Overview of the dating criteria for Middle Bronze Age Luwian hieroglyphic seals or sealings.

As far as typology is concerned, we can distinguish two distinct types of legends, one characterised by the use of the Luwian pronoun of the first person singular *amu* 'I' in combination with a personal name (Acemhöyük III-17 and Louvre AO 20.138) and the other by the sequence of personal name with title followed by the personal name of the latter's superior without title (Klavdia, Erlenmeyers' seal, Hogarth no. 154, and Tell Atchana-Alalaḫ no. 154). Both these types are represented in our periods B (Kültepe-Kanesh phases II and Ib) and C (Tell Atchana-Alalaḫ VII).

If the distinction between seal and sealing indeed informs us in the first instance about the region of origin of the owner of the seal and in the latter instance about contacts of the owner of the seal with distant regions resulting from trade or diplomatic relations, we may reasonably infer from the distribution of these two categories that the Luwian hieroglyphic script originates in western Anatolia, where it is evidenced exclusively by seals, whereas in central Anatolia this particular script, apart from one graffito on a vase from Kültepe-Kanesh, is primarily represented by sealings (see Fig. 7). This particular inference can even be further underlined by the fact that the sealings Kültepe-Kanesh no. 73 and Acemhöyük III-17 bear testimony of the personal name *Muwawalwas*, which corresponds to that of the founding father of the royal dynasty of Seḫa, *Muwawalwis*, so that we may well be dealing here with evidence for trade or diplomatic contacts of a dignitary living in the western country Seḫa with counterparts stationed in the trading centers of Acemhöyük and Kültepe-Kanesh in central Anatolia. In any case, it is clear that in the Kültepe-Kanesh texts with a bearing on the indigenous Anatolian population Hittite personal names are much more frequent than Luwian ones (Yakubovich 2010: 221).

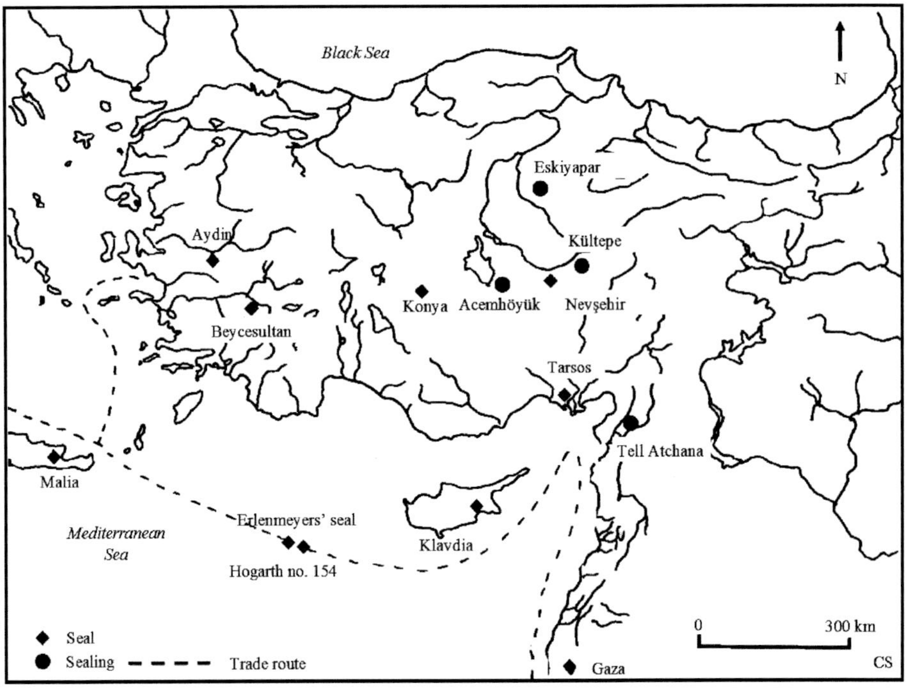

Fig. 7. Distribution of Middle Bronze Age Luwian hieroglyphic seals and sealings (design Clio Stronk).

And, for the very existence of these texts, the Hittites in question already had a vehicle to become literate at their disposal, namely the Assyrian cuneiform introduced by the traders from Assyria living in the Karum. As far as the evidence goes, the Assyrian cuneiform did not spread all the way to western Anatolia, so the Luwian population groups living there had an incentive to device their own script when getting into trade or diplomatic contacts with their already literate eastern neighbours.

But trade or diplomatic contacts were not confined to the routes overland between western and central Anatolia, such contacts also entailed routes overseas from western Anatolia via Crete and Cyprus to the Levant. It deserves attention in this connection that cylinder seals were an entry ticket into Near Eastern trade, and that the seals and sealing with a bearing on overseas trade are of this type. Now, the legend of the seals and sealing in question happen to be of the type characterised by the sequence of personal name with title mostly followed by the personal name of the latter's superior without title. In the case of the sealing from Tell Atchana-Alalaḫ (no. 154) it may, in line with our observation concerning the name Muwawalwas in the above, be argued that the owner of the seal, *Tarkuwalwas* (see Fig. 8), originates from Arzawa in western Anatolia as his name is most closely paralleled by that of a great king of the latter country as attested in lenited variant form as *Tarḫu(ndi)walwas* for a Luwian hieroglyphic seal from Thebes in Greece (see section 4.3 below).

A similar argument may also be employed in the case of the Erlenmeyers' seal and seal Hogarth no. 154 (reported to have been bought at Beirut, see note 18 above) of unknown origin but ascribed to Henri Frankfort's First Syrian Group for stylistic reasons, which are both characterised by slightly varying writing variants (one being characterised by rhotacism of the dental, which therefore represents the voiced [d] otherwise not distinguished in the script) of the same personal name, *Tarkundimuwas* (see Figs. 9-10).

TARKU-WALWA TAPAR<-na> á-mu-sà-mi$_4$
'Tarkuwalwas, governor of Ammusama'

Fig. 8. Sealing Tell-Atchana-Alalaḫ no. 154 (Collon 1975: 84-85).

ú-na-ra-á TARKU-ara-MUWA-á TAPAR-sà PIA
'Tarkunaramuwas, governor (of) Unaras, (has) give(n)'

Fig. 9. Erlenmeyers' seal (Erlenmeyer 1965: Abb. 5).

á+tì-ná TAPAR-*sà* TARKU-*ti*$_5$-*mu-wa*$_8$ PIA-*á*
'Atinas, governor (of) Tarkundimuwas, (has) give(n)'

Fig. 10. Seal Hogarth no. 154 (Hogarth 1920: 34; Pl. VI).

Now, in lenited variant form this latter name corresponds to that of a great king of Arzawa, *Tarḫu(ndi)muwas*, also attested for the aforesaid Luwian hieroglyphic seal from Thebes in Greece, whereas in shorthand variant *Tarkuwas* (< **Tarku[ndimu]was*) it is well known from the 'Tarkondemos' seal, the rock relief at Karabel, and sealings from Boğazköy as the name of one of the last kings of Mira.

	MN	ranking	seal
1.	*Unaras*	superior of *Tarkunaramuwas*	Erlenmeyers' seal
2a.	*Tarkunaramuwas*	inferior of *Unaras*	Erlenmeyers' seal
2b.	*Tarkundimuwas*	superior of *Atinas*	Hogarth no. 154
3.	*Atinas*	inferior of *Tarkundimuwas*	Hogarth no. 154

Table VII. Analysis of the legends of the Erlenmeyers' seal and seal Hogarth no. 154 from Henri Frankfort's First Syrian Group.

Close analysis of the aforesaid Middle Bronze Age seals (see Table VII) allows for the conclusion that Tarkundimuwas was a subordinate of Unaras, no doubt a dignitary stationed somewhere in the Levant, but the superior of a certain *Atinas*, whose name may be analyzed as a reflex of Greek Ἀθηνα(ῖος). But what is even more, the name of our 'middlemen' Tarkundimuwas is also attested for a Cretan hieroglyphic seal from Malia belonging to the earliest group of seals conducted in this form of writing dating to the Middle Bronze Age (Detournay, Poursat & Vandenabeele 1980: 160, Fig. 231; see Fig. 2 above). Against this backdrop, then, it may reasonably be argued that the dignitary

Tarkundimuwas, who is at home in Arzawa, had a trading station at Malia to facilitate his overseas contacts with the Levant. His henchman Atinas, if indeed a reflex of Greek Ἀθηνα(ῖος), may in that case reasonably be assumed to originate from Athens and to be involved in the transport of metal ores from the mines of Laurion in Attica, which according to Philip Betancourt were already exploited for the Cretan market from the Early Minoan III/Middle Minoan I transitional period onwards (see Betancourt 2008: 212; 214). Finally, the fact that the seal from Klavdia in Cyprus (see Fig. 3 above) as far as its contents is concerned belongs to the same type as the ones discussed in this paragraph strongly enhances our attribution of them to overseas trade between the Aegean via Crete and Cyprus to the Levant. It comes as no surprise, therefore, that our interpretation of the earliest set of seals characterised by the personal name Tarkundimuwas strikingly coincides with information from the Mari tablets dated to the reign of Zimrilim during the first half of the 18th century BC according to which, in tablet A 1270, line 28 (*a-na Kap-ta-ra-i-im* 'to the Cretan') a Cretan is staged as a participant in the tin-trade (AN.NA = *anaku-* 'tin') (Dossin 1970: 99; Bardet *e.a.* 1984: 229). As the transaction entails the mediation of an interpreter, and is explicitly stated to have taken place at Ugarit along the Levantine coast opposite to Cyprus, it may reasonably be suggested that the language of the Cretan in question was something other than Semitic (Woudhuizen 2009: 203 with note 2; Woudhuizen 2015b: 27). Although Cretan traders were involved in the international tin-trade during the Middle Bronze Age, it altogether possible that an Anatolian trader like Tarkundimuwas with a trading station in Crete was in fact identified in the Mari texts as a Cretan.

Ever since my work on the Erlenmeyers' seal and Hogarth no. 154 started in 1989, I have put forward various ideas as to come to grips with them. In first instance, I took the region of origin to which they are assigned, North Syria, as a starting point and suggested that these seals bear testimony of the fact that the region of North Syria forms an integral part of the cradle of the Luwian hieroglyphic script. Later on, the close relationship in form of the signary to counterparts in the earliest evidence of the Luwianizing Cretan hieroglyphic script encouraged me to suggest that we might be dealing here with evidence, not of Luwian hieroglyphic *per se*, but rather the related Cretan hieroglyphic (Woudhuizen 2009: 202). In the end, I countered this argument by the observation that the ductus of the signs forming the legends of the two seals is executed in an impeccably Luwian hieroglyphic style and definitely lacks the for the related Cretan hieroglyphic typical Luwianizing features (Woudhuizen 2011: 82, note 7). It deserves mention in this connection that the aforesaid Cretan hieroglyphic seal of Tarkundimuwas from Quartier Mu at Malia definitely shows Luwianizing features in the execution of the non-predatory bird LH 128 ti_5 on side 2 (it looks as if it has dropped dead) and that of the combination *m+UWA* on side 3, with the four strokes on top of the bull's head instead of on its cheek as in case of LH 107. The same verdict also applies to the seal from Klavdia in Cyprus, of which the Luwoid nature of its legend is deducible from the fact that the boar sign LH 529 ***aper***$_2$ is represented by a porcupine.[25] The solution appears to be that the seals have been inscribed by a Luwian scribe from western Anatolia, where, as we have noted in

[25] Note that we may have here a personal name of Old Indo-European type based on the onomastic element *Eburo-*, cf. Woudhuizen 2018: 76-77, note 72.

the above, Tarkundimuwas is at home, who in turn may have facilitated in this matter his henchman Ἀθηνα(ῖος) from Attica, and that these seals were subsequently used in trade and diplomatic contacts with a counterpart in the Levant. This latter inference might explain the fact that the seals ended up in North Syria—if this attribution indeed applies (as in case of Hogarth no. 154 where it may be underlined by the fact that the seal has been bought in Beirut). This solution to the problem, then, is illustrated in our Fig. 7.

The seal from Gaza, which bears testimony of the titular expression *taparsa-* in an otherwise entirely Egyptian hieroglyphic legend, seems to indicate that the overseas trade route from western Anatolia to the Levant extended to the southern part of the latter region.

3.5 Overview of Luwian Hieroglyphic Inscriptions from, or Attributable to, Assuwa/Arzawa/Mira-Kuwaliya, Seḫa-Appawiya, and Ḫapalla

Along the foregoing line of reasoning that the distinction between seal and sealing indeed informs us in the first instance about the region of origin of the owner of the seal and in the latter instance about contacts of the owner of the seal with distant regions resulting from trade or diplomatic relations, then, we would arrive at the following overview of Luwian hieroglyphic inscriptions originating from or attributable to the western Anatolian countries Assuwa or Arzawa or Mira-Kuwaliya (by and large corresponding to later Lydia) and Seḫa-Appawiya (to be situated in the Kaikos valley and the upper Makestos region):

A. **EBA III/MBA transitional period (c. 2000 BC)**	
1. stamp seal from Beycesultan (*Mira*)[26]	seal
B. **Middle Bronze Age**	
2. Erlenmeyers' seal (*Tarkunaramuwas*)	seal
3. Hogarth no. 154 (*Tarkundimuwas*)	seal
4. Acemhöyük III-17 (*Muwawalwas*)[27]	sealing
5. Kültepe-Kanesh no. 73 (*Muwawalwas*)[28]	sealing
6. Tell Atchana-Alalaḫ no. 154 (*Tarkuwalwas*)[29]	sealing
7. seal side Louvre AO 20.138 (*Tarku(ku)runtas*)[30]	seal
C. **Late 15th/early 14th century BC**	
8. Alacahöyük (*[Piyama]kuruntas of Assuwiya*)[31]	seal

[26] Mora 1987: XIIb 3.3.
[27] Özgüç 1980: 82.
[28] Matouš & Matoušová-Rajmová 1984.
[29] Collon 1975: 84-85.
[30] Mora 1987: Ia 1.3.
[31] Mora 1987: XIIb 1.1. Note that king Piyamakuruntas of Assuwa, after his defeat by the Hittite great king Tudḫaliyas II (1425-1390 BC), had been deported to Ḫatti-land, which explains the fact that his seal came to

9. stamp side Louvre AO 20.138 (*Assuwiya*)[32]	seal
10. stamp side Aydin (*Assuwiya*)[33]	seal
11. Thebes no. 25 (*Tarḫuntmuwas/Tarḫuntwalwas*)[34]	seal
12. Aydin (*URA+ḪANTAWAT* 'great king'; *á+sa*$_4^{UMINA}$ 'Assuwa')[35]	seal
13. Schimmel rhyton (*á+sa*$_4^{UTNA}$ 'Assuwa')[36]	rhyton
D. **Late 14th and 13th century BC**	
14. Ortakaraviran Höyük (prince *Masḫuiluwas*)[37]	sealing
15. Beyköy 1 (*tuḫkanti Urḫitesup*'s campaign in Ḫapalla)[38]	stone inscr.
16. 'Tarkondemos' seal (king *Tarku[ndimu]was* of *Mira*)[39]	seal
17. Karabel (king *Tarku[ndimu]was* of *Mira*, son of *Alantallis*)[40]	rock inscr.
18. Torbalı (apodosis of damnation-formula)[41]	stele/orthost.
19. Akpinar (palace official)[42]	rock inscr.
20. Latmos 1 (great prince with *Kupanta*-name)[43]	rock inscr.
21. Latmos 5 (official of *Mira*)[44]	rock inscr.
22. Latmos 2 (approval by a prince *Laḫas*)[45]	rock inscr.
23. Çivril (scribe of the god of the field)[46]	potsherd
24. Beyköy 3-4 (prince *Masḫuittas*, son of great king *Alantallis*)[47]	rock inscr.
25. Kocaoğuz-Afyon (prince *Tarpamaliawatas* of *Kuwaliya*)[48]	stele

light in Alacahöyük within the Halys bend.

[32] Mora 1987: Ia 1.3.

[33] Mora 1987: Ia 1.2; Alexander 1973-6: Pl. I, fig. 2b; Woudhuizen 2006-7.

[34] Mora 1987: IX 5.9; Porada 1981-2: 47; Güterbock 1981-2: 71-72; Woudhuizen 2009: 204-212.

[35] Mora 1987: IIIb 2.1. For the origin of this seal, see Hogarth 1920: 75 ad Fig. 79: 'Said to be first seen at Aidin in Lydia'; cf. Bossert 1942: 64 ad nos. 679-680: 'angeblich aus Lydien'. In view of this origin, the combination *á+sa*$_4^{UMINA}$ in the outer ring (anticlockwise nr. 12) more likely renders the geographic name *Assuwa* than that of *Isuwa* as suggested by Hawkins 1998a: 288. Note in this connection that Poetto & Bolatti 1994 take the variant in question of LH 402-3 for a separate sign, different from the one used in identical position in the country-name Isuwa, on account of the fact that the decoration inside the circle happens to be different.

[36] Woudhuizen 2013b.

[37] Mellaart 1954: 239-240; Mellaart 1959, 32, Fig. 1.

[38] See section 5.3 below.

[39] Mora 1987: VIII 3.1. The reading of the final sign of this personal name is assured since Herbordt 2005 as I acknowledged in Woudhuizen 2004-5: 171. Note that the first sign of this name is that of the goat head (LH 101), and not that of the donkey head (LH 100) as Hawkins and Herbordt want to have it, hence *Tarku[ndimu]was* instead of †*Tarkasnawas*.

[40] Hawkins 1998b: reconstruction of the genealogy of the king of Mira, *Tarku[ndimu]was*, presenting his father *Alantallis* and his grandfather *Kupantakuruntas*.

[41] Oreshko 2013: 384.

[42] Oreshko 2013: 368.

[43] Peschlow-Bindokat & Herbordt 2001.

[44] Peschlow-Bindokat & Herbordt 2001.

[45] Oreshko 2013: 347.

[46] Oreshko 2013: 371.

[47] Zangger & Woudhuizen 2018.

[48] Şahin & Tekoğlu 2003.

E. **Early 12th century BC**

26. Beyköy 2 (great king *Kupantakuruntas* of *Mira*, son of great king *Masḫuittas*)[49]	stone inscr.
27. Edremit (great prince *Muksas* of *Wilusa*)	stone inscr.
28. Yazılıtaş (great king *Walwamuwas* of *Seḫa*)	stone inscr.
29. Dağardı 2 (prince *Asaḫa[ ]s* of *Seḫa*, son of *Walwamuwas*)	stone inscr.
30. Dağardı 1 (prince *Masanatarḫunas* of *Masturiwanatasa*)	stone inscr.
31. Şahankaya (a.o. prince *Masanatarḫunas*)	stone inscr.

In his contribution of 2013 on Luwian hieroglyphic inscriptions from western Anatolia, Rostislav Oreshko argues against the view held by Yakubovich that the Luwian hieroglyphic script has been deviced in the capital of the Hittites, Boğazköy-Ḫattusa, in a mixed Hittite-Luwian milieu. On the contrary, he argues, the inscriptions bear testimony of a scribal tradition independent from that of the Hittite capital. It is true that the evidence he deals with dates from the period during which western Anatolia was incorporated into the Hittite empire and that as a result of numerous intermarriages between the local dynasties on the one hand and members of the Hittite royal family on the other hand the ruling elite in actual fact consisted of 'one big, happy Hittite family'. In this sense, the seals or sealings from the Hittite empire period found in western Anatolia are rightly ascribed in the literature to Hittite political influence and the same may well hold true of the rock inscription at Latmos near Miletos by a 'great prince' with a *Kupanta*-name characteristic of the royal house of Mira, the successor-state of Arzawa after its conquest by Mursilis II (1322-1295 BC) in the third and fourth year of his reign. There are indications, namely, that the most important vassal kings of the Hittite great king, those of Karkamis, Tarḫuntassa, and Mira, during the final stage of the Hittite empire rose to the preeminent status of great king—a prerequisite for our understanding of the fact that the local ruler of *Millawanda* or Miletos consisted of a 'great prince' of Mira. In any case, it seems, contrary to the opinion of Oreshko, highly likely that with the winged sun-disc at the start of the inscription from Afyon (Kocaoğuz) direct reference is made to the Hittite great king, presumably the last one, Suppiluliumas II (1205-1190 BC), as the publishers of this text, Seracettin Şahin and Recai Tekoğlu, maintain (cf. Woudhuizen 2013a: 9-12). As an alternative, it is also possible that with this sign reference is made to the great king of Mira-Kuwaliya, Kupantakuruntas III (see discussion of this text in chapter 5).

Nevertheless, Oreshko has a point in his assertion that the Luwian hieroglyphic inscriptions in western Anatolia bear the testimony of a local tradition in this class of writing. Furthermore, he presents readings of two phrases, one from the graffiti at Latmos near Miletos:

1.	*la-ḫa* ***infans***^{m}*+ḪANTAWAT* *à-wa -ma pu-pa-tá*	'prince Laḫas: I have approved (it) myself.'

[49] For this text and the following ones, see Zangger & Woudhuizen 2018.

and the other on the lower side of an orthostat or stele from Torbalı near İzmir:

1	*[à-wa] -tu* ^{MASANA}*TARḪUNT*	'Tarḫunt and queen Kubaba by
	$^{\text{[MASANA]}}$*ku<-pa-pa>* URA-***domina*** *-ḫa*	(decision) of all the gods
	^{KA}*MASANA-sa+ri ḪARSALA-li-sa-tu*	shall be angry with him!'[50]

which, in the light of the relevant parallels, are certainly conducted in the Luwian language. The question remains, however, where and when and by whom the Luwian hieroglyphic script was first deviced. In my opinion, this matter can only be decided on the basis of evidence, so far available, from western Anatolia of the Luwian hieroglyphic script dating from the period *before* the Hittite take-over and its incorporation into the Hittite empire. As a matter of fact, such evidence happens to be provided by glyptic material strangely enough entirely neglected by all participants in the discussion.[51]

In her contribution of 2013 on singers of *Lazpa* (= Lesbos), Anette Teffeteller is particularly interested in a Hittite cuneiform letter sent to the Hittite great king by his Akhaian or Mycenaean Greek colleague, KUB 26.91, in which the sender claims that the king of *Assuwa* on the occasion of a bond in marriage had granted to his ancestor certain islands—with which reference can only be made to islands in the Aegean. Now, Teffeteller assumes that the islands in the Aegean in question include *Lazpa* or Lesbos, because this north-Aegean island is situated directly opposite the coast of Assuwa, which is usually taken for a country separate from Arzawa and lying to the north of it. As we have seen in the preceding chapter, though, the province of Assuwa is not located in the Kaikos valley, but in the Hermos valley. Whatever the extent of the latter remark, it should be realized in this connection that in Egyptian texts dating from the years directly following the for northeastern Crete disastrous Santorini-eruption at the end of Late Minoan IB, *c.* 1450 BC, *i.c.* the annals of Tuthmosis III (1479-1425 BC) for the years 34 and 38-39, the Egyptian equivalent of Anatolian Assuwa, *'Isy*, occurs in association with *Keftiu*, the Egyptian name of Crete and that such associations in Egyptian texts in actual fact do reflect political realities. Furthermore, the Assuwian League is not a separate country, but a blanket term for a short-lived political coalition which was defeated by the Hittite great king Tudḫaliyas II (1425-1390 BC) sometime during the final stage of the 15th century BC and which was headed by a king, *Piyama-kuruntas*, who, owing to his name, may safely be identified as a member of the Arzawan royal house.[52] Finally, the name Assuwa itself cannot be dissociated from the Greek *Asios leimōn* 'Asian field' near Ephesos, as we have noted the capital of Arzawa. In short, the islands in the Aegean which the king of Assuwa had granted to the ancestor of the Akhaian sender of KUB 26.91 may, instead of Teffeteller's assumption that reference is made to those in the north-Aegean, with equal justice be assumed to have a bearing on those in the central and southern Aegean, up to and including Crete!

[50] Both phrases rendered here in my transliteration and translation.
[51] Yakubovich (2013: 117) even goes as far as to claim that 'The assumption that the hieroglyphic literacy in the Aegean area reflects 'the long arm o[f] the Empire' is based on the absence of hieroglyphic inscriptions in Arzawa in the period before its fall to the power of Hattusa.'
[52] Note that a son of *Uḫḫazitis*, the king of Arzawa during the reigns of Suppiluliumas I (1350-1322 BC) and Mursilis II (1322-1295 BC), bears the same name.

To return to our glyptic evidence from western Anatolia for Luwian hieroglyphic dating from the period *before* the Hittite take-over, it so happens that the seal of the Assuwian king Piyamakuruntas, who, after his defeat had been deported to Ḫatti-land, has actually been found in Alacahöyük, and that its legend in Luwian hieroglyphs reads as follows: *KURUNT ḪANTAWAT á-su-wi* '[Piyama]kuruntas, king (of) Assuwiya' (Mora 1987: XIIb 1.1; Woudhuizen 2011: 88; see Fig. 11). Alongside the evidence of this seal, mention should also be made of two seals of the stamp-cylinder type from the so-called Tyszkiewicz group, one from the Louvre in Paris (AO 20.138; Mora 1987: Ia 1.3) and the other also from the Louvre (AO 1180) but reported to have surfaced on the market in Aydin (Mora 1987: Ia 1.2), which are inscribed on the stamp side with the legend *á-su-wi* 'Assuwiya' and, as Arzawa formed the nucleus of the Assuwian League, therefore positively attributable to members of the Arzawan royal house (Woudhuizen 2006-7). Furthermore, it may be of relevance to note in this connection that yet another seal reported to have surfaced on the market in Aydin bears testimony of the title *URA+ḪANTAWAT* 'great king' and the geographic name *á+sa*$_4^{UMINA}$, which, given the context, may reasonably be argued to confront us with an alternative way of writing *Assuwa* (Mora 1987: IIIb 2.1; Woudhuizen 2013b: 335-6; see Fig. 19). However this may be, what primarily concerns us here is that the stamp-cylinder seal Louvre 20.138, apart from the legend on its stamp side, also contains a hieroglyphic inscription on its cylinder side which, in contrast to the one on the stamp side, is not added secondarily but forms part of the original design. It reads as follows: *ÁMU TARKU-KURUNT* 'I (am) Tarku(ku)runtas', and in this manner reveals to us the personal name of a late 18th or early 17th century BC forerunner of the members of the Arzawan royal house (Woudhuizen 2006-7). As it seems, then, the Luwian hieroglyphic script was already in use in western Anatolia at a time that the kingdom of the Hittites still had to be founded! Ergo: the Luwians of western Anatolia did not take over the Luwian hieroglyphic script from the Hittites, but deviced it themselves.

The latter conclusion is not premature but can even be underlined by pointing to the stamp seal from Beycesultan, situated along the upper Maiandros river. This seal came to light in a dividing line marking the transition from the Early Bronze Age (level VI) to the Middle Bronze Age (level V), which means that it is securely dated to *c.* 2000 BC (cf. Mora 1987: XIIb 3.3.). It contains a legend in Luwian hieroglyphic, which starts with the town name *mi+ra* 'Mira'. If correct, this implies that the ancient name of modern Beycesultan was *Mira* and that the successor-state of Arzawa after the latter's incorporation into the Hittite empire by Mursilis II (1322-1295 BC) in his third and fourth year was so called after this border town between Arzawa and the Hittite Lower Land, which evidently became its new capital—no doubt to assure a closer hold on the new province than possible from its former capital *Apasa* along the coastal region in the far west. The rest of the legend, which runs from right to left in the middle line and then boustrophedon from left to right in the lower line, informs us that the seal belonged to a functionary who was *1000*^{mm} '(overseer of) 1000 men' *ḪAPA i -ḫa UMINA* '(with respect to) the river and this town [viz. Mira]' (see Fig. 12). The execution of the legend is rather cursive, suggesting that the script had been in use already for some time. In any case, the language is straightforwardly Luwian and in actual fact we are dealing here not only with the earliest evidence of the Luwian hieroglyphic script and language, but with the earliest datable document in an Indo-European tongue altogether (Woudhuizen 2012b)!

Fig. 11. Seal of king Piyamakuruntas of Assuwiya (Mora 1987: XIIb 1.1).

Fig. 12. Stamp seal from Beycesultan (reconstruction of the legend by the author).

There can be no doubt, therefore, that the Luwian hieroglyphic script was used by the Luwian population groups of western Anatolia from *c.* 2000 BC as a *terminus ante quem.* With respect to the origin of Luwian hieroglyphic, then, we may safely conclude by repeating Hans Gustav Güterbock's *dictum* in answer to the question 'für welche Sprache wurde die Bilderschrift entwickelt?': 'von den Luwiern, für das Luwische, in luwischen Landen' (Güterbock 1956: 518).

Addendum

In a recent article, to which my attention was kindly drawn by Willemijn Waal, Alfonso Archi (2015) cogently argues that Indilima was a ruler of Ebla and not of Tarsos. The dating of this ruler to the period of Tell Atchana-Alalaḫ VII is not in doubt, though (Archi 2015: 23). In line with the new identification, the seal of Indilima, reported to have been acquired in Cilicia, no doubt ultimately originates from Ebla. A problem is posed, however, by the Luwian hieroglyphic legend. From our overview of the Middle Bronze Age Luwian hieroglyphic inscriptions it is clear that this class of script is indigenous in Anatolia, if not actually its southwestern part (see Fig. 7). Attestations of Luwian hieroglyphic in the coastal regions of the Levant at this early period are secondary and the result of trade connections.

Given the fact that the use of the Luwian hieroglyphic script thus far goes unrecorded for Middle Bronze Age Ebla and that this region certainly falls outside the scope of the distribution zone of this class of writing, the aforesaid Luwian hieroglyphic legend on the Indilima seal needs to be explained by special pleading.

The history of cylinder seals is often long and complex. The seal found in the Uluburun wreck was at least half a millennium old before the ship sank. In the course of their history, seals may have been inherited within the family or handed over to seal-bearers stationed in foreign countries in order to facilitate trade connections. The latter scenario may well be of relevance in the present case. At any rate, the Luwian hieroglyphic legend is likely to have been added secondarily, when the seal was used in Kizzuwatna within the frame of trade relations between Ebla and Anatolia—which are assured owing to two impressions on two tablets from Kültepe-Kanesh (Archi 2015: 22).

As we have seen, the Luwian hieroglyphic legend consists of a titular expression, indeed (cf. Archi 2015: 23), written in ligature to be read from bottom to top, LH 398 + LH 14 *ta?+PÁRANA* 'tabarnas', which is followed by a wish formula consisting of LH 369 ***vita*** and LH 370 *ASU*. The use of an animal head (in this case clearly that of a donkey, see Archi 2015: 23) with protruding tongue (in fact the distinctive feature of the sign, which allows for its identification with the man's head with protruding tongue LH 14) for the value *PÁRANA* is most closely paralleled in the related Cretan hieroglyphic on seal # 271 from Malia, where it occurs in the titular expression also written in ligature but this time reading from top to bottom LH 175 + LH 14 *la+PÁRANA* 'labarnas'—a mere writing variant of 'tabarnas' characterised by *d/l*-change (Woudhuizen 2009: 21; see Fig. 13).

It is worth noting in this connection that, as demonstrated by A. Poruciuc and acknowledged by J. Makkay (1998: 185, note 17), the titular expression *taparna-*, or its earlier variant *taparsa-*, shows the reflex a Proto-Indo-European root. The root is further represented by Old Iranian *tapara* and Slavic *topor*, both meaning 'axe', and may be reconstructed as **tapar-* 'axe'. To the group of words based on this root also belongs Lydian *labrus* 'double-axe' (Gusmani 1964: 275) and Mycenaean Greek *da-pu$_2$-ri-to-jo* (KN Gg 702) 'Labyrinth [G sg.]' or 'house of the double-axes'. Accordingly, *taparsa-* or *taparna-* confronts us with an adjectival derivative in *-sa-* or *-na-* of PIE **tapar-* 'axe', so that the titular expression literally means 'the (one) of the axe' or 'the (one who holds) the axe' and the axe obviously functions as the symbol of authority of the functionary in question.

The Indo-European nature of the titular expression *taparsa-* or *taparna-* is not exceptional for Luwian hieroglyphic inscriptions from the Middle Bronze Age (*c.* 2000-1650 BC). In fact, PIE roots are lavishly represented in this category of documents as the following overview may show (see Table VIII).

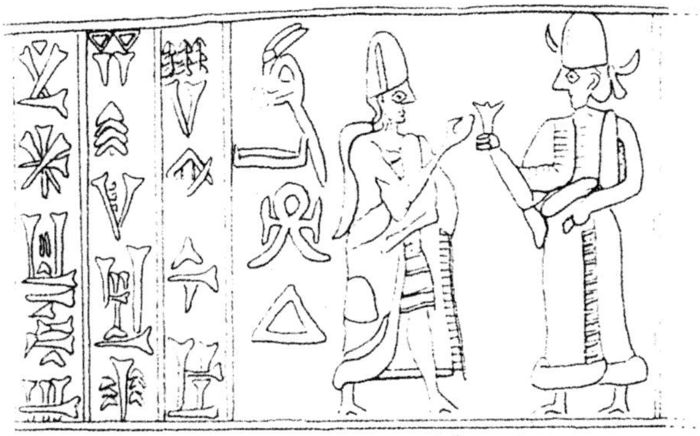

Cun. *In-di-lim-ma* DUMU *Še*$^{?}$*-ir-da-mu* ÌR ^{d}*Iš-ḫa-ra*
'Indilima, son of Sirdamu, servant of Isḫara'
Hier. *ta?+ PÁRANA* **vita** *ASU*
'tabarnas, life-health'

(a) Indilima seal (Boehmer & Güterbock 1987: 40, Abb. 26a)

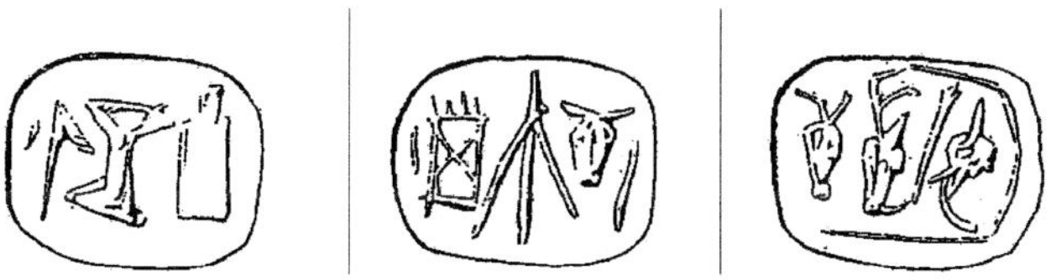

1. *SASA UTNA* 2. *sà-ḫur-*wa_9 3. *la+PÁRANA TARKU-MUWA*
'seal (with respect to) the land (of) Skheria, king Tarkumuwas'

(b) seal # 271 from Malia (Chapouthier 1930: 18)

Fig. 13. The Luwian hieroglyphic titular expression of the Indilima seal compared to its closest cognate on seal # 271 from Malia.

	LH MBA	PIE root
1.	*ÁMU*	*$h_1$me* 'me'
2.	*ARA*	*$h_2$er-/$h_3$or-* 'eagle'
3.	*ASU*	*esu* 'good'
4.	***aper$_2$*** (*Eburo-*)	*$h_1$epero-* 'boar'
5.	*-ḫa*	*-k^we* 'and'
6.	*ḪAPA*	*$h_2$eb$^{(h)}$-/$h_2$ep-* 'water, rivulet'
7.	*kasu* (< *ḫasu-*)	*$h_2$ens-* 'god, lord'
8.	*KURUNT*	*k̑erh$_1$-* 'horn'
9.	*mi* (LH 391)	*mei-* 'less' > '4'
10.	**Mida* < *Mira*	*med^{h}yos* 'middle'
11.	*ta?* (LH 398)	*dék̑m̥t-* '10'
12.	*TAPAR*	*tapar-* 'axe' (> 'rule')
13.	*TARKU* (< *Tarḫu-*)	*terh$_2$-* 'to be victorious'
14.	*USA*	*wet-* 'year'

Table VIII. Overview of Proto-Indo-European roots in Middle Bronze Age Luwian hieroglyphic.

Note finally that in the figurative scene of seal AO 1180 from Aydin the god Ea holds the double-axe as a symbol of his power (van Loon 1985: 10-11).

Postscript: In the overview of Luwian hieroglyphic inscriptions from Assuwa/Arzawa/Mira-Kuwaliya, Seḫa-Appawiya, and Ḫapalla on pages 46-48 should be included sub D the 2 sealings from Çine-Tepecik published by Sevinç Günel & Suzanne Herbordt in *Archäologischer Anzeiger* 2010/1: 1-11 and 2014/1: 1-14.

4. Luwian Hieroglyphic Evidence on the Great Kingdom of Assuwa

4.1 Introduction

In his annals, the Hittite great king Tudḫaliyas II (1425-1390 BC) commemorates the fact that he defeated the Assuwian League, headed by the Arzawan king Piyamakuruntas. Even though mentioned without much ado, this was no minor achievement as among the captives there were 10,000 foot-soldiers and 600 teams of horses for chariots. These are impressive figures for this early period. With the remainder of the booty, the captured soldiers and chariots were taken to the Hittite capital Ḫattusa or more in general Ḫatti-land, as the seal of king Piyamakuruntas (see Fig. 11) has been surfaced in Alacahöyük within the bend of the Halys. The importance of this historical event is further underlined by the fact that the Hittite great king Tudḫaliyas celebrated his victory over Assuwa with the dedication of swords to the storm-god, one of which is inscribed with a legend in Akkadian cuneiform reading as follows (cf. Gander 2015: 450):

i-nu-a ^{m}*Du-ut-ḫa-li-ia* LUGAL.GAL	'As Tudḫaliyas the great king
KUR ^{URU}*A-aš-šu-wa ú-ḫal-liq* GÍR$^{ḪI.A}$	shattered the Assuwan country,
an-nu-tim a-na ^{d}IŠKUR *be-lí ú-še-li*	he dedicated these swords to the storm-god, his Lord.'

Now, the Assuwian League consisted of a coalition of forces running from Lukka in the southwest to Wilusiya in the northwest, and hence comprised western Anatolia in its entirety. That Arzawa, whose king functioned as its leader, was indeed the core zone of the Assuwian League can be deduced from the identification of the place-names *Dura*, *Ḫalluwa*, *Ḫuwalusiya*, and *Kurupiya* with Classical *Tyrrha*, *Koloē*, *Kolossai*, and Mt. *Koruphē*, respectively (see chapter 2). According to his seal, the leader of the coalition, Piyamakuruntas of Arzawa, considered himself merely a king. However, in discussing the Luwian hieroglyphic evidence with a bearing on the Assuwian League we will see that forerunners of this ruler actually ranked themselves among the illustrious group of great kings. This latter ranking befits the impressive figures of the captives just given. Furthermore, with a view to these forerunners it may reasonably be argued that this league was not as short-lived as thus far maintained but knew a longer period of existence. The latter conclusion coincides with the fact that Assuwa in form of *'Isy* features in the annals of Tuthmosis III (1479-1425 BC) for the years 34 and 38-39 of his reign, which means 1445 BC and 1441-1440 BC when the grandfather of Tudḫaliyas II, Tudḫaliyas I (1465-1440 BC) ruled over Ḫatti (cf. Bryce 2010: 124-127; Gander 2015: 447-458).

4.2 Two Assuwian Royal Seals

Three stamp-cylinder seals, addressed to as Tyszkiewicz, Aydin (= Louvre AO 1180) and Louvre AO 20.138 in the relevant literature, are often grouped together under the blanket term 'Tyszkiewicz group', after the first mentioned and most famous representative of this set of seals.[1] Now, of these three stamp-cylinder seals, two, namely Aydin and Louvre OA 20.138, can be positively identified as Assuwian royal seals on the basis of the Luwian hieroglyphic legend of their stamp side. This is most obvious in the case of Louvre AO 20.138, where we can easily distinguish the sequence of 'man's head in profile' LH 19 *á* (middle), 'triangle' LH 370 *su* (right), and 'vine tendril' LH 160 *wi* (left), which results in the reading *á-su-wi* in sum (see Fig. 14a)—no doubt a short hand rendering of *Asuwia* 'Assuwiya' if we realise that in case of the name of a Hittite princess Luwian hieroglyphic LH 56-370-175-160 *kà-su-la-wi* as attested for two sealings from Boğazköy-Ḫattusa corresponds to cuneiform *Gassuliyawiya*.[2] Working from this reading of the stamp side of Louvre AO 20.138, the same sequence of signs can definitely be traced for the stamp side of Aydin as well, be it that the 'triangle' now appears to the left of the 'man's head in profile' and the 'vine tendril' to the right of the latter, and that the entire legend is supplemented by a wish-formula in form of the combination of LH 369 ***vita*** (below) and LH 187 'star' (on top) (see Fig. 14b).[3] As the Assuwian League, which, in view of the name of its leader, Piyamakuruntas, is likely to be taken for a conglomeration of forces from western Anatolia running from Troy in the north to Lycia in the south headed by the royal house of Arzawa (note that this name is paralleled for a son of the Arzawan king Uḫḫazitis) seated at *Apasa* 'Ephesos', figures only for a short time in Hittite texts, *in casu* the annals of Tudḫaliyas II (1425-1390 BC),[4] who defeated it so decisively that (with the exception of a later historical reflection) it is never heard of again in Hittite sources, the legends of the stamp side of Louvre AO 20.138 and Aydin can safely be assigned to the latter half of the 15th century BC (Woudhuizen 2004b).

On the basis of the decoration on its cylinder side, however, the Aydin stamp cylinder seal, together with the closely related Tyszkiewicz seal, clearly dates from a much earlier period and is usually assigned to the 18th or 17th century BC for stylistic reasons.[5] Consequently, Aydin and possibly Louvre AO 20.138 as well, for which, though it is in the main considered of later date on the basis of the style of the frieze on its cylinder side (suggested to be Mitannian by some),[6] we believe to have epigraphical reasons as presented in the following to trace it back to the 17th century BC at least, must be considered centuries old heirlooms of the Arzawan royal family at the time of their being reinscribed at the stamp side during the episode of the Assuwian League.[7] This inference can be further underlined if we take a look at the decoration of the

[1] For a detailed treatment of this group, see Alexander 1973-6.
[2] Güterbock 1940: nos. 37 and 104; cf. Laroche 1960, s.v. LH 160.
[3] Note that Laroche's interpretation of the central sequence in this legend as a theophoric name as reported by Parrot 1951: 180 must be considered erroneous.
[4] For the chronology of the Hittite kings of the New Kingdom period, see Freu 2007: 311.
[5] Boehmer & Güterbock 1987: 35, note 27; Mora 1987: 32-35.
[6] Alexander 1973-6: 153 ff.
[7] Note that Alexander (1973-6: 143) already observed that the stamp sides of Aydin and Louvre AO 20.138 were reworked.

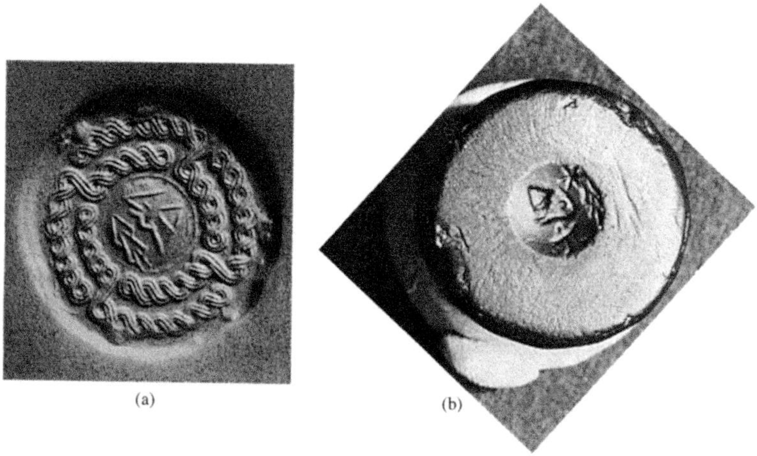

Fig. 14. Stamp side of stamp-cylinder seals Louvre AO 20.138 (a) and Aydin (b) (Alexander 1973-6: Plate I, Fig. 2c and 2b, respectively).

cylinder side of Louvre AO 20.138, which consists of two friezes framed by an upper band of repeated man's heads and a lower band featuring the repeated combination of the goat's and deer's heads (not deer's and antelope's heads, as Alexander wants to have it).[8] These upper and lower bands are, in my opinion, not strictly decorative, but bear the testimony of Luwian hieroglyphic writing in its earliest form as attested for Middle Bronze Age documents, in which the individual signs are sometimes repeated as to form columns or rows in order to fill otherwise empty space, as in case of a sealing from Tell Atchana-Alalaḫ VII *c.* 1720-1650 BC (no. 154, see Fig. 8) and one attributable to the reign of the Karkamisian king Aplaḫandas of the early 18th century BC from Acemhöyük.[9] To be more exact, we appear to be dealing here with the earliest form of the glyph LH 19 which (in contrast to the more 'modern' profile as encountered in the late 15th century BC inscription on the stamp side) still indicates the back of the head, to all probability used here logographically for *ÁMU* 'I',[10] and the combination of LH 101 *TARKU* with LH 102-3 *KURUNT*, *rú* to form the royal name *Tarku(ku)runtas*,[11] likely to be considered an

[8] Alexander 1973-6: 154.

[9] Özgüç 1980: Fig. III-17, see preceding chapter.

[10] For the derivation of the syllabic value of 'man's head' LH 19 *á* from logographic 'man pointing at himself' LH 1 and LH 2 *AMU* according to the acrophonic principle, see Woudhuizen 2015a: 345.

[11] Note that in Herbordt 2005 it is proposed that the names with the onomastic element LH 102-3 *KURUNT*, *rú* already developed into the late form *Runtias* during the Late Bronze Age, as in case with *Ḫalparuntias* (Kat. nos. 108-10), etc. In view of *Ru-wa-tí-a* and *Ru-tí-a* (Yakubovich 2010: 212) in the Kültepe-Kanesh texts, however, the typical Luwian development *kuru-* > *kru* > *ru* had taken place as early as in the Middle Bronze Age. This suggestion can be further underlined by the patently Luwian name *Rw-w-w-n-ti-i* 'Ruwantis' in an Egyptian exercise of writing *Keftiu* (= Minoan) names presumably from the period of the early 18th dynasty (*c.* 1550-1450 BC) (see Woudhuizen 2016: 80, Fig. 2). To this comes that the Cretan hieroglyphic offshoot of Luwian hieroglyphic 'deer' or 'deer's antlers' LH 102-3, E99 or CHIC028 (attested from *c.* 2000 BC onwards; for the closest Old Hittite parallel in ductus to the Cretan counterpart of this sign as rendered in Best 1996-7 [= Best 2011]: 125, Fig. 14a [below], see Beran 1967, Tafel I, no. 54), renders the value *rú*. Notwithstanding so, Hittite cuneiform ^{d}KAL still reads phonetically *Kuruntas* up to the end of the Bronze Age. Both the given Hittite and

ancestor of the leader of the Assuwian League Piyamakuruntas and one of the latter's successors, the Arzawan king Kupantakuruntas I (a contemporary of the Hittite kings Tudḫaliyas II and Arnuwandas I, of which the latter ruled from 1390 to 1370 BC).[12] For later Luwian hieroglyphic seals starting with LH 1 *AMU*, see the Nişantepe-archive from Boğazköy-Ḫattusa, cat. nos. 16 and 17 (Herbordt 2005). For double-deity names, compare, amongst others, *Sauska(ku)runtas* or *Sauska(ku)runtis* (a Hittite prince, contemporary of the Hittite king Tudḫaliyas IV [1239-1209 BC], and principal of the Luwian hieroglyphic Köylütolu text), whose name combines that of the Ḫurritic goddess *Sauska* with that of the Luwian stag god *Kurunt-*, and *Armatarḫuntas* (son of Zidas, an adversary of the Hittite king Ḫattusilis III [1264-1239 BC]), a combination of the name of the Luwian moon-god *Arma* with that of the Luwian storm-god *Tarḫunt-*.[13] It is not unthinkable that the aforesaid seal from the reign of king Aplaḫandas of Karkamis provides the closest comparative evidence for the legend of the cylinder side of Louvre AO 20.138 and should likewise be interpreted as LH 19 *ÁMU* 'I' in combination with LH 107 *MUWA* and LH 97 *WALWA* for the personal name *Muwawalwas* of an in that case Anatolian subordinate of Aplaḫandas, paralleled for the father of Manapatarḫundas, the vassal king of Seḫa during the reign of the Hittite great king Muwatallis II (1295-1272 BC).[14]

If we are right in assigning the stamp-cylinder seal Louvre AO 20.138 to a 18th or 17th century BC forerunner of later Assuwian and/or Arzawan kings, the pictorial design of its cylinder part gives us some interesting information about western Anatolia during this early period (see Fig. 15). In the first place, this region appears to be rather advanced in having the disposal of war-chariots with teams of horses apparently reigned by means of a bit or a cavasson instead of a nose-ring as still attested for seals or sealings from the Kültepe-Kanesh period (*c.* 1920-1750 BC).[15] Secondly, the depiction of a storm-god with his war-chariot driven by bulls in intimate relationship with an unveiling fertility goddess with streams of water pouring from her shoulders in true Mespotamian style in the upper frieze (note the graphical connection by means of twisted streams culminating in rudimentarily drawn vases, and the fact that only of the

Luwian forms show a reflex of PIE *$\hat{k}erh_1$-* 'horn', see Woudhuizen 2011: 401-402, note 10.

[12] Note that I have erroneously catalogued the inscription of the stamp side of the Aydin seal as evidence for Middle Bronze Age Luwian hieroglyphic in Woudhuizen 2004a: 203, Map II, which, if I am right in my interpretation of it, now can be replaced by the evidence of Middle Bronze Age Luwian hieroglyphic for western Anatolia as represented by the inscription on the cylinder side of Louvre AO 20.138.

[13] Laroche 1966: nos. 1144 and 138.

[14] Laroche 1966: no. 839. Note that the combination of 'bull' (LH 107) and 'lion' (LH 97) is also present in a sealing from Kültepe-Kanesh (Matouš & Matoušová-Rajmová 1984: no. 73; if this renders a personal name indeed, the combination on top of the column in my opinion should be emended as 'hare' LH 115 *TAPAR* + 'antelope' LH 104 *sà* for the titular expression *taparsa-* [= *labarsa-* in the Kültepe-Kanesh texts] frequently attested for Luwian hieroglyphic seals or sealings from the Middle Bronze Age period) and, reduced to heads and in association with the 'man's head' (LH 19), in the outer ring on the stamp side of the Tyszkiewicz seal; but note that in the latter case the name of the owner of the seal appears to be rendered in the center and to have LH 312-3 *ZITI* as its second element, whereas the signs in the outer ring (supplemented by the 'bird of prey' [LH 131-3], the 'antelope' [LH 104] and the 'lion's head' [LH 97] en face) might well be pseudo-hieroglyphs for decoration purposes only. At any rate, it must be admitted that the symbols on the cylinder side of Tyszkiewicz consisting of the ass's (LH 100) and bull's (LH 107) heads, the pomegranate (?) and an ear of wheat are plausibly interpretated by Alexander 1973-6: 150 as representations of offerings to the gods.

[15] Littauer & Crouwel 1979: figs. 28-29 and 32; for the earliest Syrian seals or sealings bearing testimony of innovative form of horse-control by a bit or cavasson dating from the late 18th or 17th century BC (i.e. about the same period to which we assign Louvre AO 20.138), see Littauer & Crouwel 1979: figs. 33-34 and 36.

Fig. 15. Impression of the cylinder side of stamp-cylinder seal Louvre AO 20.138 (Parrot 1951: Pl. XIII, 1).

storm god and the fertility goddess the genitalia are indicated, suggesting their sacred marriage),[16] and that of a bow-god receiving the spoils of a hunt in the lower frieze, strongly suggests that we are confronted here with the earliest pictorial representation of the Luwian trifunctional divine triad *Tarḫunt-* or *Tarku* (storm-god, F2), *Santas* (tutelary deity, F3), and *Kubaba* (fertility goddess, trans-functional) as attested for the Early Iron Age successor of Arzawa, the kingdom of Lydia, and the peripheral region of Crete in the form of a magical spell against the Asiatic pox in the language of the *Keftiu* (= Minoans) as preserved in an Egyptian hieroglyphic text probably dating back to the reign of Amenhotep III (1390-1352 BC).[17]

4.3 An Assuwian Royal Seal from Thebes

In the relevant literature on oriental imports in Mycenaean Greece, the Egyptian and Near Eastern material is abundantly represented, but that from Asia Minor lags behind to the extent that it has been considered to be either negligible or largely invisible in the material record. Thus C. Lambrou-Phillipson (1990: 428) lists only 7 imports originating from Asia Minor, and Eric Cline (1994: 271; 162) only two seals from Mycenae (no. 237) and Perati (no. 235). If we realise that Anatolian glyptic provides the most distinctive category of evidence for imports from Asia Minor, it is of relevance to our topic to note that according to oral information by Günter Neumann as referred to by Joachim Latacz in the English version of his book on Troy and Homer (2004: 71)[18] in sum 6 biconvex seals and 1 seal impression have been reported for Late Bronze Age Mycenae, Thebes, and Perati. The collection of Luwian hieroglyphic seals referred to

[16] Alexander 1973-6: 156-7.

[17] Woudhuizen 2016: 20. Note that this Luwian trifunctional divine triad is already attested for the Kültepe-Kanesh period in form of the divine name *Kubabat* and related personal names like *Tarḫu(a)la*, etc., *Sa(n)taḫsu*, etc. and *Ṣílikubabat*, see Hirsch 1961: 28 (*Kubabat*) and Laroche 1966: nos. 1255-6, 1266, 1273 (*Tarḫ-*) and 1097-8 (*Sa(n)ta-*).

[18] For reviews, see Joshua Katz 2005, Ian Morris 2005, and Jorrit Kelder 2007.

as the source, however, only lists 1 biconvex seal from Mycenae, 1 cylinder seal from Thebes, and 1 biconvex seal from Perati (Boysan, Marazzi & Nowicki 1983: 102), but note that forthcoming volumes of this work are still in progress and the missing 3 seals and 1 sealing may well await future publication.

Of these three Anatolian seals, I have recently treated the one from Perati (Lambrou-Phillipson 1990: no. 298) and argued that this is inscribed with the country name Mira in Luwian hieroglyphic (Woudhuizen 2004-5b). As it has been found in a grave of a girl dated to the transition from Late Helladic IIIB to C, it might be indicative for continuity of the realm of Mira into the earliest phase of the Dark Age, but note that this argument is to some extent undermined by the fact that the seal has been secondarily used as a bead for a necklace (Jakovidis 1964: 149). The biconvex seal discovered in a grave as well at Mycenae (Lambrou-Phillipson 1990: no. 485) is inscribed with to a large extent barely recognizable Luwian hieroglyphic signs and may perhaps be nothing but a pseudo-inscription (Boardman 1966). This leaves us with the cylinder seal from Thebes (Lambrou-Phillipson 1990: no. 350).

According to the editor of the substantial number of cylinder seals found at the palace of Thebes, Edith Porada (1981-2), there can be distinguished five groups among them in accordance with their origin. In the first place there is a Mesopotamian group with 6 seals dating from the Ur III dynasty to the Old Babylonian period. Next, there are a Mitannian group, consisting of 5 seals, and a Kassite group, consisting of 11 seals. This latter group covers the period from the reign of the Babylonian king Burna-Buriaš II (1375-1347 BC), who was a contemporary of Amenhotep IV or Akhenaten (1355-1337 BC), to that of his successors up to the destruction of Babylon in 1225 BC by the Assyrian king Tukulti-Ninurta I (1243-1207 BC). The fourth group entails 11 seals from Cyprus (nos. 1-11), among which the earliest datable seal (no. 1) is assigned by Porada to *c.* 1450 BC. Finally, the fifth and last category is formed by 1 cylinder seal (Porada's no. 25) singled out from the rest for its definite Anatolian origin.

In her publication of these seals, Porada (1981-2: 68-70) developed a special theory about the group of Kassite ones, based on the observation that the total weight of this group of seals (including the unengraved ones of the same proportions) measures 496 grams or almost the equivalent of 1 mina. Thus she argued that this group of seals had been sent to Thebes as a cache by Tukulti-Ninurta I after his conquest of Babylon in 1225 BC to provide the recipient, the king of Thebes, with 1 mina of lapis lazuli as raw material. In return, he no doubt hoped that the Thebans would continue their trade efforts with Assyria and in this manner break the ban imposed by the Hittite great king Tudḫaliyas IV (Sauskamuwa-treaty). As a *conditio sine qua non* for this theory, however, the destruction of the palace of Thebes at the end of Late Helladic IIIB1 cannot be dated earlier than *c.* 1220 BC, which is questioned by others who rather would assign this particular destruction to *c.* 1250 BC.

Whatever the merits of this theory, what primarily concerns us here is that the Cyprian cylinder seals and the Anatolian one fall outside the scope of it. In order to formulate the correlation between these seals in positive terms, it is of importance to note that two of the Cyprian seals (nos. 9 and 10) and the Anatolian one (no. 25) had originally been *gold-covered* (Porada 1981-2: 77). Presumably, therefore, these seals had been *encased in a gold container in order to facilitate their being actually worn*. Yet another connection between a Cyprian seal, in this case no. 1, and the Anatolian one no. 25 is formed by the fact that these both are inscribed with Luwian hieroglyphic signs.

In the case of the Cyprian seal, this fact has virtually remained unnoticed, but the antithetically arranged human and lion's heads are in fact Luwian hieroglyphic signs, corresponding to, respectively, LH 19 *á* and LH 97 *WALWA* (see Fig. 16). The impression that we might be dealing here with the name of the owner of the seal is indeed reinforced by the fact that the sign group in question is associated with the Cypro-Minoan sign *mi*, which represents the Luwian pronoun of the first person singular in its possessive variant *(a)mi-* in order to express the meaning 'I' of the personal counterpart in like manner as this is attested for the later west-Luwian dialects Lydian and Sidetic (Woudhuizen 2010-1a: 209; Woudhuizen 1984-5: 121-122, note 10). The name in question, moreover, which reads *WALWA-á* 'Walwas', is also of typically west-Luwian type as it corresponds to *WALWA-ā* on a 13th century BC seal from Şarhöyük-Dorylaion (Doğan-Alparslan 2015) and Lydian *Valvel*$_1$ (D sg. in -λ) as attested for late 7th century BC coins (Gusmani 1964: no. 52); cf. further composite Luwian personal names of the type *Walwazitis* and *Piḫawalwas*.

The Anatolian cylinder seal is decorated with a scene consisting of 4 deities in a procession, three of which are male and the fourth female (see Fig. 17). To all probability, the deity which heads the procession is the male one with the lituus and a captured hare in his left hand, whereas he is brandishing a spear in his right hand.

Fig. 16. Cyprian cylinder seal from Thebes (Porada 1981-2: 9, no. 1).

This particular deity has been convincingly identified by Porada (1981-2: 48) as the tutelary deity, also known as ^{d}KAL or *Kuruntas* (F3). The following deity, which appears to hold a bolt of lightning in his left hand, seems nonetheless to be identifiable as the sun-god, ^{d}UTU or *Tiwatas* (F1), owing to the winged sun-disc (LH 190) above his head. If so, the third deity of the procession who is carrying a lance in his left hand likely represents the storm-god, ^{d}U or *Tarḫunt* (F2). The final deity in the procession, then, is a goddess who seems to hold up a shield in protection of her adorant whose name, as we will see shortly, is added in Luwian hieroglyphic in front of her. This goddess may be identified as Kubaba or *Ištar* or the like (= trans-functional goddess in Puhvel's terminology).

Now, according to Porada (1981-2: 46) this procession of deities formed the original design of the cylinder seal, and the hieroglyphic legends as well as the small seated figure with a lance in his left hand were added later, presumably by another artist. However this may be, it is of vital importance for our understanding of the composition in its entirety that the hieroglyphs and decorative motifs are added to the *front* of the deity with which these are associated. Thus, the tutelary deity at the head of the procession is associated with the wish-formula consisting of the combination of LH 369 ***vita*** with LH 370 *ASU* in front of him, so that the wish pertains to the state or community involved as a whole. Next, the sun-god is associated with the legend in form of the combination of the symbol of lightning LH 199 *TARḪUNT*, *ḫà* with what at first sight appears to be the ox-sign LH 107 *MUWA*, *mu*. Below this, we are confronted with a second instance of the wish-formula. In similar vein, the third deity in the procession, the storm-god, is associated with the seated figure in front of him. Finally, then, the goddess holding up what appears to be a shield is associated with the Luwian hieroglyphic legend above and in front of the shield as well as the third instance of the wish-formula below the supposed shield.

In his treatment of the Luwian hieroglyphic legends, Hans Gustav Güterbock (1981-2: 71-72) has rightly identified the sequence in front of the goddess at the top side of

Fig. 17. Luwian hieroglyphic cylinder seal from Thebes (Porada 1981-2: 47, no. 25).

the supposed shield as a combination of a title, expressed by the spear-sign (with an arm-grip?), with a personal name rendered by the sequence of LH 369-90-312-376, presumably reading *wa*$_{12}$-*ti*-ZITI-*i* 'Wastizitis'—no doubt a speaking name for town-official. In any case, personal names in *-ziti-* are frequently encountered in Anatolian glyptic, and also the use of the spear for the indication of a magistracy below the rank of a king is ascertained (LH 173 ***hastarius*** '(member of the) body guard'). In deviation of this latter identification, Güterbock next suggests that the legend in front of the sun-god has a bearing on this god and, under due consideration of the fact that this god holds a bolt of lightning, renders the notion 'the storm-god's (male) calf'. In reality, however, we appear to be dealing here with a personal name as well, reading, if the second sign indeed renders a bull, *TARḪUNT-MUWA*, i.e. a personal name of the well-known Luwian type of *Tarḫundi-muwas* 'Tarkondemos'! The problem with the identification of the second sign is a real one, though, and it seems most likely that, as in glyptic a sign can only be changed into a larger one, the original bull (LH 107), has been secondarily altered in a lion (LH 97) by changing its head into a lion's head and adding manes on its neck and breast while leaving the hooves in tact. If this analysis is correct, the original personal name *TARḪUNT-MUWA* 'Tarkondemos' has been changed by a secondary intervention into *TARḪUNT-WALWA*, i.e. a composite name of the type *Walwazitis* and *Piḫawalwas* referred to in the above, most closely paralleled by *TARKU-WALWA* of Tell Atchana-Alalaḫ VII no. 154 as discussed in the preceding chapter.

The consequences of our adjustment of Güterbock's treatment of the Luwian hieroglyphic legends in this respect are twofold: (1) all deities, except the first one who represents the entire community, are directly associated with a personal name and as such staged as protective deities of the person in question; (2) the personal name(s) associated with the sun-god, for the use of the symbol of winged sun-disc (LH 190), can only be surmised to refer to (a) great king(s). If we are right in these inferences, it follows in the first place that the seated figure associated with the storm-god denotes a person as well, no doubt a dignitary, in like manner as the Luwian hieroglyphic legends associated with the sun-god on the one hand and the goddess presumably holding a shield on the other hand. Secondly, it may reasonably be inferred that the personal name(s) associated with the sun-god can only refer to (an) Anatolian or, more in specific, Luwian, great king(s), which inevitably leads us to the conclusion that we are dealing here with (a) ruler(s) of the one time illustrious realm of Arzawa, known to have been headed by great king Tarḫundaradus in the early phase of the Amarna period (*c.* 1360-1350 BC), or the latter realm's predecessor, the Assuwian League, a political entity rising to prominence during the latter half of the 15th century BC. Now, if we realise that all rulers of Arzawa from Piyamakuruntas, the leader of the Assuwian League defeated by Tudḫaliyas II (1425-1390 BC) presumably sometime during the beginning of the latter's reign, onwards are known (see Table IX), the great kings *Tarḫundimuwas* and *Tarḫundiwalwas* as recorded for the Thebes seal are definitely to be situated in the period before *c.* 1425 BC and hence to be identified as contemporaries of the Hittite great kings Tudḫaliyas I (1465-1440 BC) and Ḫattusilis II (1440-1425 BC).

Accordingly, the cylinder seal likely dates, just like the earliest Cyprian one, to about the middle or the latter half of the 15th century BC. If we are right in our analysis, then, the persons mentioned in the legends associated with the deities are likely to be enumerated in diminishing importance, from the great kings associated with the sun-god, via what may be a king seated on a throne associated with the storm-god, to a lower functionary, 'spear-man', associated with his protective female deity.

The answer to the question who the king associated with the storm-god might be is, in view of the fact that the seal had once been encased in gold in order to facilitate it to be actually worn, likely to be answered as follows: none other than the king of Thebes (note that his use of an icon instead of hieroglyphs betrays him as someone unfamiliar with Luwian hieroglyphic). This answer necessarily leads us to the assumption that the king of Thebes in question was a vassal of the great kings mentioned in association with the sun-god, which, as we have seen, means the rulers of Assuwa during the period of *c.* 1450-1425 BC.

At this point, it becomes expedient to refer to the findings by Frank Starke as ventilated in a press interview and incorporated by Latacz in the English version of his book on Troy and Homer (2004: 243-4).[19] According to Starke, then, a passage in a Hittite letter (KUB 26.91, line 8) reads *ka-ta-mu-* instead of *ka-ga-mu-*, which, in the opinion of Joshua Katz (2005: 424), is not unlikely because the signs for *ga* and *ta* in Hittite cuneiform are very similar, the difference being made by one extra *cuneus* only (see Rüster & Neu 1989: 166, no. 159 [ga]; 167, no. 160 [ta]). In line with this adjustment of the reading of the letter involved, it follows that an ancestor of the sender of the letter in the third degree (*A-BI A-BI A-BI̥[-YA]*), so great-grand-father, named *Kadmos*, had received disputed islands (*gursawara* according to Starke's interpretation since 1981) in the Aegean from the king of Assuwa at the event of the betrothal of his daughter to the latter king. As the sender of this message is likely to be identified with the Aḫḫiyawan dignitary active in the region of Millawanda or Miletos, *Tawagalawas*, who, as first realised by Emil Forrer, is none other than the Theban king *Eteoklēs*, it lies at hand that we are confronted here with information about the Theban royal family which fits the information about it in Greek literary tradition to the extent that Eteokles is indeed a successor of the founding father, Kadmos (Schachermeyr 1983: 231). It must be admitted in this connection, however, that the mythical Kadmos is situated at the very outset of the foundation of Thebes as a palatial site, datable to the beginning of Late Helladic I, *c.* 1600 BC, whereas, if the genealogical information of KUB 26.91 is exact (note in this connection that the *Tawagalawas*-letter [KUB 14.3] according to Smit 1990-1 and Gurney 2002 more likely dates from the reign of Muwatallis II, *c.* 1280 BC, than that of Ḫattusilis III as commonly assumed), we rather would be dealing here with a Kadmos ruling at Thebes in the period of *c.* 1450-1425 BC, so that we must assume it to be a hereditary royal name which is not specified as such by the literary tradition. However this may be, the relative sequence from *Katamu* or *Kadmos* to *Tawagalawas* or *Eteoklēs* as far as the Theban royal house is concerned fits the information from the literary tradition to the extent that it is hard to resist.

[19] I like to thank my friend and colleague Jorrit Kelder for drawing my attention to Starke's new reading of KUB 26.91, line 8.

Against the backdrop of Starke's new reading, then, our reconstruction of events would be as follows: as a result of marrying his daughter to a great king of Assuwa a Theban ruler named Kadmos received islands in the Aegean in loan from the aforesaid great king. In order to facilitate administration of the islands in question, the great king of Assuwa handed over to this Kadmos a cylinder seal by means of which he in effect could exercise his power there through the means of the former's henchman (perhaps, as we have seen, a member of his body guard), Wastizitis.

In his dissertation on *The Kingdom of Mycenae: A Great Kingdom in the Late Bronze Age Aegean* of 2009 (= market edition of 2010), Jorrit Kelder cogently argued that the highest percentage in mainland Greece of Egyptiaca at Mycenae strongly militates in favor of Mycenae's dominant position in the region. Similarly, he duly stressed the fact that the destruction layers at Thebes at the end of Late Helladic IIIA1 and that of Late Helladic IIIB1, whatever their precise dating in absolute terms, patently illustrates the instability in this region during the period in question and as such rules Thebes out as the seat of an Aḫḫiyawan great king.[20] On the other hand, however, it must be admitted that as far as orientalia from Anatolia are concerned, the palace of Thebes produced the largest extant Late Bronze Age Luwian hieroglyphic text from the Greek mainland and therefore must be attributed with a crucial role as an intermediary in Aḫḫiyawan affairs concerning western Anatolia, duly expressed in the mention of Theban royal names like Kadmos and Eteokles in connection with Mycenaean relations with Assuwa and Millawanda or Miletos. Note in this connection that the ethnic adjective *mi-ra-ti-jo* 'the Milesian' occurs exceptionally frequent in the Theban Linear B tablets, see Aravantinos, Godart & Sacconi 2001; note also that the Euboian places *a-ma-ru-to* 'Amarynthos' and *ka-ru-to* 'Karystos' mentioned in the Theban Linear B texts are located 'en route' from Thebes to Miletos, and may therefore well have been drawn within the Theban sphere of influence during the period in question, as suggested by Latacz (2003: 288).

I am aware, of course, of the fact that the readings by some colleagues and me of the text on the Phaistos disc have been received with much skepticism (Achterberg, Best, Enzler, Rietveld & Woudhuizen 2004), but would like to point out to those skeptics that the vassalage of the king of Thebes to the great king of Assuwa as recorded by the combined evidence of KUB 26.91 and the Anatolian cylinder seal from Thebes, while this Theban king no doubt was at the same time a vassal king of the Akhaian great king seated at the capital of Mycenae, reflects exactly the political situation in Crete of which the text of the discus bears testimony and according to which the king of Pylos, Nestor, no doubt a vassal of his Mycenaean overlord, had territories in Crete in loan from a great king who is likely to be identified as Tarḫundaradus of Arzawa, ruling sometime during the middle of the 14th century BC. As a matter of fact, therefore, from now on the *onus probandi* to the contrary, in my opinion at least, lies with these skeptics.

[20] It is true that Eteokles is referred to in the Tawagalawas-letter as the brother of the king of Aḫḫiyawa, but this does not necessarily mean that he is considered a great king like the latter; it merely indicates that he was of royal stature or, in Mycenaean Greek terms, a *wanaks*, ruling to all probability as a vassal of the Mycenaean great king over the Thebaid. In similar vein, namely, the king of Alasiya is also addressed as 'brother' by the Egyptian pharaoh in the Amarna correspondence, whereas at the same time he (or his predecessors and successors) was (were) considered (a) mere vassal(s) by the latter's Hittite colleagues.

It deserves our attention, finally, that in the figurative scene on the seal from Thebes, we came across the trifunctional divine triad consisting of the sun-god (F1), the storm-god (F2), and the tutelary deity (F3). Now, if we are right in our attribution of the seal to Assuwian great kings, it lies at hand to correlate this evidence on western Anatolian religion with that presented by yet another Assuwian royal seal, Louvre AO 20.138. In the aforegoing treatment of this seal we came across a divine triad as well, but this time consisting of the storm-god Tarḫunt or Tarku (F2), the tutelary deity Santas (F3), and the fertility goddess Kubaba (trans-functional). In actual fact, however, the Dumézilian or Old Indo-European trifunctional triad can be reconstructed if we realise that the part of the scene to the extreme right of the storm-god shows two personified mountains and a crawling figure crowned by what appear to be flower leaves. The last mentioned figure has been convincingly identified by Joseph Azize in 2005(: 133) as a representation of *the sun-god or sun-goddess rising between twin peaks*. In line with this identification, then, we appear to be confronted in the scene of Louvre AO 20.138 with the sun-god(dess) (F1),[21] the storm-god (F2), and the tutelary deity (F3)—the latter, true to his nature, hunting deer in the open field—in like manner as in the scene of the Thebes seal. For a discussion of the Dumézilian trifunctional divine triad of Old Indo-European type, which apparently is still worshipped by the Luwians of western Anatolia during the Middle and early phase of the Late Bronze Age as evidenced by the Thebes seal and, in a rudimentary way, Louvre AO 20.138, see Woudhuizen 2010b.

4.4 On the Reading of the Luwian Hieroglyphic Legends of the Schimmel Rhyton[22]

Since its publication by Oscar Muscarella in 1974 (as no. 123), the scene on the silver stag-rhyton from the collection of Norbert Schimmel has been treated by various scholars. Most important among these treatments are the ones by Hans Gustav Güterbock, Sedat Alp, and John David Hawkins.

In his discussion of the intriguing object, Alp (1988) focuses on the order of the scene, which is a running one, and the question of its date. As to the order, which is convincingly established by Alp, his colleague Güterbock (already in 1977, but see esp. 1989a) draws attention to three Late Bronze Age seals with a Luwian hieroglyphic legend in the center, one from the British Museum in London (Mora 1987: IIIb 3.1), another from Dresden (not included in Mora 1987), and the third from Adana (Mora 1987: IIIb 3.3). All these three seals are in the outer band decorated with a scene depicting in varying detail more or less the following sequence:

(1) a seated goddess with a bird perched on her outstretched left hand and an altar in front of her;

(2) worshippers to the right of the altar, the first one of which is pouring a libation and the third and last one represents the so-called 'cupbearer of squatting'; and

[21] Note that the lack of a beard, duly noted by Azize and explained by him in terms of a *female* deity, may alternatively indicate that the rising sun is considered a *youthful* deity.

[22] This is a reworked version of Woudhuizen 2013b.

Fig. 18. Drawing of the scene on the Schimmel rhyton (Hawkins 2006: 71, Fig. 5).

(3) behind the seated goddess the head and hoofs of a stag, a hunting bag, a quiver, two spears and the *eya*-tree.

As the scene of the first two seals is characterised by a part focusing on a winged sun-disc on top of a triangle which is supported on either side by a mythological being in between the *eya*-tree on the one hand and the row of worshippers on the other hand, the order as depicted in our Fig. 18, which is first suggested by Güterbock and further underlined by Alp, who had the aforesaid figure drawn on the basis of these observations, may safely be assumed to be correct.

As far as the dating of the silver stag-rhyton from the Schimmel collection is concerned, Muscarella preferred its assignment to the Hittite empire period, which presumably boils down to a dating to the 14th and 13th centuries BC. In any case, Alp contrasts this dating with the one by the former leader of the excavations at Boğazköy, Kurt Bittel, who rather suggests a dating to the period around or just after *c.* 1400 BC. Finally, Alp himself dates the object to the Old Hittite period, which covers the earliest phase of the Late Bronze Age, from *c.* 1650 to 1500 BC (Alp 1988: 21-23). It is of relevance to note in this connection that the seals used by Güterbock in his reconstruction of the order of the scene (see above) most certainly date prior to the Hittite empire period, at least in the sense as used here (i.e. dating from the reign of Suppiluliumas I, *c.* 1350-1322 BC, onwards), the one from the British Museum in London being assigned by Clelia Mora to the period of the second half of the 16th to 15th century BC (see Mora 1987: discussion of IIIb 3.1). Notwithstanding so, Hawkins (2006: 50) sides with Muscarella and considers the silver rhyton a cult object dating from the reign of Tudḫaliyas IV (1239-1209 BC).

What primarily concerns us here are the Luwian hieroglyphic legends added to the scene, one on top of the seated goddess with a bird perched on her outstretched left hand (our no. 1) and the other also at the upper margin, but this time in between the tutelary god standing on a stag and the first worshipper pouring a libation (our no. 2).

According to Hawkins (2006: 52; 56), the legends in question are to be read in the reverse order as ***cervus***$_x$***-deus***$_x$ and *á-x-**deus***$_x$***-filia***. In his interpretation of the last sign in our legend no. 1 as ***filia*** he bases himself on Güterbock 1989b: 115, who suggests this as one of two options, both of which he considers insecure. The feminine nature of what simply seems to be an early variant of LH 45 ***infans***^{m} (note that the sign attached to the lower side of the hand is not an oval indicative of female gender [LH 408 ^{f} or ***femina***], but a rectangular and hence more likely to be considered a shorthand variant of LH 386, 1 ^{m} or ***vir***$_{2}$) is in fact an inference from Güterbock's identification of the seated deity with which the legend is associated as a goddess, in which he, in my opinion, is correct. But does the legend have a bearing on this particular deity? In the opinion of Hawkins it does, and in this manner he arrives at the interpretation of the legend as the GN *Ala*, the consort of the stag-god mentioned in the other legend, our no. 2. As corroborating evidence for the fact that there is a consort of the stag-god named Ala, Hawkins draws attention to Emirgazi § 26, which he reads as *á **(femina.deus)**.*461* 'the goddess Ala' (so also Hawkins 2004: 366). Along this line of approach, finally, Hawkins is quite certain about the identification of the enigmatic sign which occurs in both legends as an odd variant of LH 360 *MASANA* (= ***deus***).

In actual fact, however, the given reading of the section of the Emirgazi text in question is highly questionable. In my treatment of this text it concerns § 27 and reads *á-ya* ^{MASANA}*pá<+r+tì>* 'the heroic stag-god' (reconstruction on the basis of Malatya 5, where the divine name of the deity in question, standing on a male deer with prominent antlers, is written out in full and owing to this fact can be traced back to PIE **b*^{h}*rent-* 'stag', see Woudhuizen 2011: 119, note 2). But much more important than that is the fact that what Hawkins takes as an unidentified sign in legend no. 1 and without proper foundation assumes to render the value *la* much more likely consists of the sign for 'land', LH 228 *UTNA* (= ***regio***) — this identification being only slightly hampered by the fact that the two triangles of which the sign is composed are set apart and are not connected at the lower side as is normally the case. If so, we may well be dealing here with the name of a country. Working along this alternative line of approach, the comparison with a combination on the Baltimore seal (Mora 1987: IIIb 2.1; see our Fig. 19),[23] anticlockwise no. 12 of the outer ring, comes to mind for the direct association of LH 19 *á* with LH 225 *UMINA* (= ***urbs***) — especially so if we realise that the latter sign for 'town' is in fact interchangeable with LH 228 *UTNA*. If allowance be made for the possibility that LH 402, which appears in ligature here with LH 19 *á*, already in texts from the Late Bronze Age expresses the value sa_4 as attested for Early Iron Age documents because its circular form suggests a value acrophonically derived from PIE **seh*$_{2}$*wōl-* 'sun' (see Woudhuizen 2011: 423), the combination in question reads *á+sa*$_{4}^{UMINA}$ in sum. Now, although this same combination is used to express the country name *Isuwa* at the *eastern* confines of the Hittite empire (Hawkins 1998a: 294-295, Figs. 2-3), in this particular case, in my opinion at least, it rather confronts us with an abbreviated variant of the geographic name *Assuwa* (lit. *As[uw]a*) as used for a league of nations along the *western* confines of the Hittite empire featuring in Hittite history during the late 15th century BC.

This opinion is based on two facts, namely:

[23] Note that this seal is from the same group as the seal from London and the seal from Adana mentioned in the foregoing in the context of scenes comparable to the one of the Schimmel rhyton.

Fig. 19. Baltimore seal (Mora 1987: IIIb 2.1).

(1) the seal in question has surfaced on the market in Aydin in Lydia, i.e. exactly in the region where the nucleus of the Assuwian League is situated (see further below), and

(2) the combination in second position anticlockwise consists of the titular expression LH 18 *URA+ḪANTAWAT* (= ***magnus rex***) 'geat king', which is conceivable for a country along the western border of the Hittite empire, as exemplified by the case of the Arzawan king Tarḫundaradus rising to this preeminent status during the Amarna period in the earlier part of the 14th century BC, but entirely without parallel for the country of Isuwa, which as far as the evidence goes was ruled by functionaries addressed as LH 17 *ḪANTAWAT* (= ***rex***) 'king' (cf. Woudhuizen 2011: 83, note 10; *contra* Hawkins 1998a: 288).

Against this backdrop, then, it may reasonably be argued that the enigmatic sign, which takes the place of LH 402 *sa*$_4$ in the sequence from the Baltimore seal, renders a sibilant value as well. In actual fact, this latter suggestion can even be further emphasized from an epigraphical corner of incidence, as the sign in question happens to be so closely related in form to LH 430 *sa* as used in the inscriptions of great king Ḫartapus conducted in Late Bronze Age scribal tradition and dating from the earliest stage of the Early Iron Age that it may well come into consideration as an earlier variant of it (see Fig. 21). If so, the legend under discussion reads *á-sa*^{UTNA} ***infans***^{m} in sum and bears reference to a son, or, in political terms, representative of the land of Assuwa (see Fig. 20). The validity of our present reading of legend no. 1 can even be further enhanced by the observation that on the Baltimore seal the combination *á+sa*$_4^{UMINA}$ is followed by ***infans***^{m}+*UMINA* (anticlockwise no. 13)!

If we next turn to legend no. 2, it should be acknowledged that the first sign of this legend is correctly identified by Hawkins as a variant of LH 103 *KURUNT* (= ***cervus***$_3$; note that the given phonetic value originates from PIE *$\hat{k}$*erh*$_1$- 'head, horn') and as a rendering

Fig. 20. Luwian hieroglyphic legend no. 1 (Hawkins 2006: 71, Fig. 5) with comparison from the Baltimore seal (cf. Mora 1987: IIIb 2.1).

Fig. 21. Thus far enigmatic sign from the Luwian hieroglyphic legends with suggested equivalent of later date, LH 430 *sa*.

of the name of the stag-god. This leads us to the question: how does the additional sign, which we have just suggested to render a sibilant value, fit into our framework so far? The answer to this question is in my opinion to be found in the association of the, of origin, Ḫurritic goddess *Šauška* with the adjective *(a)pára-* 'of the field' in Südburg § 3 (the combination reads ^{MASANA}*(a)pá+r(a)-sà-us-ka* in full, see Woudhuizen 2015a: 27; 43), as this latter adjective is, as generally acknowledged, typical for the tutelary deity or stag-god *Kurunt* in the Yalburt (§ 3) and Emirgazi (§§ 27, 30, 37, 39) texts (see Woudhuizen 2015a: 17; 22-24; 43)![24] It seems not unreasonable, therefore, to assume that the sign with in our view a sibilant value associated with the GN *Kurunt* in our legend no. 2 confronts us with an abbreviation of the GN *Šauška*, who, as evidenced by the Yalburt and Emirgazi texts, really is the consort of the stag-god (see Fig. 22).

In this connection it is further of relevance to note that the close association of the god Kurunt with the goddess Sauska is underlined by the 'double-deity' type of MN *Sà-us-*

[24] I am aware of the fact that it is currently suggested that the related group of signs LH 461-3 should be read as *ma*$_x$ instead of *pá*, because the sequence LH 209-463-383, 2 according to this opinion reads *i-ma*$_x$*+ra/i* and as such provides us with a perfect match of cuneiform Luwian *imra-* 'field, countryside', with regular loss of the voiced velar as compared to Hittite *gimra-* < PIE **ĝ^{h}eym-/ĝ^{h}im-* 'winter, snow'. It should be realised in this connection, however, that the new reading of LH 209 as *i* instead of *a* is definitely ruled out by the correspondence of **209-la-pa-* to the TN *a-le-p-* 'Aleppo' and of **209-ma-tu-* to the TN *a-mat-* 'Hamath' and numerous other of such examples (see Woudhuizen 2011: 89-91), whereas the value *pá*, as we have already preluded upon in the case of the GN *pá+r-tì* for the stag-god in Malatya 5, is ascertained. Therefore I suggest that the labial [p] actually represents [mb] and that, as far as the initial vowel [a] is concerned — if only we realise that this corresponds to Lycian [e] — the closest comparable evidence is provided by the Lycian MN *Hẽ[p]ruma*, which occurs in Greek writing in form of *Embromos*, see Woudhuizen 2011: 399-400.

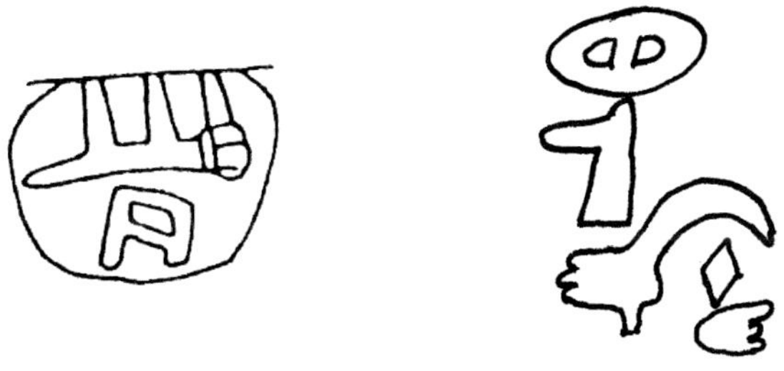

Fig. 22. Luwian hieroglyphic legend no. 2 (Hawkins 2006: 71, Fig. 5) with comparison from Südburg § 3 (cf. Hawkins 1995: Abb 35).

ka-rú-ti 'Sauskaruntias' as attested for Köylütolu § 8 (see Woudhuizen 2015a: 26; 49 and note that, in line with Woudhuizen 2011: 80, *Runtias* is the developed form of *Kurunti-* according to the phonetic development *Kuruntiyas* > *Kruntiyas* > *Runtiyas*).

If we are right, then, in our aforegoing interpretation of the Luwian hieroglyphic legends of the silver stag-rhyton, it necessarily follows that, conform legend no. 1, the object is a dedication by a functionary of the land of Assuwa and that, conform legend no. 2, the deities involved are the stag-god Kurunt and his consort Sauska. Now, it so happens that especially the identification of a functionary of the land of Assuwa has chronological repercussions. The land of Assuwa, namely, which is mostly addressed in conformity with the information in Hittite texts as the Assuwian League, first turns up in Egyptian hieroglyphic sources in form of *'Isy* 'Asia' as attested for the annals of pharaoh Tuthmosis III (1479-1425 BC) of the 18th dynasty for the years 34 and 38-39, which means in terms of absolute chronology 1445 BC and 1441-1440 BC, respectively (Sethe 1907: IV, 707, 719, and 724; cf. its discussion by Vercoutter 1956: 179-182). In one text from the latter's reign, the so-called poetic stele, it is directly associated with *K3fty* 'Crete' (Vercoutter 1956: 51, doc. 5). From the Hittite side, on the other hand, we are informed that great king Tudḫaliyas II (1425-1390 BC), presumably early in his reign, defeated a confederation known as the Assuwian League, which entailed the entire west coast of Anatolia, running from the *Lukka* 'Lycians' in the south to *Wilusa* 'Ilion' and *Tarwisa* 'Troy' in the north. As I have argued in various publications, the nucleus of the Assuwian League is formed by the kingdom of Arzawa with its capital *Apasa* 'Ephesos' for three reasons:

(1) its king Piyamakuruntas bears a name which is a hereditary one among the Arzawan royal house;

(2) Homeros in his *Iliad* II, 461 situates the 'Asian field' ('Ἀσίῳ ἐν λειμῶνι) in the neighbourhood of Ephesos, as we have just noted the capital of Arzawa; and

(3) although the province of Assuwa, as we have seen, is located in the Hermos valley, as much as four toponyms featuring in the list with a bearing on the blanket term Assuwian League can positively be situated in the realm of Arzawa (see above).

But what primarily concerns us here: in the contemporary Egyptian and Hittite sources the country name Assuwa only features during the latter half of the 15th century BC, which, by implication, provides us with a similar date for the silver stag-rhyton from the Schimmel collection! Note, however, in this context that posterior to this date the Mycenaean Linear B tablets both from Knossos (*c.* 1350 BC) and from Pylos (*c.* 1200 BC) are still referring to inhabitants of the region of Ephesos by the ethnic adjective *a-si-wi-jo* (m) and *a-si-wi-ja* (f), respectively (Woudhuizen 2009: 190). Similarly, in a list of country names of the Egyptian pharaoh of the 19th dynasty, Ramesses II (1279-1213 BC), *'Isy* still features in close association with *Kftỉw* 'Crete', presumably as a repetition from texts of his predecessors (Vercoutter 1956: 87, doc. 17).

Within the present framework, a final remark on the religion of the Luwians inhabiting the region of western Anatolia seems in order, especially in view of the fact that the writing of the country name Assuwa is, as we have seen in the above, identical with that of Isuwa and the 'awkward confusion' (Hawkins 1998a: 288) needs to be ruled out. As far as the religion of the Luwians of western Anatolia can be reconstructed, then, it is patently of the original Indo-European trifunctional type (cf. Woudhuizen 2010b). Thus, the stamp-cylinder seal Louvre AO 20.138 (Mora 1987: Ia 1.3), which on the stamp side bears the secondarily inscribed Luwian hieroglyphic legend *á-su-wi* 'Assuwiya', on the cylinder side shows us, alongside the Luwian hieroglyphic legend *amu Tarkukuruntas* 'I (am) Tarku(ku)runtas' as part of the original design, a highly informative scene in which we can discern:

(1) the sun-god (F1) rising between twin peaks at right of the top row;

(2) the storm-god (F2) mounted in his chariot in the center of the top row;

(3) the tutelary deity or stag-god (F3) mounted on a lion at the left of the lower row consisting of a hunting scene; note that this god is depicted with sacrificial slaughtered animals (the spoils of the hunt) in front of him and an *eya*-tree with a bird on top of it behind him;

(4) the sun-maiden or goddess of love (= trans-functional goddess), who is in the act of throwing off her cloths in order to prepare herself for making love with the storm-god (see above).

Furthermore, the cylinder seal discovered in Mycenaean Thebes, but which is of Anatolian origin (Mora 1987: IX 5.9) and in my opinion can be attributed to two successive Assuwian great kings, named *Tarḫundimuwas* and *Tarḫundiwalwas*, respectively, bears the testimony of a figurative scene consisting of:

(1) the tutelary deity (F3), with a lituus and a hare (the spoils of the hunt) in his left hand and brandishing a spear in the right hand;

(2) the sun-god (F1), whose identity, notwithstanding the fact that he carries the attribute of the storm-god, a bolt of lightning, in his left hand, can definitely be determined by the symbol of winged sun-disc above his head;

(3) the storm-god (F2) carrying a lance in his left hand;

(4) the sun-maiden or goddess of love (= trans-functional goddess), here depicted in her martial aspect with a shield in her left hand.

The identifications of the deities as presented here can be underlined by the Luwian hieroglyphic legends associated with them. Thus the tutelary deity is associated with the wish-formula LH 369 ***vita*** and LH 370 ASU (= ***bonus***$_2$) pertaining to the state or community as a whole, the sun-god with the names of the Assuwian or Arzawan great kings, the storm-god with the emblem of a king seated on a throne, and the sun-maiden with the name *Wastizitis* of a lower functionary, the ***hastarius*** 'spear-man' or more in specific '(member of the) body guard'. Note that from the sun-god onwards the images of the deities are associated with indications of functionaries of diminishing rank, ranging from great king via king to a lower functionary, which enhances the validity of our analysis to a great deal (Woudhuizen 2009: 204-212). Note also that, like in the case of the Schimmel rhyton, the lower functionary is directly associated with the goddess and that this latter, presumably, as we have seen, to be identified as Sauska, is a hypostase of the Assyrian goddess *Ištar* (Aro 2003: 305) or her Phoenician equivalent *Aštarte*, in other words of the Indo-European sun-maiden (< PIE *$h_2$stḗr- 'star').

Against this backdrop, then, there can be little doubt that the silver stag-rhyton from the Schimmel collection represents the third function (F3) in Dumézilian terms, abundantly attested, as we have just seen, for the clearly trifunctional religion of the Luwians of western Anatolia — which diminishes the possibility that the object is from Isuwa of which region similar detailed evidence on the religion of the population to the best of my knowledge is lacking. In addition, it will probably no longer come as a surprise if we remark that the *eya*-tree, associated with the stag-god, originates from PIE *$h_a$eig- 'oak' or, more in specific, the ever-green 'Turkey-oak' (*Quercus curris*) by the for Luwian regular loss of the voiced velar *[g] (see Mallory & Adams 2007: 161; cf. Woudhuizen 2011: 410-412).

5. Western Anatolia under Hittite Rule

5.1 Introduction

In a campaign during the 3rd and 4th year of his reign, the Hittite great king Mursilis II (1322-1295 BC) defeated the Arzawan king Uḫḫazitis, who was aided in the field by his sons Piyamakuruntas and Tapalazunawalis, and incorporated western Anatolia into his realm. In the wake of his victory, Mursilis II deported as much as 65,000 inhabitants of Arzawa to Ḫatti-land for resettlement in areas to the north and northeast of his homeland devastated by the ongoing wars with the Kaska. Moreover, the kingdom of Arzawa with its capital Apasa or Ephesos was replaced by that of Mira, named after the new capital identifiable, as we have seen in chapter 3, with present-day Beycesultan. No doubt the easternmost Mira was preferred by the Hittites to the westernmost Apasa in order to facilitate their military and political hold on the new kingdom. At any rate, its geographical extent, as proved by Hawkins readings of the Karabel inscriptions of 1998, remained in tact. As king of Mira Mursilis II appointed a prince of Mira, named Masḫuiluwas (see below), who also ruled over Kuwaliya in the region of present-day Afyon. Notwithstanding the fact that he had sided with the Arzawan king Uḫḫazitis, Mursilis II reinstated Manapatarḫundas as king of Seḫa, the region of the Kaikos valley to which also Appawiya, the upper Makestos region or Classical Abbaitis, belonged. The mildness of this measure was enhanced by the fact that according to the Hittites he owed his kingship in the first place to the intervention of Suppiluliumas I (1350-1322 BC) on his behalf in the conflict with his brother Uratarḫundas. Just like Manapatarḫundas, the king of the third 'Arzawa land', Targasnallis of Ḫapalla, situated in the region of the confluence of the Classical Sangarios river with that of the Porsuk, also maintained his position (Bryce 2010: 193-197). In year 12 of Mursilis II's reign, Masḫuiluwas joint a rebellion against his Hittite overlord and, as soon as the uprising was cut down, was replaced by his nephew and adopted son Kupantakuruntas II (Bryce 2010: 212-214).

In the subsequent reign of Muwatallis II (1295-1272 BC) we are informed about Hittite rule in western Anatolia by three documents which all bear reference to the Hittite intervention on behalf of Wilusa, located in the Troad, to ward off an attack by the Aḫḫiyawans or Mycenaean Greeks. This intervention took place *c.* 1280 BC (= end of Troy VIh in archaeological terms), just prior to the Hittite conflict with its rival great power in the Near East, Egypt, which culminated in the famous battle of Kadesh (1274 BC). The documents in question are the Manapatarḫundas-letter, the treaty with Alaksandus of Wilusa, and the Tawagalawas-letter (cf. chapter 7). In the Alaksandus-treaty, as much as four lands are grouped together as Arzawa lands (instead of the three mentioned earlier), each represented by its king, namely: Wilusa of Alaksandus, Mira-Kuwaliya of Kupantakuruntas, Seḫa-Appawiya of Manatarḫundas, and Ḫapalla of Uraḫattusas (Latacz 2010: 165, Alaksandus-treaty § 17). Of these four vassal kings, Manapatarḫundas was subsequently, but at an otherwise unspecified point in the reign of Muwatallis II, replaced by his son Masturis (Bryce 2010: 227). As it seems, this *status quo* was maintained during the reigns of Mursilis III (1272-1265 BC) and Ḫattusilis III (1265-1239 BC).

In the subsequent reign of Tudḫaliyas IV (1239-1209 BC) there are a few mutations. In the first place it deserves our attention that nothing is heard anymore about the kingdom of Ḫapalla, which may have succumbed to the ongoing infiltration of Thracian and Phrygian population groups from the European continent—a movement which, as we have noted in chapter 1, had already set in as early as the end of the 16th century BC. Next, Kupantakuruntas II of Mira-Kuwaliya was succeeded by his son Alantallis, who features in the text of the bronze tablet from the beginning of Tudḫaliyas IV's reign (Gander 2010: 164-165). Furthermore, later on in Tudḫaliyas IV's reign Masturis of Seḫa-Appawiya, who is still present as a witness in the text of the bronze tablet, was replaced by a certain Tarḫunaradus in a violent upsurge. This Tarḫunaradus subsequently rebelled against his Hittite overlord and was decisively defeated, Tudḫaliyas IV taking, amongst others, as much as 500 teams of horses for chariots as booty back to Ḫattusa (Bryce 2010: 304-305). Finally, in the Milawata-letter mention is made of a certain Walmus as king of Wilusa (Bryce 2010: 306-308).

At this point it may be instructive to present an overview of the events with a bearing on Tudḫaliyas IV's policy in the west and to try to determine their sequential order more in specific (cf. Bryce 2010: 295-326).

It is generally asssumed, that the treaty between Tudḫaliyas IV and his uncle Kuruntas as recorded for a bronze tablet from the Hittite capital Boğazköy-Ḫattusa, in which the borders of the realm of the latter, the province of Tarḫuntassa, are meticulously described, may plausibly be situated at or near the start of Tudhaliyas IV's reign (Otten 1988). In this treaty, a future campaign against Parḫa along the Kastaraya (= Pamphylian Perge along the Kestros) is announced, after the successful completion of which, so it is stipulated, the spoils will fall to Tarḫuntassa (Otten 1988: VIII, 60-2). The Lycian campaign as recorded for the Luwian hieroglyphic texts from Yalburt and Emirgazi could be a natural corollary to the inclusion of the Lycian borderland of Parḫa into the empire. At any rate, it is clear that Tudḫaliyas IV could not have attempted to exchange hostages from Pina(tí) and Awarna (= Pinara and Arna in the Xanthos valley) against those from Utima and Atriya with the father of the ruler of Milawata or Millawanda (= Miletos) as recorded for the Milawata-letter *before* his conquest of these places as commemorated in the Yalburt and Emirgazi texts—the more so because he goes at great length to stress that he is the first Hittite king to have campaigned in this region—, and hence we can be sure that the Milawata-letter postdates the aforesaid Lycian campaign (Woudhuizen 2004a: sections 3 and 4).

Now, the Milawata-letter informs us that the Hittite great king established the border of Milawata with the addressee of the letter, who is called 'his son' and therefore must be a regular vassal, whereas the father of the addressee had been a declared enemy, who refused to give the hostages from Utima and Atriya in return for the ones by Tudḫaliyas from Pina(tí) and Awarna.[1] The hostile behaviour by the father of the addressee of the Milawata-letter can only be explained by the fact that Milawata at that time is still in the sphere of influence of the king of Aḫḫiyawa (= Akhaia or Mycenaean Greece), as it had been before and after its destruction by Mursilis II in the third year of his reign (Niemeier 1998a: 38; Niemeier 1998b: 150-151). The last we hear about the king of Aḫḫiyawa, however, is that, according to the chronicle of Tudḫaliyas IV, Tarḫunaradus of the Seḫa river land—the successor of Masturis who is still present as a witness in the text of the aforesaid bronze tablet—relied on him when he transgressed against his Hittite overlord and was subsequently defeated, in the course of which event the Hittite great king captured as much as 500 chariots and an unfortunately lost number of troops—apart from taking into captivity Tarḫunaradus himself with his wives, children, and possessions.[2] As Milawata was the main Aḫḫiyawan stronghold on the Anatolian continent, it seems likely to assume that the recovery of Milawata within the Hittite sphere of influence postdates the insurrection by Tarḫunaradus of the Seḫa river land. At any rate, the immediate consequence of the volte face of Milawata was that the role of Aḫḫiyawa as a military factor in western Anatolia had effectively been ended, and, as cogently argued by Wolf-Dietrich Niemeier, this allowed the Hittite great king to erase the king of Aḫḫiyawa among his peers as attested for the Sauskamuwa-treaty, in which a ban on traffic between Aḫḫiyawa and Assyria is proclaimed.[3] In this manner, then, we arrive at the conclusion that the campaign against Tarḫunaradus of the Seḫa river land is most likely to be situated in between the Lycian campaign and the recovery of Milawata within the Hittite sphere of influence as attested for the Milawata-letter.

Tudḫaliyas IV's western policy culminates in his conquest of Alasiya (= Cyprus), which must have occurred near the very end of his reign, because, as explicitly stated by his successor, Suppiluliumas II (1205-1190 BC), contrary to standard procedures, he did not manage to set up a memorial for his victory—which omission was redressed by his devoted son after the latter's reconquest of Alasiya early in the latter's reign (Güterbock 1967; Woudhuizen 2004a: 72-74).

All in all, we arrive at the following sequence of events concerning Tudḫaliyas IV's policy in the west:

1. treaty with Kuruntas of Tarḫuntassa (bronze tablet);
2. conquest of Parḫa along the Kastaraya (preluded upon in the text of the bronze tablet);

[1] Hoffner 1982; translation improved by Güterbock 1986: 38, note 17. Note that the hostile nature of the father of the addressee precludes the possibility that the addressee is a king of Mira, as Hawkins 1998b: 19 wants to have it, because there is no evidence of a disloyal one in the reign of Tudḫaliyas IV.

[2] Güterbock 1992; note that Tarḫunaradus is explicitly stated to have been replaced by a descendant of Muwawalwis, the ruler of the Seḫa river land at the time of Suppiluliumas I (1350-1322 BC).

[3] Niemeier 1998b; for the Sauskamuwa-treaty, see Beckman 1996: 98-102. Note, however, that Tudḫaliyas IV is still preoccupied in this text with the misbehaviour of Masturis, who sided with Ḫattusilis III in his coup d'état against Urḫitesup or Mursilis III (1272-1264 BC), whereas that of his successor Tarḫunaradus was of a much more serious nature. Yet, to assume alternatively that Tarḫunaradus relied on the king of Aḫḫiyawa after the change of sides by Milawata seems highly unlikely, not to mention the fact that Masturis, who was appointed by Muwatallis II probably already before the battle of Kadesh (1274 BC), can hardly be assumed to have lived until an advanced stage of Tudḫaliyas IV's reign.

3. Lycian campaign (Yalburt, Emirgazi);
4. campaign against Tarḫunaradus of the Seḫa river land, who relied on the support of Aḫḫiyawa (Chronicle of Tudḫaliyas IV, KUB XXII 13);
5. recovery of Millawanda from the sphere of influence of Aḫḫiyawa (Milawata-letter, KUB XIX 55 + XLVIII 90);
6. ban on traffic between Aḫḫiyawa and Assyria (Sauskamuwa-treaty, KUB XXIII 1 (+)); and
7. Alasiya campaign (KBo XII 38; Nişantaş).

If this reconstruction of the events applies, it seems most likely that the Luwian hieroglyphic Köylütolu text, which commemorates the capture of Attarima somewhere in the hinterland of Miletos by prince Sauska(ku)runtis (Woudhuizen 2004a: section 2), took place in the course of Tudḫaliyas IV's recovery of Millawanda. Accordingly, it postdates the Yalburt and Emirgazi texts set up in commemoration of Tudḫaliyas IV's Lycian campaign.

It is interesting to note in this connection that according to the Milawata-letter, the king of Wilusa (= (W)ilion), Walmus, fell under the supervision of the governor of Miletos, to whiom he took refuge after his deposition by his own people. Now, as evidenced by a Luwian hieroglyphic inscription from Latmos, the region of Miletos was ruled by a great prince with the hypercoristic form *Kupaā* of a *Kupanta*-name characteristic of the royal house of Mira, probably near the very end of the Late Bronze Age (see Fig. 23; for the variant of LH 334 *pa* without handles, cf. Herbordt 2005: Kat. no. 208). Yet another inscription at the same location actually mentions the land of Mira (Peschlow-Bindokat & Herbordt 2001). As it seems, then, the region of Miletos fell under the supervision of Mira in an advanced stage of the reign of Suppiluliumas II. But the title of great prince presupposes subordination to a great king, hence the king of Mira may well have reached this preeminent status in the given period. The latter inference ties in with the fact that in a fragmentarily preserved letter (KBo XVIII 18) presumably by Suppiluliumas II, dealing with affairs concerning Wilusa, the addressee, Masḫuittas, is greeted by the extensive formula only reserved for great kings. This evidence for a great king of Mira would tie in with that for Kuruntas of Tarḫuntassa and Talmitesup of Karkamis suggesting that the Hittite empire in its latest stage was ruled by a tetrarchy of four great kings among which the one from Ḫatti functioned as *primus inter pares* (see Woudhuizen 2015d). As noted by Hawkins, it may in the given context plausibly be suggested that Masḫuittas actually was, as far as the Hittite cuneiform texts are concerned, the latest recorded king of Mira,[4] who, I would add, through his vassal residing in the region of Miletos, exercised power over the Troad. Indeed, this particular political constellation forms the proper background for the fact that in a Cypro-Minoan text from Ras Shamra-Ugarit (RS 20.25) dating from the reign of Suppiluliumas II the Trojan trader Akamas is staged as a representative of both Malos in the southern Troad and Apasa (= Ephesos), one of the main coastal cities of Mira (Woudhuizen 1994; Woudhuizen 2017: Part I, chapter 4)!

4 Hawkins 1998a: 20-21. For the text, see Hagenbuchner 1989, 2: 316-318, for the greeting formula, Hagenbuchner 1989, 1: 51-52.

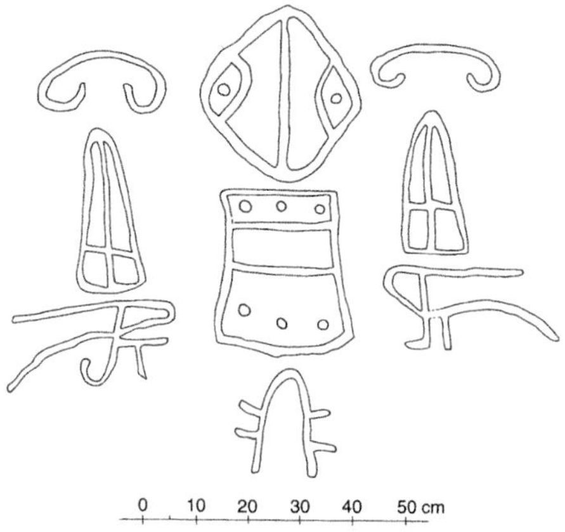

Fig. 23. Rock inscription of great prince *Kupaā* (Peschlow-Bindokat & Herbordt 2001: 373, Abb. 7a).

Concerning the reign of Suppiluliumas II (1205-1190 BC) we can distinguish two phases. In the first, of which we are informed by KBo XII 38 and the Luwian hieroglyphic Nişantaş text, this ruler was still preoccupied with keeping up the memory of his father, no doubt to legitimize his own rule. He finished the Alasiya campaign of his father and arranged a settlement which lasted up to the end of his reign. To this period belong the texts in Linear C of the cylinder seals from Enkomi and Kalavassos in Cyprus and of tablet RS 20.25 from Ras Shamra-Ugarit in which maritime trade was recorded for taxation (Woudhuizen 2017: Part I, chapters 2-4). Near the end of his reign, from which the Luwian hieroglyphic Südburg inscription stems—a monument which was left unfinished—, Suppiluliumas II no longer showed the zealous piety towards his father, who in fact is not even mentioned. According to the Südburg text, then, in this latter period he campaigned against *Wiyanawanda*, *Tamána*, *Masa*, *Lukka*, and *Ākuna*. As opposed to this, in the time of these campaigns the infrastructure of the province of Pala is stated to have been reinforced, whereas of the provinces of Walma and Tarḫuntassa it is said that these remained loyal (Woudhuizen 2004a: 76-90).[5] Accordingly, Suppiluliumas II demonstrates that he was fully in control of his realm (though the regions of Karkamis in North Syria and Mira in western Anatolia, headed by separate great kings, are not mentioned) just before its breakdown which apparently came like a bolt of lightning in a clear sky.

Of the regions against which Suppiluliumas II's campaigns were directed, *Tamána* likely corresponds to Hittite cuneiform *Tumana*. This is situated to the northeast of Pala (see Fig. 6), and in it the Kaska were traditionally active, so no doubt likewise at this time. Of the remaining four regions, *Masa*, *Wiyanawanda*, and *Lukka* are definitely located in the west. Thus *Wiyanawanda* is identical to Classical *Oinoanda* and in the Yalburt

[5] According to Südburg §§ 12-14 Tarḫuntassa had fallen to the crown, presumably after Kuruntas had died without an heir, and was placed under the authority of a governor, all this just before the demise of the empire.

Fig. 24. Sealing of prince Mašḫuiluwas (Mellaart 1959: 32, Fig. 1).

text functions as a military headquarters for Tudḫaliyas IV's Lycian campaign. Next, *Lukka* corresponds to Classical *Lycia*, whereas *Masa* bears reference to Classical *Mysia* situated to the east of the Troad. Now, a glance at our map suffices to show that *Masa* and *Lukka* border on the sea. Therefore, it seems likely that we are dealing here with Suppiluliumas II's reflection of the upheavals of the Sea Peoples, which ultimately caused the breakdown of his rule. If so, it may reasonably be argued that the remaining and somewhat puzzling *Ākuna* confronts us with a derivative in *-na* of a reflex of PIE *ak^wa- 'water', used here in lieu of Hittite *aruna-* 'sea'. In any case, as the Ugaritic letters inform us, Suppiluliumas II lost the sea battle in the waters of Lycia and his troops on land were, according to the Egyptian evidence, also decisively defeated (cf. van Binsbergen & Woudhuizen 2011: 226-230).

5.2 The Sealing of Prince Mašḫuiluwas

In Ortakaraviran Höyük, located to the southeast of Beyceltan-Mira in the province of Tarḫuntassa, a bulla has been found of a sealing of a prince whose name was suggested by James Mellaart to be that of the later king of Mira, Mašḫuiluwas (Mellaart 1954: 239-240). As we have seen, Mašḫuiluwas was appointed as king of Mira by Mursilis II (1322-1295 BC) after his defeat of Arzawa in the third and fourth year of his reign. The distinguished British archaeologist was followed in this identification by the French historian Jacques Freu (1980: 284). The identification of the MN Mašḫuiluwas, however, happens to be based on the flawed reading of LH 209, 3 *ā*, which follows the first sign LH 110 *ma* in the column to the right, as †*sa*.

In actual fact, then, the reading on this bulla of the personal name Mašḫuiluwas in the part of the legend between the antithetically arranged titular expression ***infans***^{m}-ḪANTAWAT 'prince' is problematic. According to the epigraphically correct order the name reads *ma-ḫú-wa-sa-ā-*UMINA+*li* (cf. Mora 1987: XIIa 2.17; see Fig. 24), which, however, makes no sense at all. The solution to the problem seems to be that the third sign of the column to the left, LH 415 *sa*, must be read before the first sign in this same column, LH 342 *ḫú*, that this sequence is followed by the signs in the right column, LH

209, 3 *ā* and LH 225 *UMINA* + LH 278 *li* which only makes sense as an alternative writing form of syllabic *lu*, and that LH 439 *wa* in the middle of the column to the left is to be taken as the last sign. In this manner, at least, we arrive at the reading: *ma-sa-ḫú-ā-l+u-wa* 'Masḫuiluwas'.

The problems posed by the reading of the name of the bulla from Ortakaraviran Höyük might be considered to be indicative of the fact that we are dealing with the product of an inexperienced scribe. In my opinion, however, the opposite conclusion should be drawn: even in this playful hotchpotch form the correct reading of the legend is immediately clear to an experienced reader. Especially the seemingly *ad hoc* solution of using *UMINA+li* for the expression of the syllabic value *lu* may be instigated by its close resemblance to LH 227 *um+r+li*, the writing of the name Mursilis—the king who eventually promoted Masḫuiluwas from mere prince to king of Mira. If so, the sealing can be dated to the period of 1322 BC to 1318 BC.

5.3 The Stone Inscription of *tuḫkanti* Urḫitesup

In Beyköy, which is located in the southwestern part of Ḫapalla (see Meriggi 1975: Carte geografiche), a stone inscription with a Luwian hieroglyphic legend has been found. This fragmentarily preserved stone inscription, which, against the backdrop of the other inscriptions from the same site, is to be labelled Beyköy 1, most recently received treatment by Emilia Masson (1980: 119-122). She was able to read in the second line the subject *KULANA* 'army' and the verbal form *tá-ta+r-ḫa-tá* 'it continued to be victorious' (note the reduplication of the verbal root *tarḫ-* 'to be victorious', which is used to render a frequentative aspect). The combination in the middle of these two elements can now be clarified thanks to the discovery of the bilingual sealings of Urḫitesup in his function as *tuḫkanti* 'heir elect' from the Nişantepe-archive at Boğazköy-Ḫattusa (Herbordt 2005: Kat. 504-505). At any rate, the lower sign clearly confronts us with an instance of LH 526 *TUḪKANTI*, which is related in form to LH 300 and LH 490. If this identification applies, the upper sign is not an instance of LH 423 *ku* but the lozenge for the expression of the first element of Urḫitesup's name, *URḪI*, on the aforesaid seals (see Fig. 25). Accordingly, the inscription dates from the latest phase of the reign of Muwatallis II (1295-1272 BC), when Urḫitesup had succeeded his half-brother Kuruntas as *tuḫkanti* 'heir elect' after the latter's premature death sometime after the period of the Tawagalawas-letter of *c.* 1280 BC (Woudhuizen 2005d; see p. 110, esp. note 14).

5.4 The Seal and Rock Relief of Tarku(ndimu)was

The famous Tarkondemos seal with a bilingual inscription, the one in Akkadian around the border and the other in Luwian hieroglyphic in the center, played a notorious role in the deciphering process of Luwian hieroglyphic, its exact reading being contested until recently (see Fig. 26). Nevertheless, it may reasonably be argued that the cuneiform legend should be emended as follows: ^{m}*Tar-qu-u-tim-me* LUGAL KUR ^{URU}*Me-ra-a*. Furthermore, the Luwian hieroglyphic version, considering the fact that David Hawkins has recently shown that LH 320 is a mere variant of LH 165 *wá* owing to its interchange with regular LH 439 *wa* on sealings from the Nişantepe-archive, definitely

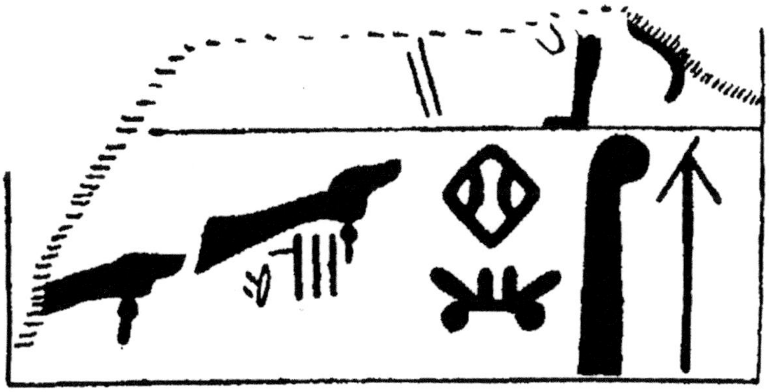

KULANA URḪI<-TESUP> TUḪKANTI tá-ta+r-ḫa-tá

'The army (of) Urḫitesup, the heir elect, continued to be victorious'

Fig. 25. Stone inscription Beyköy 1 (Masson 1980: 119, Fig. 5).

Cun. ^{m}*Tar-qu-u-tim-me* LUGAL KUR ^{URU}*Me-ra-a*

Hier. *TARKU-wá ḪANTAWAT mi+r(a)-à*^{UTNA}

'Tarku(ndimu)was, king (of) the land Mira'

Fig. 26. Seal of 'Tarkondemos' (Doblhofer 2008: 192, Abb. 64).

Fig. 27. Rock relief at Karabel (Hawkins 1998b: 7, Fig. 5b).

reads *TARKU-wá ḪANTAWAT mi+r(a)-à*^UTNA^.[6] The translation of both variants of the legend remains the same: 'Tarkondemos, king (of) the land Mira'.

The difference in form of the royal name between the two versions of the bilingual inscription can plausibly be explained by the fact that the Luwian hieroglyphic variant, on the analogy of short hand versions like *ḫá+li* and *um+r+li* of the Hittite royal names Ḫattusilis and Mursilis as attested for numerous sealings, constitutes an abbreviation of **Tarkundimuwas*. In variant writing *TARKU-wa*, this same abbreviation is traceable on sealings of the same king of Mira from Boğazköy-Ḫattusa (Güterbock 1975: 51, nos. 6-7).

We also owe it to the merit of Hawkins (this time in 1998) that *Tarku(ndimu)was* of Mira can be identified as the penultimate ruler of Mira (in actual fact he is the last but two). In the legend added to the rock relief at Karabel, namely, the name *Tarkuwas* features together with that of his father and grandfather. Of the latter two names, only the first is readable as *ARA+li*, which Hawkins likely identified with cuneiform *Alantallis*. If this is correct, the no longer readable name of the grandfather may be restored as *Kupantakuruntas* (= Kupantakuruntas II) (see Fig. 27).

According to these stunning readings, Tarkuwas of Mira can be positively identified as the successor of Alantallis, who, as we have noted in the above, is mentioned as king of Mira among the witnesses in the text of the bronze tablet from the beginning of the reign of Tudḫaliyas IV (1239-1209 BC). Against this backdrop, the reign of Tarkuwas over Mira is likely to be situated at an advanced stage of that of Tudḫaliyas IV and during the beginning of that of Suppiluliumas II (1205-1190 BC). In this scenario, then, Tarkuwas is succeeded by Masḫuittas who ruled over Mira in the final years of the Bronze Age just anterior to the demise of the Hittite empire in the period of the upheavals of the Sea Peoples. For the latter's successor, Kupantakuruntas III, who ruled in the period of the upheavals of the Sea Peoples, see discussion of Beyköy 2 in chapter 6.

[6] Hawkins in Herbordt 2005: 257 with reference to the correspondence of Kat. 281-286 to Kat. 287-289. Note that Hawkins is mistaken, though, in taking the goat's head LH 101 *TARKU* as a mere variant of the donkey's head LH 100 *TARKASNA* on account of their interchange as a result of a scribal error in the Assur letter f-g, §§ 21-22.

5.5 The Stone Inscription of Prince Masḫuittas

On a 'Phrygian throne' stone monument at Beyköy have been found fragmentarily preserved inscriptions bearing the reference to prince Masḫuittas. The inscriptions in question are numbered here Beyköy 3-4 (see Fig. 32, A-B). According to their legends prince Masḫuittas is, like Tarkuwas of the rock relief at Karabel, the son of Alantallis. So he and Tarkuwas must have been brothers or half-brothers.

Beyköy 3-4

(A)	***infans***^{m}*+ḪANTAWAT* *ma-sa-<ḫù>+i-ti URA+ḪANTAWAT* *á-la-na-ta*$_6$*+li*	'prince Masḫuittas, (son of) great king Alantallis'
(B)	*á-la-na-ta*$_6$*+li* ***infans***^{m}	'son (of) Alantallis'

As we know from the combined evidence of the Hittite letter KBo XVIII 18 (Hagenbuchner 1989, 2: 317) and the Luwian hieroglyphic inscription Beyköy 2 (see section 6.1), Masḫuittas ultimately became great king of Mira. According to the present texts, the same status had already been achieved by his father Alantallis.

5.6 The Luwian Hieroglyphic Stele from Afyon

In 2003, Seracettin Şahin and Recai Tekoğlu have published a stele with a Luwian hieroglyphic inscription which had come to light four years before as a result of illegal diggings in the province of Afyon (Şahin & Tekoğlu 2003).[7] The hieroglyphic inscription on this stele, presently exhibited in the museum of Afyon, runs boustrophedon from top to bottom over 5 clearly indicated lines (see Fig. 28). It consists of two phrases in sum, governed by a verb form lacking a proper ending, in like manner as this happens to be the case for the Südburg text from an advanced stage of the reign of the last known Hittite great king, Suppiluliumas II (1205-1190 BC).[8]

Nevertheless, owing to the use of the dative of the enclitic pronoun of the 1st person singular, *-mi*, it may safely be deduced that the endingless verbal forms render the 1st person singular of the past tense in *-ḫa*. Contrary to the opinion of the editors of the text, however, I do not think that the given form of the enclitic pronoun is used for the expression of the nominative, as such a use is (apart from an example in a Luwianizing inscription on a seal from Cyprus dated to the 15th century BC, reading *mi* WALWA-*á* 'I (am) Walwas')[9] only attested for related forms in the later Luwian dialects Lydian (*-m* 'I') and Sidetic (*m*$_1$*i* 'I').[10] It is a characteristic feature of the inscription under discussion, namely, that the enclitic pronoun *-mi* occurs twice in coordinative phrases directly associated with the GN Tarḫunt, thanks to whom the accomplishment of phrase 1 is

[7] Cf. Ehringhaus 2005: 48-49.
[8] Hawkins 1995; Woudhuizen 2004a: 76-90.
[9] See chapter 4, Fig. 16.
[10] Woudhuizen 2010-1a: 209; Woudhuizen 1984-5: 121-22.

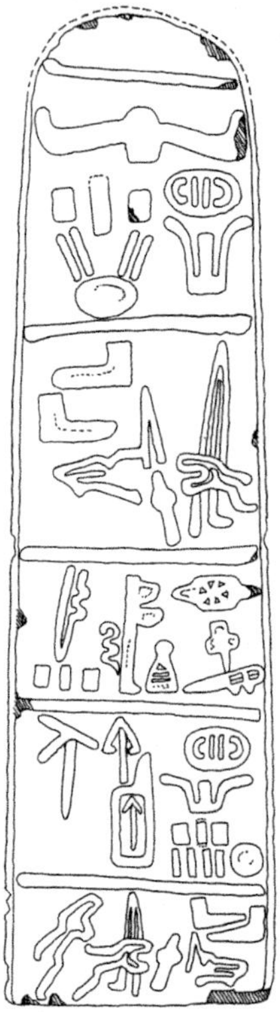

Fig. 28. Stele from Afyon (Ehringhaus 2005: 48, Abb. 90).

achieved and to whom the monument is dedicated in the second phrase. In this manner, the dedicator of the monument wants to express that the accomplishment of phrase 1 *also* results from his own involvement, and that the dedication of phrase 2 *also* has a bearing on himself, while at the same time, by using a chain of enclitics, he is trying to avoid the impression to be presumptuous.

Another salient point concerns the region mentioned in the first phrase in which the verbal root *warpa-* (as expressed by the 'uraeus'-sign LH 273, on which see Woudhuizen 2007: 717) informs us that the dedicator 'represented the crown' in the region in which the stele has been dedicated, presumably its find-spot, the region of Afyon. With a view to this find-spot of the stele, it has been reasonably argued by the editors of the text that reference may well be made here to the region of *Kuwaliya*, the annex to the realm of Mira with its capital *Apasa* 'Ephesos' in Hittite texts and therefore likely situated inland of the latter realm, which means precisely in the region of Afyon. In my opinion, the first sign of the geographic name in question is not LH 286 *wa*$_7$, as the editors want to have it, but LH 329, 4, also catalogued as LH 460 and, redundantly, LH 508,[11] consisting of a helmet with cheek-piece and expressing the value *ḪWÁ*. If we add to this that the sign below it is likely to be analyzed as a ligature of LH 278 *li* with LH 450 *à*, we arrive as a lenited variant *Ḫwáliyà* of the geographic name Kuwaliya!

If we allow for the aforegoing adjustments, we arrive at the following transliteration (in the system of my series on Luwian hieroglyphic)[12] and translation:

Afyon

1. ^{1}***sol suus*** ^{MASANA}*TARḪUNT*	'(On behalf of) his majesty,
-wa -mi -ḫa ^{2}*TARPA-MALIA-WATA*	(thanks to) Tarḫunt as well
infans^{m}*+ḪANTAWAT*	as by my (own effort), (I),
^{3}*TASḪUWAR+WÁSU ḪWÁ-li+à*^{UMINA}	Tarpamaliawatas, prince,
WARPA	(have) represent(ed) the
	crown (in) the blessed
	land (of the town of)

[11] Numbering according to Hawkins 2000: 24, Table 1.

[12] Woudhuizen 2013a: 9-12; most recently, see Woudhuizen 2015a: 29-30.

	Kuwaliya.'
2. *à-wa* [4]*i* *scalprum*WANA MASANATARḪUNT -*wa* -*mi* -*ḫa* [5]TARPA-MALIA-WATA ***infans***m+ḪANTAWAT TUWA	'And this inscribed stele (I), Tarpamaliawatas, prince, (have) erecte(d for) Tarḫunt as well as for my(self).'

Two remaining points are of relevance to elaborate on: the date of the inscription and the nature of the personal name of its dedicator. To start with the dating, I am inclined to ascribe this text to an advanced stage of the reign of the last Hittite great king, Suppiluliumas II. In any case, the use of the winged sun-disc (LH 190) at the start of the text suggests that it dates to the Hittite empire period (it seems unlikely that the realm of great king Ḫartapus, the Early Iron Age successor of the 'Sekundogenitur' in Tarḫuntassa, included the region of Afyon), whereas we have already noted that the lack of verbal endings is a characteristic feature of the Südburg text, dating from an advanced stage of Suppiluliumas II's reign. But what in my view really tips the balance in favor of this latter dating is the fact that the region of Afyon entails a border zone located precisely in between the provinces of Pala and Walma on the one hand, mentioned in the Südburg texts as being under a governor 'serving well', and the more westerly regions of Wiyanawanda, Lukka, and Masa on the other hand, against which Suppiluliumas II's military actions as commemorated in the Südburg text are directed (see Fig. 6). It seems highly conceivable, therefore, that one of Suppiluliumas II's subordinates, in this case a prince, had been engaged in some sort of preparatory actions in the given border zone (either of a consolidating or of an extending nature) in order to pave the way for the great king's military interventions further to the west.

As an alternative historical reconstruction, with ***sol suus*** 'his majesty' reference may be made to the great king of Mira, to the realm of whom the province of Kuwaliya belonged. It so happens, namely, that at least from the times of Masḫuittas onwards Mira is governed by a great king, whose rank is acknowledged by the Hittites in the greeting formula of KBo XVIII 18 (Hagenbuchner 1989, 1: 317). In the text from the reign of Kupantakuruntas III, the son of Masḫuittas, Beyköy 2, § 12, the latter great king states to have built roads in Kuwaliya which connected this province with Pitassa (to the southeast), Sallapa (to the southwest), and Masa (to the northwest).[13] Apparently, the region of Afyon already functioned as a crossroads in the final stage of the Late Bronze Age, and Tarpamaliawatas may have served great king Masḫuittas of Mira by representing the crown (endingless form of the verb *warpa-*) of the latter in the province of Kuwaliya.

Finally, about the name of the dedicator, it might, considering the fact that the first element *tarpa-* means 'to trample' (Woudhuizen 2015a: indices s.v.), whereas the further elements *malia-wata-* refer to 'sacred water, pool' (Woudhuizen 2004a: 37-38),[14] at first

[13] See section 6.1 below.

[14] The titular expression on seal Mora 1990: XII 2.64 from Mersin, as referred to by Hawkins 2006: Fig. 10, does

sight be frowned upon as an incompatible compound. But it should be borne in mind in this connection that the mythical horse *Pegasos*, whose name originates from the Luwian epithet of the storm-god, *piḫaššašši-* (Haas 1994: 78), caused springs to well up wherever one of his hooves trampled upon the earth.

Ḫatti	**date**	**Assuwa/Arzawa/Mira**	**Seḫa**
KÜLTEPE/KANESH			
Pitḫanas	1790-1770		
Anittas	1770-1750	Tarkundimuwas	
Peruwas			
		Tarku(ku)runtas	
OLD KINGDOM			
Ḫuzziya I	1680-1670		
Labarnas I	1670-1650		
Ḫattusilis I	1650-1620		
Mursilis I	1620-1590		
Ḫantilis I	1590-1560		
Zidantas I	1560-1550		
Ammunas	1550-1530		
Ḫuzziyas II	1530-1525		
Telipinus	1525-1500		
Alluwamnas			
Ḫantilis II			
Taḫurwailis			
Zidantas			
Ḫuzziya III			
Muwatallis I			
EMPIRE			
Tudḫaliyas I	1465-1440	Tarḫundimuwas	
Ḫattusilis II	1440-1425	Tarḫundiwalwas	
Tudḫaliyas II	1425-1390	Piyamakuruntas	
Arnuwandas I	1400-1370	Kukkulis	
		Kupantakuruntas I	
Tudḫaliyas III	1370-1350	Tarḫundaradus	

not concern the combination under discussion, but correctly reads, as is especially clear for the variant on side b, MALIA-*509 'sacred lancer'.

Suppiluliumas I	1350-1322	Uḫḫazitis	Muwawalwis
		Piyamakuruntas	Uratarḫundas
		Tapalazunawalis	
Mursilis II	1322-1295	Masḫuiluwas	Manapatarḫundas
		Kupantakuruntas II	
Muwatallis II	1295-1272		Masturis
Mursilis III	1272-1265		
Ḫattusilis III	1265-1239		
Tudḫaliyas IV	1239-1209	Alantallis	Tarḫunaradus
		Tarku(ndimu)was	unspec. descendant of
Arnuwandas III	1209-1205	Masḫuittas	Muwawalwis
Suppiluliumas II	1205-1190	Kupantakuruntas III	
			Walwamuwas

Table IX. Synchronisms between the dynasties of Ḫattusa, Arzawa, and Seḫa (based on Gurney 1990: 181, Woudhuizen 2005a: 112-113, and Freu 2007: 25-26).

6. Western Anatolia in the Final Stage of Bronze Age

6.1 Introduction

It is thanks to the intervention of Eberhard Zangger and his foundation Luwian Studies that recently a set of Luwian hieroglyphic inscriptions from western Anatolia has been rediscovered (Zangger & Woudhuizen 2018). The texts, of which the publication as planned for the early 1980s for some reason came to no avail, were found in a pile of papers on the so-called 'Beyköy Text' belonging to the inheritance of the British archaeologist James Mellaart (1925-2012), acquired by Zangger and his foundation in June of 2017. Most important among them is the one labelled Beyköy 2 here, which amounts 50 phrases in sum and as such confronts us with the longest Luwian hieroglyphic text from the Late Bronze Age and the most significant find within the discipline since that of the Karatepe bilingual in 1947. The remaining texts are shorter, the one from Edremit entailing 4 phrases in sum, the one from Yazılıtaş consisting of 1 verbless phrase, whereas the ones from Dağardı (1-2) are only fragmentarily preserved. Finally, there are some fragments from Beyköy (Beyköy 3-4), again, and from Şahankaya.

The inscription from Yazılıtaş (‹inscribed stone›) in the region of Classical Pergamon was found as early as in 1854. At that time the Luwian hieroglyphic script was not yet known, and so the inscription was thought of as being conducted in Egyptian hieroglyphic writing. The inscription is stated to be in high relief, which remark may well be valid for the other inscriptions as well. Next, the inscription from Edremit in the southern Troad is stated to have been found in 1871 and the local authorities had kept the blocks at Belediye ('municipality') Garden until Georges Perrot (as the story goes) copied them in 1878. The longest text, Beyköy 2, was found in 1878 and copied (according to the same story) by Perrot in the same year, together with the other two inscriptions. There is no information about the date and find circumstances of the remaining fragments other than that one from Beyköy (Beyköy 3) was found on a Phrygian 'throne' and that the ones from Dağardı and Şahankaya are rock reliefs found in the mountains.

The longest text, Beyköy 2, is a dedication by the great king of Mira, Kupantakuruntas III, who was the son of Masḫuittas and ruled in the period of the upheavals of the Sea Peoples during the first decades of the 12th century BC. Even though this king maintains to have respected Hittite interests, he only mentions Arnuwandas III (1209-1205 BC) and that this king had died. If his silence about the successor of Arnuwandas III, Suppiluliumas II (1205-1190 BC), means that he did not recognize the latter as the legitimate heir to the Hittite throne, presumably because Suppiluliumas was a younger brother and not the eldest son of Arnuwandas III, the Hittites surely had a problem along their western borders! At any rate, the realm of Kupantakuruntas III consisted of the great kingdom of Mira-Kuwaliya or Arzawa, ruled directly by himself, and further entailed the kingdoms of Assuwa, Seḫa, Ḫapalla, and Wilusa, each headed by a vassal king. Furthermore, the western part of Ḫapalla formed a separate province called Atapali, in which the town of modern Beyköy was situated, and was also headed by a vassal king. The most outstanding achievement commemorated in the text is the maritime conquest of Ashkelon in Philistia, executed under the command of the great prince of Wilusa, Muksus, together with some of his colleagues. The memory of this historical feat is preserved in Greek myth in the legendary tales about Mopsos whose conquests led him all the way to Ashkelon in the Levant (Houwink ten Cate 1961: 44-50, esp. 45). Great prince Muksus is rewarded with the realm of Wilusa and his seat is specified here as *Apassawa* 'Apaisos', whereas one of his colleagues, Kulanamuwas, received the realm of Masa as his dominion. As a result of the maritime conquests up to the border of Egypt in the Levant kings in the region, like the ones from Kizzuwatna in southeast Anatolia and Karkamis in North Syria, are stated to have brought gifts to Kupantakuruntas III as a token of their appreciation or even submission.

The inscription from Edremit is a dedication by the great prince of Mira and Wilusa, Muksas. As Muksas is a writing variant of Muksus as recorded for Beyköy 2, we are dealing here with the same vassal of Kupantakuruntas III and both inscriptions are therefore no doubt from the same chronological horizon. In the text, Muksas provides us with an overview of the extent of his realm, summing up as many as 43 place-names. This overview begins in the west, with the islands of Lesbos, Imbros, Lemnos, and Tenedos. It then continues clockwise with a series of place-names situated to the north-east of Troy, like Abydos, Arisbe, Perkote, Pityeia, and Parion. The enumeration ends with localities in the southeast of the Troad, like Gargara, the town of mount Leleges, and Adramyttion or Edremit itself. The last mentioned region is known by Homeros (*Iliad* XX, 92-96; XXI, 86) as the territory of the Leleges, who are likely to be identified as an Indo-European Anatolian if not actually Luwian population group on the basis of the place-names in *-ss-* (*Lyrnēssos*) and *-nth-* (*Sminthē*) found here (see chapter 1). In this part of Muksas' realm, then, the inhabitants were presumably able to read a Luwian hieroglyphic text like the present one. However, this does not necessarily mean that the dominant language of the entire Troad was Luwian. The personal name *Muksas* or *Muksus* itself is definitely of non-Luwian type and most likely to be identified as Phrygian on account of its attestation in form of *Muksos* for a Phrygian inscription from tumulus MM at Gordion, dating to the 8th century BC (Liebhart & Brixhe 2009: 145; 155, Fig. 5). This tallies with the fact that the place-name *Adrasteia* is derived from the Phrygian MN *Adrastos* (Woudhuizen 2018: 36-37). Moreover, among the place-names mentioned in the text there can be found some definite Thracian ones among those situated to the northeast of Troy, like most certainly *Pityeia*, derived from the Thracian vocabulary word πιτύη 'treasury' (Detschew 1976: 372), but presumably also *Arisbe* and *Perkote* (Detschew 1976: 364; 25). As a consequence, the dominant language in the Troad may well have been of Thraco-Phrygian type (see further chapter 9).

The inscription from Yazılıtaş is a dedication by a great king of Seẖa, called Walwamuwas, who specifies himself as the son of Kupantakuruntas III. Apparently, therefore, this inscription dates from about a generation later in time as Beyköy 2 and Edremit. As it seems, the status of the ruler of Seẖa at this time had risen to that of great king. At any rate, what primarily concerns us here is that Walwamuwas also presents us an overview of his realm and that among the place-names enumerated by him we can easily identify Lesbos, Adramyttion, Atarneus, and the town of mount Leleges. The overlap in this enumeration with the one concerning the southeastern Troad in the Edremit inscription may well be explained by the fact that Yazılıtaş postdates Edremit and that the status of the ruler of Seḫa has been upgraded to that of great king at this time and his realm may have been enlarged at the expense of that of the Troad. However this may be, the mention of Atarneus clearly indicates that the river land of Seḫa is to be located in the Kaikos valley.

The latter inference is further enhanced by the evidence from Dağardı 2. This inscription is a dedication by prince Asaḫ[ ]s of Seḫa, who specifies himself as the son of Walwamuwas. Accordingly, this inscription may postdate the one from Yazılıtaş by one generation, or alternatively, prince Asaḫ[ ]s may have been seated in the eastern part of Seḫa as a Sekundogenitur by his father already during the latter's lifetime. In any case, among the place-names enumerated in the by now familiar practice of the dedicator to present an overview of his realm we can easily identify Pergamon, Thyateira, Pitane, and Adramyttion. In snooker terms, this clinches the frame and there can be no doubt about the location of Seḫa in the Kaikos valley.

Finally, from the fragmentarily preserved inscription Dağardı 2, which is a dedication by an otherwise unrelated prince Masanatarḫunas, it is clear that the site of Dağardı was called Masturiwantasa at the time, after Masturis, the ruler of Seḫa from the period of the reign of the Hittite great king Muwatallis II (1295-1272 BC) onwards. Moreover, it seems likely that the eastern part of Seḫa from which Dağardı 1-2 originate and which in the main consisted of the upper Makestos region was called Appawiya in the Late Bronze Age, a name subsequently reflected in Classical Abbaitis.

The Luwian hieroglyphic inscriptions rediscovered from the files of Mellaart are highly informative about a period and a region shrouded in darkness until recently. Owing to these inscriptions, there can be no doubt any more about the location of Seḫa in the Kaikos valley and of Wilusa in the Troad. Furthermore, because of their date to the first half of the 12th century BC they shed light on a period formerly known as the Dark Age. Clearly, therefore, our thanks are due to Eberhard Zangger and his foundation Luwian Studies, without the intervention of whom these texts would still be hidden in the files of Mellaart's inheritance. It is thanks to the kind gesture of Zangger that I am able to present in the following photographs of the drawings of these texts and to render them in transliteration and translation (for a comprehensive linguistic commentary, see Zangger & Woudhuizen 2018).

6.2 The Rediscovered Luwian Hieroglyphic Inscriptions from Western Anatolia in Transliteration and Translation

Beyköy 2

1.	***sol suus*** *URA+ḪANTAWAT* *la+PÁRNA ku-pa-tá-KURUNT* *la+PÁRNA URA+ḪANTAWAT* *mi+r(a)-à*^{UTNA} *URA+ḪANTAWAT* *ma-sa-ḫù+i-ti* ***infans***^{m} *URA+ḪANTAWAT á-la-na-ti+li* ***infans***^{m} *ku-pa-tá-KURUNT* *URA+ḪANTAWAT mi+r(a)-à*^{UTNA} <***infans***^{m}>	'His Majesty, great king, labarnas Kupantakuruntas, labarnas, great king (of) Mira, son (of) great king Masḫuittas, son (of) great great king Alantallis, son (of) Kupantakuruntas, great king of Mira.'
2.	*à-wa PÁRANA-na wa-la-mu-sa* *ḪANTAWAT wi-lu-sa*^{UTNA} *[ ]*	'On behalf of Walmus, king (of) Wilusa [ ].'
3.	*[ ] i pa-ti [ ] UMINA*	'[ ] this for him [ ] town.'
4.	*à-wa mi+r(a)-à*^{UTNA} *à+ta* *mi-ti-sa UMINA ARḪA* *PARNA(+r)-ta*$_{6}$	'In Mira (the enemy) destroyed the town of a servant.'
5.	*à-wa ma-sa-ḫù+i-ti* *URA+ḪANTAWAT wi-lu-sa*^{UTNA} *[ ]*	'Great king Masḫuittas [supported] Wilusa.'
6.	*i[-wa] PARNA+r-ti ARḪA* *UMINA-mi-na*^{UMINA} *[ ]*	'(If the enemy) will destroy this town,'
7.	*à-wa [ ]*	
8.	*ta*$_{4}$*-pa*<*+r*>*-sa*$_{7}$*-la UMINA na*$_{4}$ *ta*$_{4}$*-pa*<*+r*>*-sa*$_{7}$*-la* *ā-wi-sa-nà*^{UMINA} *PARNA(+r)-na-sa-nà*^{UMINA} *ta+r-wi-sa*^{UMINA} *TAPAR-wi-sa*^{UMINA} *ki+r-su-sa*^{UMINA} *[ ]*^{UMINA} *na*$_{4}$ *há+r-na*^{UTNA} *pu-ru-sú-wa*^{UMINA}	'Towns of the government (and) not (directly) of the government (total 25): Awisana, Parnasana, Troy, Taparwisa, Kirsusa, [ ]; not (directly): the land (of) Ḫarna, Purusuwa, Suruta, the land (of)

	su-ru-ti^{UMINA} *wí/zu-sà-na-ti*^{UTNA} *APA-sa-sa-wa*^{UTNA} *ā-ta+r-ma-sa*^{UMINA} *lu+r-sa-na-saUMINA ā-ti-tu+r(a)*^{UMINA} *ā-su-wa*^{UMINA} *UTNA* *TIWATA-ru-sa*^{UMINA} *sá-wi-sa*^{UMINA} *ku-ru-ti-sa*^{UMINA} *wa-sa-ta+r-nà*^{UMINA} *pa-la-na-sa*^{UMINA} *ti-wa-lú-sa*^{UMINA} *KWA-pa-na-sa*^{UMINA} *na*$_{4}$ *-pu -la* *ti-wa ka-wa-sa-ká+r(i)*^{UMINA} *ku-su+r-ā*^{UTNA} *ḫa-pu-ru-sa*^{UMINA}	Wi/Zusanati, the land (of) Apaisos, Atarmasa, Lursanasa, Atitura, the land (of) Assuwa-town, Tiwatarusa, Sawisa, Kurtisa, Wastarna, Palanasa, Tiwalusa, Kwapanasa; formerly not go(ing along) with him: in Kawasaka, the land (of) Kusura, Ḫapurusa.'
9.	*à-wa ī ÁMU ta-sa -ḫa* *mi+r(a)-à*^{UTNA} *tà-ḫa*	'I placed this stele also (for/in) Mira.'
[ ]		
10.	*à-wa ā-la-na-ti -li* ***infans***^{m}*+ḪANTAWAT URA+PARNA* ***infans***^{m} *TUZI-mi wi-lu-sa*^{UTNA} *á URA+ḪANTAWAT* *mi[+r(a)]-à*$^{[UTNA]}$	'The prince (or) palace official (who) will covet (it) for himself: may you guard Wilusa (like) the great king (of) Mira (did)!'
[ ]		
11.	*à-wa URA+ḪANTAWAT* *mi[+r(a)]-à*^{UTNA}	'Great king (of) Mira,'
12.	*URA+ḪANTAWAT ku-wa-lú-à*^{UTNA} *à+ta pi-ta*$_{6}$*-sa*^{UTNA} *à ḫa*$_{6}$*+r-wa-na* *KWA UTNA sa-la-pa*^{UTNA} *ma-sa*^{UMINA}	'(I), great king, made a road in Kuwaliya (to) Pitassa (and) what(ever) land: Sallapa (and) Masa-town,'
13.	*à-wa ḪARWAN ma-sa-na-ti*^{UTNA}	'and a road into the divine land.'
14.	*à-wa -mu URA+ḪANTAWAT* *mi+r(a)-à*^{UTNA} *TIWA*$_{2}$*-TIWA*$_{2}$*-wa* *ḪÁ(TI)-sa*^{UTNA} **202 à-wa*	'I, great king (of) Mira, will continue to provide (for) the sanctuarie(s) of Ḫatti, (and) I will make (use of them).'
15.	*à-wa ḪÁ(TI)*^{UTNA} *sá-sá-ḫa*	'I continuously rendered

		support (to) Ḫatti.'
16.	*à-wa mi+r(a) ta-ta$_6$ UTNA i-i 6000* *ma ma*	'Mira has placed (in) the land these 6000 rams.'
17.	*à-wa 10 UMINA+mi TAMA-ḫa* *mi+r(a)-à-ti^{UTNA}* *mi+r(a)-à^{UMIN}A PÁRA-ASA^{UMINA}* *[?-?]-wa^{UMINA} TARKU-wa^{UMINA}* *á+r-TARKU-nà^{UMINA} wa-ḫa$_4$-ma^{UMINA}* *ā-mu-wa^{UMINA} mi-ta$_6$-sa^{UMINA}* *ḫá-pa-nu^{UMINA} ma-TARKU -ḫa$^{[UMINA]}$*	'I have built 10 citadel(s) in Mira: Mira-town, Parasa, [ ]wa, Tarkuwa, Artarkuna, Waḫama, Amuwa, Mitasa, Ḫapanu, and Matarku.'
18.	*à-wa URA+PARNA* *^{MASANA}PARNA i-ā-i* *^{MASANA}TARḪUNT ^{MASANA}(a)pá+r(a)* *^{MASANA}ku-*128 URA+**domina*** *PÁRA-ASA^{UMINA} TAMA-ḫa wa-[ā]*	'I have built a palace (and) a temple for these (3 gods): Tarḫunt, the god of the field, (and) Kupapa, the queen (of) Parasa, (while) pray(ing).'
19.	*à-wa ḪANTAWAT ḫá-pa-la^{UTNA}* *ā[ ]* *ta$_4$-la+r(i)^{UMINA} á+r-ma-ta$_6$^{UMINA}* *ḫi-li-?+r^{UMINA} la-la-ta^{UMINA}* *sa$_5$+r-tu-wa^{UMINA} la+r(i)-ma^{UMINA}* *PARNA(+r)-ta$_6$ ARḪA*	'The king (of) Ḫapalla [ ] destroyed (6 towns): in Tala, Armata, Ḫili[..]r, Lalanda, Sartuwa, (and) Larima.'
20.	*à-wa ḪANTAWAT á-ta$_6$-pa-li^{UTNA}* *PARNA-su-ḫa-na-ti^{UMINA} ā-la-?^{UMINA}* *na-ḫi-ta$_6$^{UMINA} ḫu-ta-na^{UMINA}* *PARNA(+r)-ta$_6$ ī **infans**^{m}na-na^{UMINA}*	'The king (of) Atapali fortified (5 towns): in Parnasuḫana, Ala[..], Naḫita, Ḫutana, (and) this town (of) a son (= junior official) [= Beyköy].'
21.	*à-wa 6 ḪANTAWAT^{i}* *ḪANTAWAT wa-lu-sa^{UTNA}* *ḪANTAWAT ḫá-pa-la^{UTNA}* *ḪANTAWAT URA-WALWA^{UTNA}* *ḪANTAWAT AS[UW]A -ḫa^{UTNA}*	'(There are in sum) 6 king(s): the king (of) Wilusa, the king (of) Ḫapalla, the king (of) Urawalwas' land (= Seḫa), and the king (of) Assuwa,'

22.	*à-wa URA+ḪANTAWAT* *mi+r(a)-à*^{UTNA}	'and the great king (of) Mira,'
23.	*à-wa i URA-ḪANTAWAT ARA-wa*	'(and) this (one is also) the great king (of) Arzawa.'
24.	*à-wa á+ya ḪANTAWAT ḪÁ(TI)*^{UTNA} *URA+UMINA ta*$_6$ *ta+r-sa*^{UMINA} *ā-ti-na*^{UMINA} *la-wa-ta*$_4$*-ti*^{UMINA} *na*$_4$ *à-ma-na mu-ka-sa +ḫa*^{UTNA} *ha-la-pa*^{UTNA} *ká+r-ka-mi+sa*^{UTNA} *wa-ka+r-tá*^{UTNA} *[ ]*^{UTNA} *ā-ma-tu*^{UTNA} *ku-pi-la*^{UTNA}	'The hero, king (of) Ḫatti, provides the capital (for the towns): Tarsos, Adana, (and) Lawazantiya; (and) not (directly): the lands (of) Amanos and Mukish, Ḫalpa, Karkamis, Ugarit, [ ], Hamath, (and) Byblos.'
25.	*à-wa mi+r(a)-à*^{UTNA} ***navis***$_2$ ***navis***$_2$ *URA+UMINA wa* *PÁRA-há*^{UTNA} *pi+?-?*^{UMINA} *pu-la-sà-ti*^{UTNA} *la-sà-ti-na*^{UTNA} *URA*^{UMINA} *wa-lu-KATA*^{UTNA} *sà* *KATA-sa*^{UTNA} *la-mi-á*^{UMINA}	'(Owing to its) fleet Mira (provides) the capital (for): Parḫa, Pi[ ], Philistia, Lasatina, Ura, Walukata of the Lower Land, (and) Lamiya.'
26.	*à-wa [-mu]* *URA+ḪANTAWAT+**infans***^{m} *ʹmu-ku-su-sa ā-nà UTNA* *UMINA -wa MI WI*	'For me Muksus, great prince in the land(s) and town(s of) Mi(ra and) Wi(lusa),'
27.	*à-wa **infans***^{m} *KULANA* *URA+ḪANTAWAT **infans***^{m} *tu*$^{?}$*-wa-ta*$_6$ *URA+ḪANTAWAT* ***infans***^{m} *PIA-ma-KURUNT* *URA+ḪANTAWAT*	'great prince Kulana(muwa)s, great prince Tuwatas, (and) great prince Piyamakuruntas,'
28.	*à-wa ARḪA mi-zi+r(i)*^{UTNA} *ā-sa-ka-lú-na*^{UMINA} *ka-?-?-ḫa*$_6$ ***navis***$_2$ *ā-ta*$_6$ *ḪARNAS*	'they made Ashkelon (along) the border (of) Egypt (by) war(?) ship (into) a fortress.'
29.	*à-wa [ ] URA+ḪANTAWAT á-i-wa*	'[ ] I, great king, will

	UTNA ASATAR ya 40 *? (= weight)	sacrifice (from that) land (for) a throne these 40 (metal units),'
30.	*à-wa URA+ḪANTAWAT* ^{MASANA}*TARḪUNT* ^{MASANA}*PARNA* *TAMA* ^{MASANA}*(a)pá+r(a)* *[ka]-ta-WATA-na*^{UTNA} ^{MASANA}*ku-*128 [ ]*^{UTNA} ^{MASANA}*WANTI [ ]* ^{MASANA}*[ ]* *[? -?]*$^{\text{UTNA MASANA}}$*[ ] á-pa-sa*^{UTNA}	'and I, great king, have built a temple (for the gods) Tarḫunt, the god of the field of Kizzuwatna, Kupapa of the land [ ], the god of the divine mountain [ ], god [ ] of the land [ ], god [ ] of the land Ephesos.'
31.	*à-wa URA+ḪANTAWAT* *UMINA+mi TAMA-mu-ḫa ASU* *à+ta ARA-wa*^{UTNA} *á-pa-sa*^{UMINA} *ā-lú-pa-na*^{UMINA} *ku-ru-pi*^{UMINA} *la-pa-tí*^{UMINA} *[sa]-mu+r-na*^{UMINA} *ā-ku-ma-na*^{UMINA} *ASA-ru-ti*^{UMINA} *na*$_4$ *ti*$_4$*-ma-la*$^{\text{URA+ḪARNAS}}$ *ḫu-wa-la-?-?*^{UMINA} *ku-ka-wa-mi-sa*^{UMINA} *ku-wa-li-sa-sa*^{UMINA} *nà-nú-wa-sa*^{UMINA} *ḫa*$_6$*+r-pa-hi-li*^{UMINA} *na*$_4$ *ḫu-na-sa*^{ḪARNAS} *PÁRA-ASA-ā-na-sa*^{UMINA} *sa*$_5$*-la-á-pa-sa*^{UMINA} *URA-na-sa-sa*^{UMINA} *ā-la-wa-sa*^{UMINA} *ā-ti-pa-li-à*^{UMINA} *[ ]*^{UMINA} *[ ]*^{UMINA} *[ ]*^{UMINA}	'I, great king, built lavishly citadel(s) in Arzawa (total 25): 'Ephesos, Alupana, Kurupi, Lapati, Smyrna, Akumana, Sardis, not (in a town) the great fortress (of) Timala, Ḫuwala[ ], Kukawamisa, Kuwalissa, Nanuwasa, Ḫarpaḫili, not (in a town) the fortress (of) Ḫunasa, Parasanasa, Salapasa, Uranassa, Alawasa, Atipaliya-town, [ ], [ ], (and) [ ],'
32.	*à-wa PÁRA-la-à-wi-sa*^{UMINA} *ku-wa+r-?*^{UMINA} *pu+r-sa-ta-na*^{UMINA}	'and Paralawisa, Kuwar[..], (and) Pursatana.'
33.	*na*$_4$ *á-na-ma wa-na ī-na* *ḫá-pa-la*^{UMINA}	'Not (included those) with a name-stele in Ḫapalla (total 14):'

34.	*à-wa APAMI-mi*^{UMINA} *ā-lu-sa*^{UMINA} *á-na-sà+r(i)*^{UMINA} *ḪARNAS* *TARKU-na-sa*^{UMINA} *mi+r(a)-wa-na-ī*^{UMINA} *ḫu*$_{4}$*-pa-ka-tì*^{UMINA} *pá+r-sa-tí*$^{?}$*-na*^{UTNA} *ḫu*$_{4}$*-ta+r-ā-li*^{UMINA} *á-pa+r-ā*$_{4}$*-ti*^{UMINA}	'West-town, Alusa, in the fortress (of) Anasa, Tarkunasa, Mirawanai, Ḫupakati, the land of Parsatina, Ḫutarali, (and) Aparati,'
35.	*à-wa mu-la-wa-sa*^{UMINA} *ī-ká+r(i)*^{UTNA} *lu-KATA-na-sa*^{UMINA} *ki-na-tu-wa*^{UMINA} *na-sa-sa*$^{[UMINA]}$	'and Mulawasa, in the land (of) Ika, Lukatanasa, Kinatuwa, (and) Nassa.'
36.	*à-wa URA+ḪANTAWAT la+PÁRNA* *mu-ku[-su-sa] [APA-sa-sa]-wa*^{UTNA} *à [ ]* ^{MASANA}*TARḪUNT* ^{MASANA}*(a)pá+r(a)* ^{MASANA}*[ ]* ^{MASANA}*ku-*128* ^{MASANA}*[ ]* ^{MASANA}*[ ]* ^{MASANA}*[ ]* ^{MASANA}*[ ]*	'(On behalf of) the great king, labarnas, Muksus will sacrifice (in) the land (of) Apaisos (to) Tarḫunt, the god of the field, the god [ ], Kupapa, the god [ ], the god [ ], the god [ ], (and) the god [ ],'
37.	*wa-à KWA PÁRA-na i-ā*	'and (he will do) what(ever else) for the benefit of these.'
38.	*URA+ḪANTAWAT [ ]* *[mu-ku-su]-sa [APA-sa-sa]-wa*^{UTNA}	'(So on behalf of) the great king [ ] [Muksu]s (in) the land (of) [Apaiso]s.'
39.	*à-wa KULANA-MUWA* ***infans***^{m} *MA URA+ḪANTAWAT* ^{MASANA}*KULANA[ ] mu-ka-sa<+r>* *lu-lu-ti -li*	'Kulanamuwas, great prince (of) Ma(sa), will placate for himself the god of the army (by) invocation.'
40.	*ASATAR [ASA]-wa ARA*^{UTNA} *URA+ḪANTAWAT*	'I, great king, will [remain seated] (on) the throne (of) Arzawa.'
41.	*à-wa* ^{MASANA}*TARḪUNT-ti-sa-sa*^{UMINA}	'I regularly campaigned (in)

	UTNA AMU TIWA-TIWA *ka-sa-ka*^{UMINA} *UTNA AMU* *TIWA-TIWA ma-sa*^{UMINA} *UTNA*	the divine land (of) Tarḫuntassa, I regularly campaigned (in) the land (of) Kaska, (and so also) in the land (of) Masa.'
42.	*à-wa ḪANTAWAT á-ti-pa-li*^{UTNA} *ḪANTAWAT KATA-WATA-na*^{UTNA} *ḪANTAWAT ká+r-ka-mi+sa*^{UTNA} *ḪANTAWAT ā-la-sá-?*^{UTNA} *ḪANTAWAT* a_5*-lu-sa-?*^{UTNA} *ḪANTAWAT ka-ta-ta+r-?*^{UTNA} *TALMI-*ma_4 *[ ] UTNA *?* (gift bearing person)	'The king (of) Atapali, the king (of) Kizzuwatna, the king (of) Karkamis, the king (of) Alasiya(?), the king (of) (W)ilusiya(?), the king (of) lower Tar[..](?), (the kings of) all land(s) brought gifts.'
43.	*à-wa ā ma-sa-sa UMINA+mi* *mi*$^{?}$*-ā-na URA+ḪANTAWAT UTNA*	'(I), great king, made the citadel of Masa (into) my (own) land.'
44.	*à-wa URA+ḪANTAWAT [ ]* *mu-ku-su-sa* ^{MASANA}*TARḪUNT [ ]* ^{MASANA}*[ ]*	'(On behalf of) the great king, Muksus [ ] (to) Tarḫunt, the god [ ].'
[ ]		
45.	*ku-pa-tá-KURUNT la+PÁRNA* a_5*-wa-na-*$ta_6$$^{ḪAPA-UTNA}$ *wa-ta+r-wa*^{UMINA} *ḫu-la-na*$^{ḪAPA-UTNA}$ ha_6*+r-KWA-wa-na*^{UTNA} *TARKASNA-la+r(i)*^{UTNA} *sa-la-pa*^{UTNA} *ka-la-sa-ma*^{UTNA} *la-la-ḫa-sa*^{UMINA} *[ ]* $^{ḪAPA-UTNA}$ **?-na*$^{ḪAPA-UTNA}$ *AMU-ru-sa*^{UMINA} *pi-*ta_6*-sa*^{UTNA} ^{MASANA}*TARḪUNT-sa*^{UTNA} *la-la-na-*ta_6^{UMINA} *ā-na-*ta_6^{UMINA} *sa-i-ma-*ta_6^{UMINA} na_4 *lu-la-sa*^{UTNA}	'Labarnas Kupantakuruntas, the Awanata river-land, the town (of) Watarwa, the Ḫulana river-land, the land (of) Ḫarkwawana, in the land (of) Tarkasnala, the land (of) Sallapa, the land (of) Kalasma, the town (of) Lalaḫasa, the river-land (of) [ ], the riverland (of) [..]na, the town (of) Amurusa, the land (of) Pitassa, the divine land (of) Tarḫuntassa, the town (of) Lalanda, the town (of)

		Anata, the town (of) Saimata (total 16 towns and lands), (but) not the land (of) Lulasa,'
46.	à-wa UTNA sa-ta+r-ḫa-ta$_6$ ḫá-pa-la^{UTNA} á+r-wa-na-ta$_6$ 8000 [ ]	'he continued to be victorious over the land(s) (and to) Ḫapalla he sent 8000 (troops) [ ].'
47.	mi+r(a)-à^{UTNA} à-ta [ ]^{UMINA} [ ]^{UMINA} [ ]^{UMINA} [ ]^{UMINA} [ ]^{UMINA} [ ]^{UMINA} pa-li-i^{UMINA} mi<+r(a)>-à^{UMINA} TARKU-wa$^{\text{ḪARNAS-UMINA}}$ ma-na-ḫu-sa^{UMINA} ku-wa-ta$_6$-na^{UMINA} pa-wí/zu-na-i^{UMINA} mi-ta$_6$-sa^{UMINA} wa-sa-ta$_6$-sa^{UMINA} mi-tu-wa-na^{UMINA} i-ta-pa-li^{UMINA} ḫu-wa-li-i^{UMINA} wí/zu-na-ta+r-wa^{UMINA} a$_5$-la-na^{UMINA} á-wa-na-sa^{UMINA} URA-wa-na^{UMINA} ta+r-wa-li-i^{UMINA} pa-la-na-sa^{UMINA}	'In Mira (total 23 towns): [ ], [ ], [ ], [ ], [ ], [ ], Pali, Mira, Tarkuwa, Manaḫusa, Kuwatana, Pawi/zunai, Mitasa, Wasatasa, Mituwana, Itapali, Ḫuwali, Wi/Zunatarwa, Alana, Awanasa, Urawana, Tarwali, Palanasa,'
48.	à-wa [ ] ḪARNAS sa mi+r(a)-à^{UTNA} 6000 ta-ta$_6$ á+r-wa-na [ ]	'he placed (at) the [ ] fortress of Mira 6000 (troops for) missions.'
49.	à-wa á+r-nú-wa-na-ta$_6$ ḪANTAWAT ḪÁ(TI)^{UTNA} MASANA <á-i-mi>	'Arnuwandas, king (of) Ḫatti, having become god,'
50.	à-wa -tá ^{MASANA}TARḪUNT+UMINA URA^{UMINA} wa-su la-wa^{UMINA} la-mi-i$^{\text{ḪAPA-UTNA}}$ WARPA ḪÁ(TI)^{UTNA} ā-ru-na-sa WARPA i-ku-wa-na^{UTNA} ḫu+r-nà-i^{UTNA} na$_4$ ḫu-wa-ta$_6$ nú-wa-ta$_6$ UTNA	'because of this he did not run into (and) renew (his hold on) the(se) land(s): Tarḫuntassa, Ura, holy Lawa(zantiya), Lamiya, crown domain(s of) Ḫatti

of the sea, (further) crown domain(s of Ḫatti): Ikkuwaniya (and) Ḫurna.'

Edremit

1. *URA+ḪANTAWAT+***infans**^{m}
mu-ka-sa ā-nà MI WI
*UTNA-***dominus** *ḪARNAS-sa*
ta+r-ḫa-ta$_6$ *a*$_5$*-la-na-ta*$_6$^{UTNA}
um+li-wa-na-ta$_6$^{UTNA}

wa-na-ta$_6$*-sa*^{UMINA} *[la-sa]-pa*$^{\underline{\text{UMINA}}}$
um+mi-tu-mi-na^{UMINA}
mu-ti-li-na^{UMINA} *[?-?-?]*$^{\underline{\text{UMINA}}}$
[?-?]-sa$^{\underline{\text{UMINA}}}$ *[ā]-pa+r(a)*$^{\underline{\text{UMINA}}}$
la-mi-na$^{\underline{\text{UMINA}}}$ *ta*$_6$*-na-ta*$_6$$^{\underline{\text{UMINA}}}$
a$_5$*-la-na-ta*$_6$^{UMINA} *ku-ru-sa*^{UMINA}
wa-ta$_6$*-ma*^{UMINA} *ā-ta+r*^{UMINA}
[ ] ka-mu-sa^{UMINA}
á-sa-tu+r(a)^{UMINA}
ta$_6$*-tu-wa-na-sa*^{UMINA}
ki-li-pa-nà^{UMINA} *pi+r-wí/zu-na*^{UMINA}
wa-ḫa-pa-ta-sa^{UMINA}
ā-ta$_6$*-pa-wa-sa*^{UMINA}
ā-wí/zu-na-la-sa^{UMINA}
^{WANTI}*wí/zu-mi-wa-sa*^{UMINA}
ka-ma-na-ta$_6$^{UMINA}
um+li-wa-na-ta$_6$^{UTNA}
wa-na-ta$_6$*-sa-ta+r*^{UMINA}
ā+r-sa-pa^{UMINA} *pa-ru-ki-ta*$_6$^{UMINA}
pi-tu[-?]^{UMINA} *la[-?-?-?]*^{UMINA}
ā-pa+r-tu+r^{UMINA} *[?-?]-sa*^{UMINA}
nà-nà[-?-?]^{UMINA} *pa+r-mu-sa*^{UMINA}
sa-ma-ta$_6$*-sa*^{UMINA} *[?-?-?]*^{UMINA}
ā-ta+r-sa-ta$_6$^{UMINA} *wi-nà-ta*$_6$*-sa*^{UMINA}
ká+r-ka$^{!}$*-la-sa*^{UMINA}

'Great prince Muksas, country-lord in Mi(ra and) Wi(lusa), conquered the (following) fortress(es in the lands of) Alanda (and) Muliwanda (total 43): Antissa, the island (of) Lesbos, Methymna, Mitylene, the islands (of) [ ], [ ]sa, Imbros, Lemnos, Tenedos, Alanda-town, Chryse, Watama, Atar, [ ], Kamusa, Astyra, Tatuwanasa, Kilipana, Pirwi/zuna, Waḫapatasa, Abydos, Awi/zunalasa, mount Wi/Zumiwasa, Kamanata, the land (of) Muliwanda, Wanatasatar, Arisbe, Perkote, Pityeia, La[ ], Apartur, [ ]sa, Nana[ ], Parion, Samatasa, [ ], Adrasteia, Winatasa, Gargara, the land (of) mount Leleges, Atarnatur, Adramyttion [= Edremit], (and) Matarsa.'

^{WANTI}*la-la-ka<-sa>*^{UTNA}
ā-ta+r-na-tu+r^{UMINA}
ā-ta+r-mu-ta_6^{UMINA} *ma-ta+r-sa*^{UMINA}

2. *à-wa á-*ta_6*-la-wa-sa*
um+li-wa-ta_6^{UMINA} *á-*$sa_4^{?}$*-wa*^{UTNA}
WARPA-ta_6

'And Atalawas represented the crown (in) Muliwanda-town (and) the land (of) Asa$^{?}$wa.'

3. *'ma-la-mu-sa tu-ḫa-pi-sa* ***infans***^{m}
'á-ka-tár-ḫa-sa la-ku-pa<-sa>
infans^{m} *pi-ḫá-sa-ta [?-?-?]*^{UTNA}

'Malamus, son of Tuḫapis, (and) Akatarḫas, son (of) Lakupas, continued to be glorious (in) the land [ ].'

4. *[ ]*^{MASANA}*[ ]*^{MASANA}*[ ]*

(dedication to the gods)

Yazılıtaş

1. *[ ] la-sa-pa*$^{\underline{UTNA}}$ *ā-ru-na*
^{WANTI}*ā-ḫu-wa-na-*ta_6^{UTNA}
á-pa-wi-sa^{UMINA} *ku-ti-nà-sa*^{UMINA}
a_5*-la-na-*ta_6^{UMINA}
á-ta+r-mu-ta_6^{UMINA} *ā-*ta_6*-pa*^{UMINA}
^{WANTI}*sa+r-wa-na-*ta_6 ^{WANTI}a_5*-*ta_6*-ā*
pa-li-nà-ta_6^{UMINA} *á-wa+r-na*^{UMINA}
su-wi-sa^{UMINA} *wa-la+r(i)-ma*^{UMINA}
ma+r$^{?}$*-wa-na-sa*^{UMINA}
ta_6*-*ta_6*+r-na-sa*^{UMINA} *wí/zu-ru-ā*^{UMINA}
á+r(i)-na-sa^{UMINA}
wí/zu-ma+r-na^{UMINA}
ā-wa-ta_6*-nà-sa*^{UMINA} *ā-ru-nà*^{UMINA}
^{WANTI}*la-la-ka-sa*^{UMINA}
wi-na-ta_6^{UMINA} *mu-*ta_6*-la*$^{\underline{UTNA}}$
wí/zu-ma-na-ta_6^{UTNA}
^{WANTI}*ḫá+r-na*^{ḪARNAS}
ma-sa-tu+r(i)-wa-na-ta_6*-sa*^{UMINA}
ASA+ḫa^{UTNA} *URA+ḪANTAWAT*
WALWA-MUWA ***infans***^{m}
URA+ḪANTAWAT
ku-pa-tá-KURUNT [ ]

'Lesbos, the sea, the land (of) mount Aḫuwanda, Apawisa, Kutinasa, Alanda-town, Adramyttion, Atapa, mount Sarwanda, mount Ida, Palinata, Awarna, Suwisa, Hyllarima, Mar$^{?}$wanasa, Atarneus, Wi/Zurua, Arinasa, Wi/Zumarna, Awatanasa, the sea, the town (of) mount Leleges, Winata, the island(s of) Muwatallis, the land (of) Wi/Zumanda, the fortress (of) mount Ḫarna, Masturiwantasa: great king (of) the land (of) Seḫa Walwamuwas, great king, son (of) great king Kupantakuruntas [ ].'

Dağardı 1

(D)	*ḪANTAWAT+**infans**^{m}* *MASANA-TARḪU(NT)-na* *ḪANTAWAT+**infans**^{m} **dominus*** *ma-sa-tu+r-wa-na-ta$_6$-sa^{UMINA}* ***dominus***	'Prince Masanatarḫunas, prince, lord (of) Masturiwantasa [= Dağardı], lord.'

Dağardı 2

(E)	***infans**^{m}+ḪANTAWAT ASA+ḫa^{UTNA}* *á-sa-há[-?] ASA+ḫa^{UTNA}* ***infans**m+ḪANTAWAT* *WALWA[-MUWA **infans**^{m}]*	'Prince (of) Seḫa Asaha[ ]s, prince (of) Seḫa, [son (of)] Walwa[muwa]s.'
(F)	*ā-ta+r-na^{UMINA} PÁRA-ḫá-ma^{UMINA}* *TIWATA-ta+r(a)^{UMINA}* *á-ta+r-sa-ta$_6$-i$^{?UMINA}$ sa-ta-la^{UMINA}* *ku-ru-ta$_6$-sa^{UMINA}* *wí/zu-na-ta+r-ha^{UMINA}* *ka-la-wa-sa^{UMINA} pi-ta$_6$-na-sa^{UMINA}* *ā-ta+r-mu-ta^{UMINA}* *^{WANTI}ta$_6$-mi-na-sa^{UTNA}*	'Atarna, Pergamon, Thyateira, Adrasteia, Satala, Kurtasa, Wi/Zunatarha, Kalawasa, Pitane, Adramyttion, the land (of) mount Taminasa.'
(G)	*á-na[-?] wí/zu-ma-na-ta$_6$^{UTNA}* *ā-ru-tu-na^{UMINA} ā-ta+r-na^{UMINA}* *^{WANTI}ḫá+r-na$^{[ḪARNAS]}$ki-la-sa^{UMINA}* *ki-su[-?]^{UMINA} ma-sa-pa$^{?[UMINA]}$* *[?]-wa-na-sa^{UTNA} [?]-ta$_6$-mi[-?]*	'Ana[ ], the land (of) Wi/Zumanda, Artuna, Atarna, the fortress (of) mount Ḫarna, Kilasa, Kisu[ ], Masapa, the land (of) [ ]wana, [ ]tami[ ].'

Şahankaya

(C)	*URA+ḪANTAWAT TARKU-ta$_6$+li* ***infans**^{m}+ḪANTAWAT+ ku-ku-li* ***infans**^{m}+ḪANTAWAT wa-pa+r-mu* ***infans**^{m}+ḪANTAWAT* *MASANA-TARḪU(NT)-na*	'great king Tarkutallis' 'prince Kukulis' 'prince Waparmus' 'prince Masanatarḫunas'

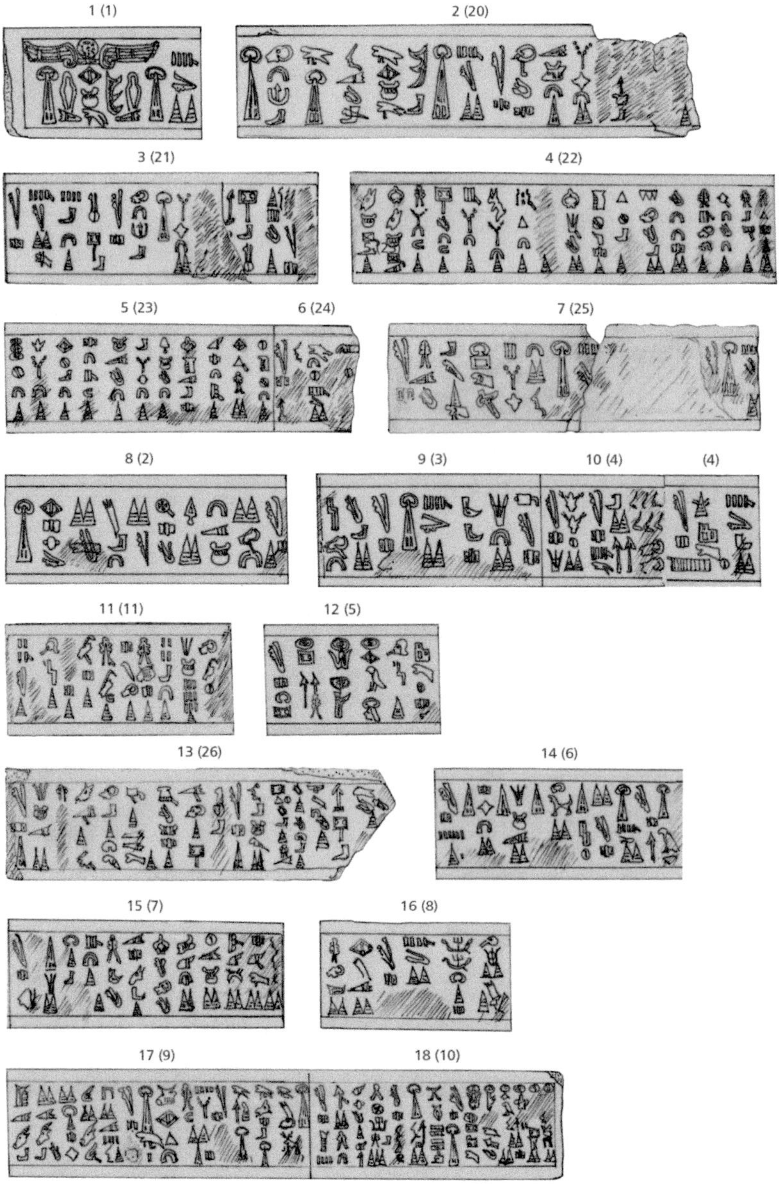
1 (1)
2 (20)
3 (21)
4 (22)
5 (23)
6 (24)
7 (25)
8 (2)
9 (3)
10 (4)
(4)
11 (11)
12 (5)
13 (26)
14 (6)
15 (7)
16 (8)
17 (9)
18 (10)

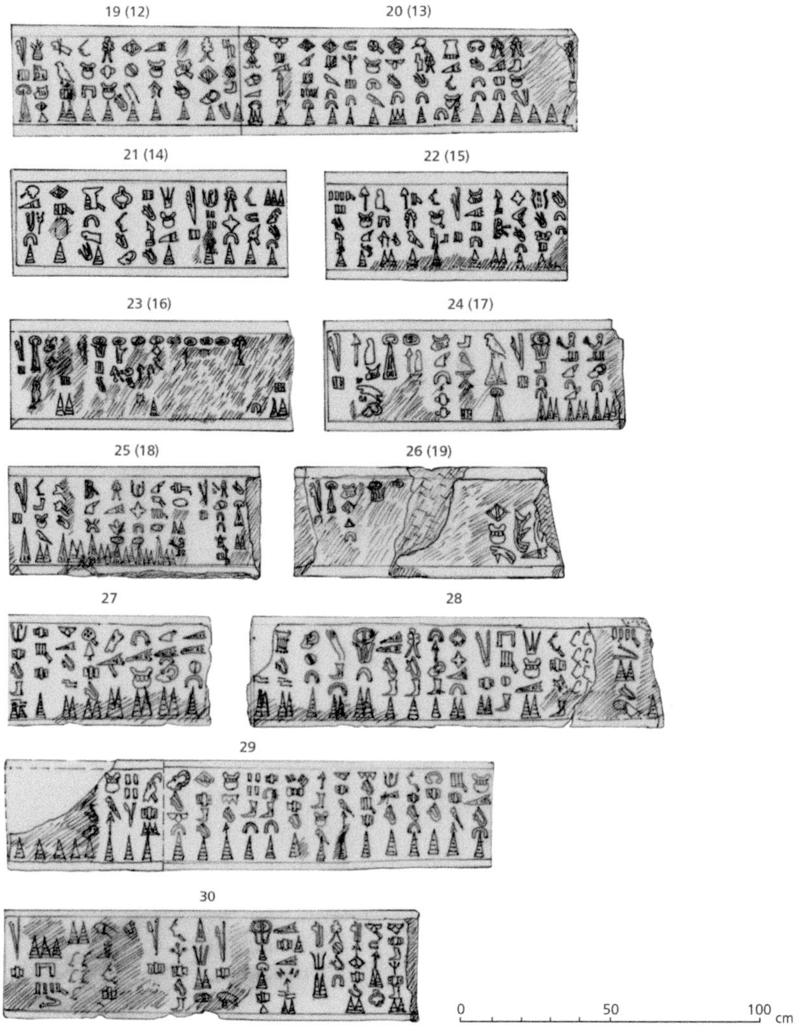

Fig. 29. Beyköy 2 (design Eberhard Zangger).

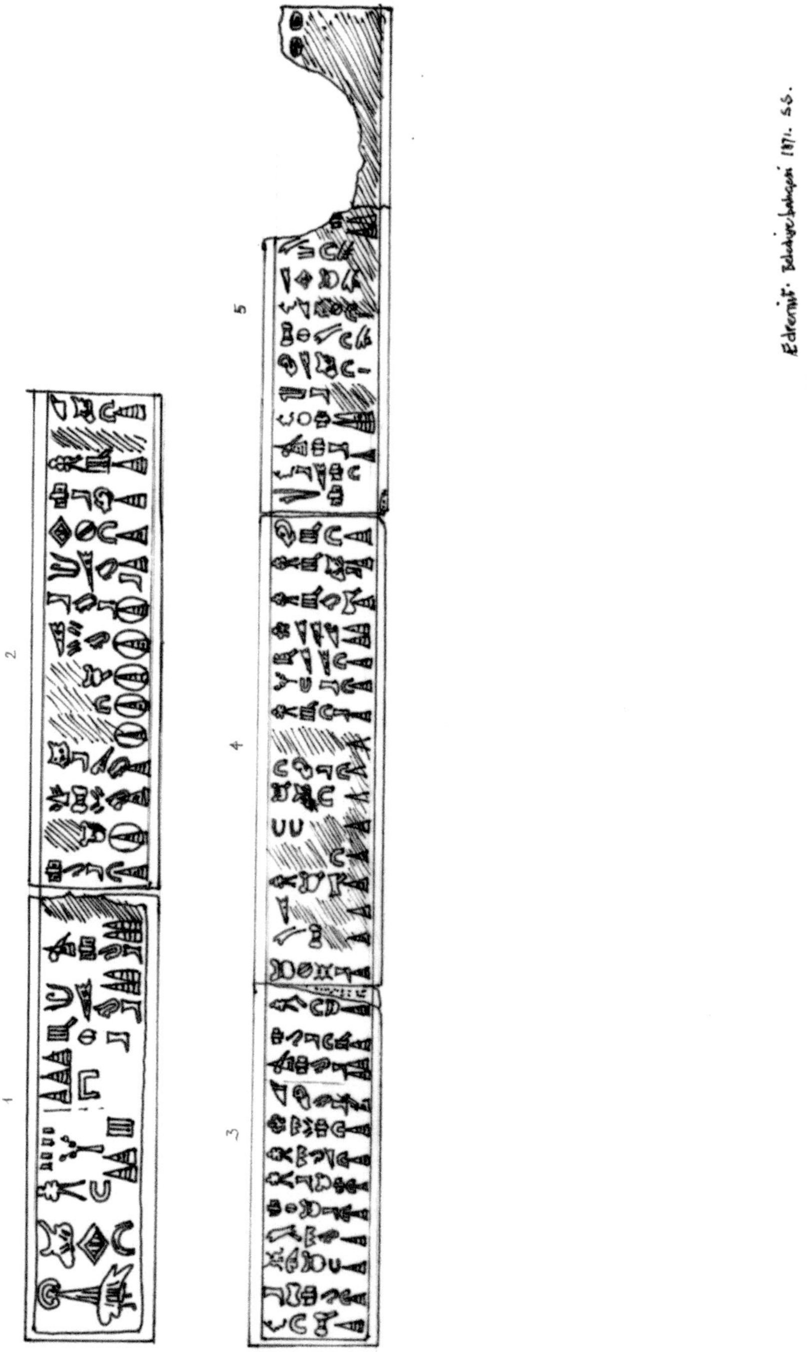

Fig. 30. Edremit.

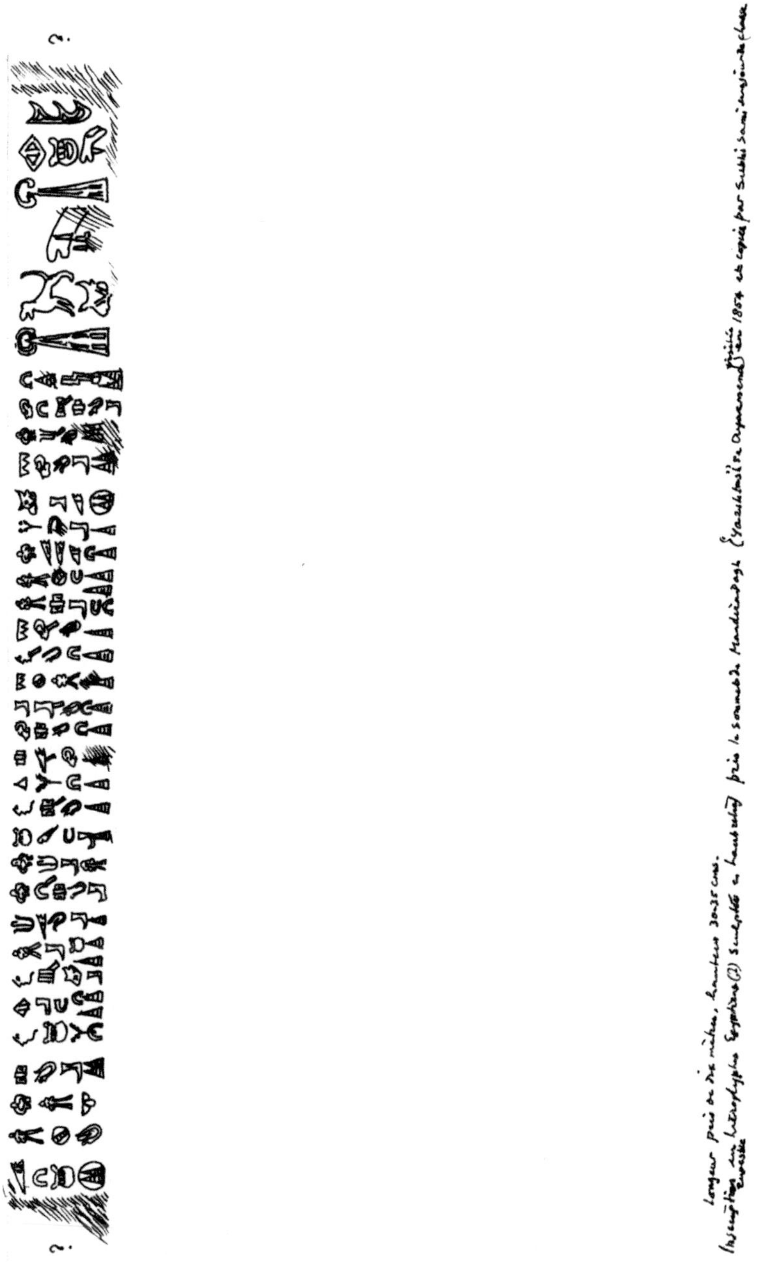

Fig. 31. Yazılıtaş.

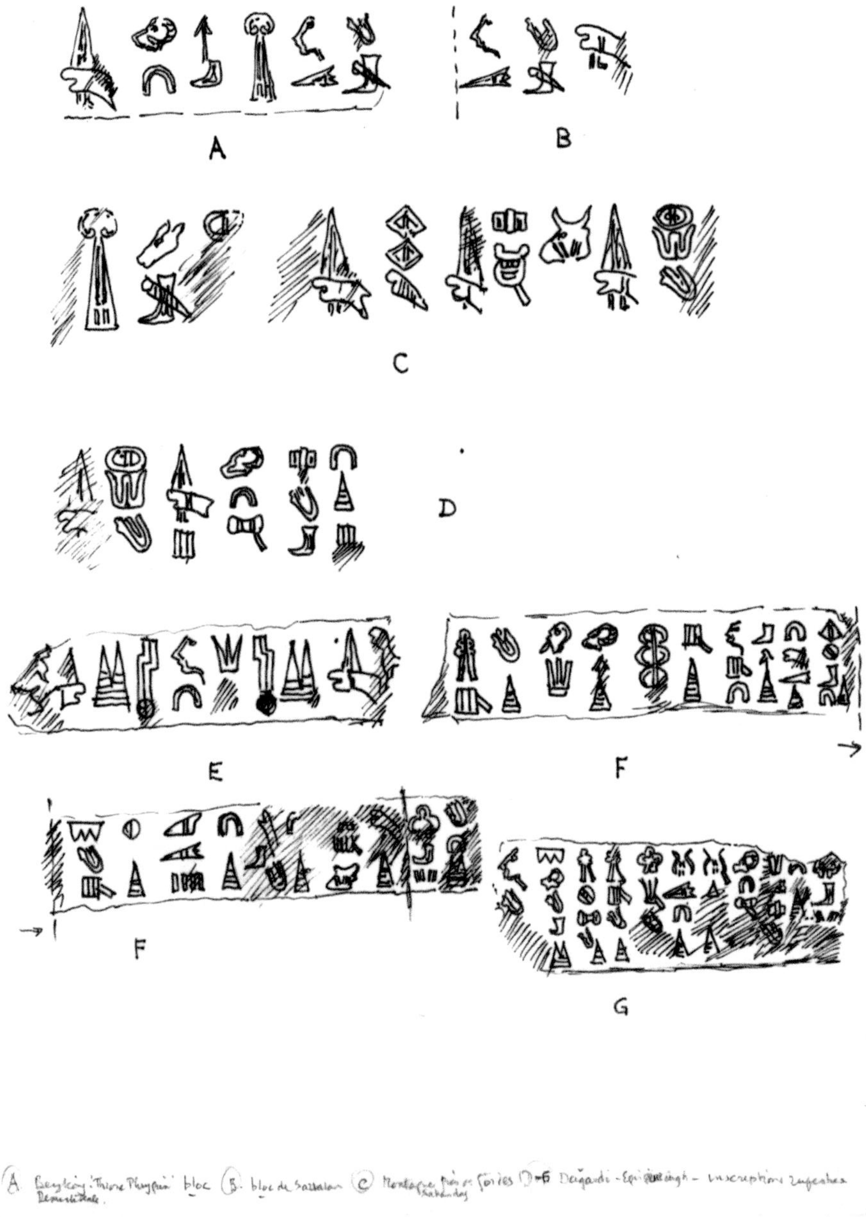

Fig. 32. Beyköy 3-4 (A-B), Şahankaya (C), Dağardı 1 (D), Dağardı 2 (E-G).

7. Amenhotep III: Historical Background to his Aegean Policy

7.1 Introduction

Scarabs of Amenhotep III have been discovered at Ialysos in Rhodes (O'Connor & Cline 2004: Fig. 7.4) and at Panaztepe in western Anatolia (Jaeger & Krauss 1990: 154, Abb. 1), in both instances in a grave dated to Late Helladic III or IIIA more in specific. Further scarabs of this particular pharaoh came to light at Ayios Elias in Aitolia (chamber tomb dated to Late Helladic IIB-IIIA2 [early]), Knossos (tomb dated to Late Minoan IIIA1) and Kydonia (Late Minoan IIIA-B context) in Crete, whereas a faience vase and faience plaques with the cartouche of this pharaoh have been dug up at Mycenae in the Peloponnesos (chamber tomb dated to Late Helladic IIIA and settlement contexts dated to Late Helladic IIIB or even B2, respectively), see Cline 1987: 24-26, Table I.

Fig. 33. Throne-name of Amenhotep III (Newberry 1906: Pl. XXXI, 5 [detail]).

With the noted exception of the faience vase from Mycenae, in which case only the lower section of the proper name (= name 5) of the pharaoh, *'Imn-ḥtp ḥq3-W3st* 'Amenhotep, ruler of Thebes',[1] occurs, it so happens that in the remaining eight cases in sum, the throne-name of Amenhotep III, *nb-M3ʿt-Rʿ*, is written with C10 *m3ʿt* instead of its *pars pro toto* the feather sign H6 as attested for scarabs with the cursive variant of this pharaoh's throne-name (see Figs. 33-34).[2]

Fig. 34. Cursive variant of the throne-name of Amenhotep III (Newberry 1906: Pl. XXXI, 2).

To the objects with the throne- and proper names of Amenhotep III in Greece, the Aegean, and western Anatolia should be added those with the name of his wife, queen Tiyi (cf. Fig. 35). These entail a stamp seal from a grave at Hagia Triada assigned to Late Minoan IIIA and two scarabs from Mycenae found in Late Helladic IIIB or IIIB2 contexts. There has also been found a scarab of queen Tiyi in grave 93 at Enkomi, Cyprus, but this was found together with a silver ring of Amenhotep IV or Akhenaten and may therefore well date to the Amarna period following that of the reign of Amenhotep III.[3]

1 This proper name is also attested for the faience plaque fragments, see Phillips 2007: 483, Fig. 3; 488.
2 Numbering of the Egyptian hieroglyphic signs according to Gardiner 1994.
3 See Murray e.a. 1900: 36; Pl. IV, nos. 608 and 617 and cf. Fimmen 1924: 177-178.

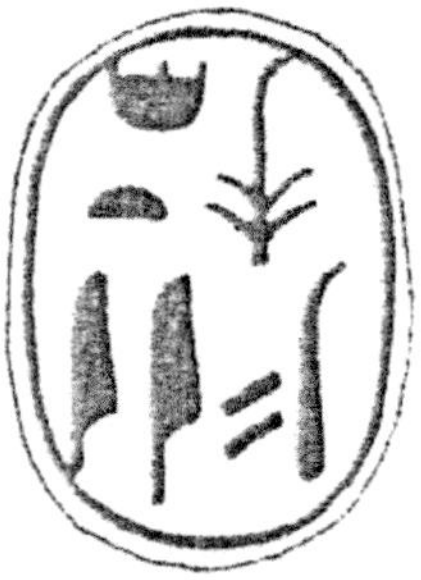

Fig. 35. Scarab of queen Tiyi (Newberry 1906: Pl. XXXI, 8).

According to Reeves (2002: 59), queen Tiyi outlived her husband by about a decennium.

Now, in this manner we arrive at the total number of 12 objects in sum from the Aegean region with the names of Amenhotep III and his consort Tiyi. This number of exports to the Aegean is unparalleled for Egyptian Bronze Age history. In comparison, only two scarabs with the cartouche of Ramesses II (1279-1213 BC) have been found at Perati in the Attica, Greece (Lambrou-Phillipson 1990: 284-285, nos. 267-268), one vase and one scarab with the cartouche of Tuthmosis III (Lambrou-Phillipson 1990: 208-209, no. 63 and 357-358, no. 489), and one figurine of an ape with the cartouche of Amenhotep II (Lambrou-Phillipson 1990: 343-344, no. 437).

What was the reason behind these visible remains of Egyptian activity in the Aegean? As a matter of fact, the aforesaid objects with the names of Amenhotep III and his wife queen Tiyi have been explained within the frame of an active policy by Amenhotep III of containment of the Hittites, in principle his most serious adversaries in the Levantine theatre. However, at the time of this active diplomatic intervention, which presumably dates *c.* 1370-1350 BC, the Hittites under the rule of great king Tudḫaliyas III (1370-1350 BC) were at a low ebb both politically and militarily, to such an extent that in the correspondence between Amenhotep III and Tarḫundaradus of Arzawa, the El Amarna letters 31 and 32, it is stated that 'the country of Ḫattusa is paralysed' (EA 31, line 27, cf. Stavi 2015: 56-60). Nevertheless, Amenhotep III thought it politically expedient, so it seems, to launch his containment policy of the Hittites, which aimed at solidifying a coalition with the enemies of the Hittites, the Luwians in western Anatolia and the Mycenaeans in Greece.

If this historical reconstruction holds water, one may wonder: how effective could Egyptian diplomatic intervention in the period of *c.* 1370-1350 BC be in solidifying a coalition between the Luwians of western Anatolia and the Mycenaean Greeks or Akhaians? To answer this question, it is instructive to briefly review the relevant evidence on the relationship between the Luwians of western Anatolia and the Akhaians of the Greek mainland.

7.2 KUB 26.91 & the Tawagalawas-letter

The first document which comes to mind in this context is the Hittite text KUB 26.91 (Beckman e.a. 2011: 134-139) which belongs to the dossier of the so-called Aḫḫiyawa texts. According to the reading of Frank Starke as referred to by Joachim Latacz (2004: 243-244), the sequence *ka-ga-mu-* in this document actually should be read *ka-ta-mu-*. If this is correct, it follows that the great-grandfather of the sender of this letter (A-

BA A-BA A-BỊ-[-YA]) is named *Kadmos*, who according to Greek literary tradition was the founding father of the royal house of Thebes. In any case, the sender is plausibly identified as *Tawagalawas*, after whom another of the Aḫḫiyawan letters is named (KUB 14.3). The name *Tawagalawas*, then, has been identified since the times of Emil Forrer with Greek *Eteoklēs*, also known from Greek literary tradition as a king of Thebes and successor of Kadmos. The identification of two kings of Thebes in the right order is in my opinion not to be dismissed as merely coincidental.

About the Tawagalawas-letter two issues are presently of relevance, namely (1) its date and (2) whether Tawagalawas is himself a great king of Aḫḫiyawa.

(1) As far as dating is concerned, the Tawagalawas-letter is usually assigned to the reign of Ḫattusilis III (1264-1239 BC). However, there is a direct reference in it to the Trojan War (iv 7-10): LUGAL ^{KUR}*Ḫa-at-ti-wa-an-na-aš-kán ú-uk* 8. *ku-e-da-ni* A.NA [INI]M ^{URU}*Wi$_5$-l[u]-[š]a še-er ku-ru-ur* 9. *e-šu-u-en nu-ụa-[m]u a-p[e]-e-[d]a-ni* INIM-*ni la-ak-nu-ut* 10. *nu-wa ták-šu-la-u-en* X (X) X-*wa-an-na-aš ku-ru-ur* UL *a-a-ra* 'In der Angelegenheit von Wilusa, der entwegen der König des Landes Hattusa und ich uns feind waren, in der hat er mich umgestimmt, und wir haben uns vertragen. Ein ... Krieg ist Unrecht für uns.'[4] This reference is repeated in the following lines 19-20: 19. *[nu] Š[A* ^{URU}*Wi$_5$-lu-ša ku-e-da-ni me]-mi-ni še-er ku-ru-ri-iḫ-ḫu-e-en* 20. *nu-za-k[án ku-it ták-šu-la-u-en nu na]m-ma ku-it* 'And concerning the matter of Wilusa about which we were hostile—because we have made peace, what then?'.[5] A similar reference can be found in the Manapatarḫundas-letter KUB 19.5 + KBo 19.79, § 3, 3-4: 3. *[^{m}Kaš-šú-ú-uš] ú-it* ÉRIN.^{MEŠ} ^{KUR}*Ḫat-ti-ya ú-wa-te-et* 4. *[na-at* GIM*]-an* EGIR-*pa* ^{KUR}*Wi$_5$-lu-ša* GUL-*u-wa-an-zi pa-a-ir* 5. *[am-mu-uk-m]a iš-tar-ak-zi* 'Kassu came (here) and brought troops from Hatti. And when they went back to attack Wilusa, I was ill'.[6] This letter certainly dates from the reign of Muwatallis II (1295-1271 BC), as Manapatarḫundas was succeeded on the throne of Seḫa by Masturis during the reign of this Hittite great king. Now, a third document of relevance in this connection is the Alaksandus-treaty drafted by Muwatallis II after his intervention in the region and his defeat of an otherwise unspecified enemy of Alaksandus (KUB 19.6 + KUB 21.1-5, § 6). From the preamble of this text (§§ 3-4), it is absolutely clear that Wilusa had remained a loyal vassal after its subjection by the first Hittite great king *Labarnas*, even if this loyalty only consisted of sending messengers 'from afar'.[7] Accordingly, the 'Wilusa attack' from the Manapatarḫundas-letter was not a Hittite attack *on* Wilusa, but an intervention to *support* it against the attack by an enemy, no doubt to be identified as the Aḫḫiyawans or Mycenaean Greeks as referred to in our citation from the Tawagalawas-letter. All three documents, then, have a bearing on *one and the same* conflict in the region of Wilusa which is likely to be identified with the Trojan War of *c.* 1280 BC (end of Troy VIh). Accordingly, the Tawagalawas-letter dates from the reign of Muwatallis II.[8]

4 See Sommer 1932: 16-17; cf. Beckman e.a. 2011: 116-117.
5 Beckman e.a. 2011: 116-117; cf. Sommer 1932: 16-17.
6 Beckman e.a. 2011: 140-141.
7 Latacz 2010: 161-162 (translation into German by Frank Starke).
8 Cf. Smit 1990-1; Gurney 2002: 136.

(2) Tawagalawas or Eteokles is the *brother* of the addressed person, the great king of Aḫḫiyawa or Akhaia, in KUB 14.3 ii 61. He cannot possibly be *great king himself*, as suggested by Metin Alparslan (2005) and Jared Miller (2006: 243-244, with note 31; 2010) on the basis of KUB 14.3 i 71-74, because the house of Kadmos in Thebes is destroyed *c.* 1350 BC by Mycenae and an Argive vassal king named Thersander has subsequently been put on the throne.[9] The critical section runs as follows: 71. *[nu-za* U*]*L *me-ma-aš* ^{m}*Ta-wa-ga-la-wa-aš-pát-kán ku-wa-pí* LUGAL.GAL *[*I-NA $^{U]RU}$*Mi-il$_5$-la-wa-an-da ta-pu-ša ú-it* 73. *[-*Y*]*A*-ma* ^{md}LAMMA*-aš ka-a e-eš-ta nu-ut-ta* LUGAL.GAL 74. *[*IGI*-an-d]a u-un-né-eš-ta Ú-*UL*-aš šar-ku-uš* LUGAL*-uš e-eš-ta*[10] 'When Tawagalawas himself, *(on behalf of)* the great king, crossed over to Millawanda, my (...) Kuruntas was here. *For you*, the great king, he drove to meet [him, i.e. Kuruntas!]—wasn't he a mighty king?'. In the given translation, I assume with Beckman e.a. 2011: 105 on account of their addition of '(as the representative of?)' in the translation of line 71, that in the given phrase of the Tawagalawas-letter *ANA* 'on behalf of'[11] or *INA* 'on behalf of'[12] needs to be emended.[13] In any case, crucial for a proper understanding of the following lines 73-74, in my view at least, is the fact that Tawagalawas meets, not the great king of Aḫḫiyawa as commonly assumed, but *on behalf of* the latter the delegate of the Hittite great king Muwatallis II, his son and heir elect Kuruntas.[14] In other words: the enclitic pronoun of the 2nd person singular *-ta* does not render the accusative but the *dative*![15]

The same solution as used in the translation of KUB 14.3 i 71-74, namely the assumption that *ANA* or *INA* needs to be emended, may well apply as well to the opening phrase of KUB 26.91, obv. § 1, 1: *[*UM-MA ^{m} o o o o o o o LUGAL.GAL LUGA*]*L ^{KUR}*Aḫ-ḫi-ya-w[a-ma* A-NA ^{d}UTU^{Š} LUGAL KUR ^{URU}*Ḫat-ti* QÍ-BI-MA*]* '[Thus says Tawagalawas *on behalf of* the great king, king] of Aḫḫiyawa: [Say to His Majesty, King of Ḫatti]:'.[16]

Now Tawagalawas' predecessor by three generations, Kadmos, must therefore be situated in the late 15th or early 14th century BC. At any rate, KUB 26.91 informs us that the king of Assuwa had bound himself to Kadmos by marrying the daughter of the latter and had bestowed upon him the rule of islands in the Aegean in return.

The critical section (obv. §3, 7-9) reads according to Starke as follows: LUGAL ^{KUR}*A-aš[-šu-wa ... n]u-za* ^{m}*Ka-ta-mu-na-aš-za-kán* A-BA A-BA A-BỊ*[-*YA *...] pí-ra-an ḫa-ma-ak-ta* 'The king of Assuwa [...]. He tied himself in marriage to my great-grandfather Kadmos (by taking the

---

[9] Woudhuizen 2013c: 7-8.

[10] Transliteration according to Miller 2010: 162.

[11] Madduwattas-text obv. § 59, see Beckman e.a. 2011: 78-79. For Luwian hieroglyphic, see Beyköy 2, § 26 and Edremit § 1.

[12] Luwian hieroglyphic Köylütolu text § 2, see Woudhuizen 2015a: 25, and Beyköy 2, § 33; in Hittite cuneiform this would entail the omission of only one horizontal *cuneus*.

[13] For the frequent omission of the prepositions *ANA* and *INA* in Hittite texts, see Friedrich 1960: 179-180, § 361.

[14] According to Gurney 2002: 139-140, this Kuruntas is an older brother of Ulmitesup, who was the crown prince at the time and presumably died before his succession to the throne was called for. In this scenario, Ulmitesup took Kuruntas as his throne-name at the time of his accession to the throne of Tarḫuntassa sometime in the reign of Ḫattusilis III, in commemoration of his deceased elderly brother.

[15] Friedrich 1960: 63, § 100.

[16] Beckman e.a. 2011: 134-135.

hand of the latter's daughter).' According to Katz (2005: 423-424) the analysis of *-aš* as the N(m/f) sg. of the enclitic pronoun of the 3rd person being attached to the A(m/f) sg. in *-na* of the personal name *Ka-ta-mu-* instead of to the preceding sentence introductory particle *nu-* is 'grammatically impossible'. This may be true, but it should on the other hand be acknowledged that we are dealing with a letter from an Aḫḫiyawan dignitary whose competence in writing Hittite cuneiform may be not up to the standard.

Whatever the merits of this latter suggestion, what concerns us here is that for the exercise of his rule over the Aegean islands in question the king of Thebes received a seal inscribed in Luwian hieroglyphic actually found at Thebes (see Fig. 17).

In summary, king Kadmos of Thebes had in loan from the king of Assuwa the rule over islands in the Aegean and hence in this respect was a vassal of the king of Assuwa. KUB 26.91 further informs us that a king of Assuwa, named Piyamakuruntas in the annals of Tudḫaliyas II (Bryce 2010: 124-127), was defeated by the Hittite great king Tudḫaliyas II (1425-1390 BC) and, as we know from the annals, deported to Ḫatti-land (his seal has actually been found in Alacahöyük, see Fig. 11). As a result of this, at the time of writing of the letter the ownership of the islands in the Aegean is disputed. The Hittite king is of the opinion that the islands in the Aegean, which formerly belonged to the king of Aḫḫiyawa in his capacity as overlord of the king of Thebes, because of his great-grandfather's defeat of the king of Assuwa, now belong to him, whereas the king of Aḫḫiyawa seems to be of the opinion that, in his capacity as overlord of the king Thebes, the islands in question naturally are an integral part of his realm. A typically feudal dispute.

7.3 The Phaistos Disc

The second document of relevance in this context is the text of the discus of Phaistos, which is the only extant letter that has come to light in the wider Aegean. According to this text, Nestor, known as king of Pylos in the Homeric epic poetry, has various regions in central Crete in loan from a great king who is only mentioned by his title ***sol suus*** 'his majesty' but likely to be identified as Tarḫundaradus of Arzawa, a contemporary, as we have seen, of the Egyptian pharaoh Amenhotep III. With respect to this loan there are distinguished two types of regions, the ones falling directly under the authority of Nestor, namely Knossos in the Lasithi and Saḫarwa or Skheria (= Hagia Triada) in the Mesara as mentioned on side A, and the ones where the latter's control is only indirect and exercised through the medium of his great intendant Idomeneus, namely Phaistos, the land behind Phaistos (= Gortyns), and Rhytion in the Mesara as mentioned on side B (see Achterberg e.a. 2004: 94-95). The title attributed to Nestor in the text of the Phaistos disc, 'great (man) in Akhaia' (A3-5), is vague; according to his own Cretan seal (CHIC # 295), he was 'prince (of) the Mesara' (Woudhuizen 2016: 117, Fig. 29). Whatever the specifics of the title, it is clear that the Pylian king Nestor, just like his Theban colleague Kadmos, had in loan territory in central Crete from great king Tarḫundaradus of Arzawa and likewise in this respect was a vassal of this Luwian great king.[17]

[17] Even after the take-over by Mycenae of power in Crete *c.* 1350 BC, Pylos remained in control of some

Text of the Phaistos disk in transliteration and translation

Side A

1-2	*á-tu*$_6$ *mi*$_1$-SARU *sa*$_6$*+ti pa*$_5$*-ya*$_1$*-tu*$_6$	'In the Mesara is Phaistos.'
3-5	*ú´ná-sa*$_2$*+ti ú ú-ri á-tu*$_6$ *ḫì-ya*$_1$*-wa*$_8$	'To Nestor, great (man) in Akhaia.'
6-7	*ku ná-sa*$_2$*-tu*$_6$ *ku tí* KATA*[+ti]*	'What Nestor (has), what you (have) under [you],'
8-9	*á-tu*$_6$ *mi*$_4$*-sa*$_6$ *[sa*$_2$*] ra-sú-ta*	'in my (territory) concerning the Lasithi,'
10-11	*á-tu*$_6$ *ti*$_2$*-sa*$_1$ *ta* SARU *ti*$_2$*-ya*$_1$*-sa*$_2$	'in your (territory) and of your kings.'
12-13	*á-tu*$_6$ *-ti*$_5$ *ti*$_1$*-wa*$_{10}$*+ti* TARḪU(NT) ***sol suus****+*WÁ SU	'To you brings Tarḫunt, his majesty [= Tarḫundaradus], 'hail'.'
14-16	*á ku-na-sa*$_3$ *ti*$_1$*-sa*$_6$ ^{LI}SARU*+ti* *á-tu*$_6$ *ra-sú+ti*	'Knossos (is) part of your sworn kingship in the Lasithi,'
17-19	*á-tu*$_6$ *ku-ku-ta* ^{DU}***jugum+aratrum*** *wa*$_8$*-ti*$_1$ *á-tu*$_6$ *ra-sú+ti*	'in (the territory) wherever a team of oxen ploughs for the town in the Lasithi.'
20-22	*á ku-na-sa*$_3$ *ti*$_1$*-sa*$_6$ ^{LI}SARU*+ti* *á-tu*$_6$ *ra-sú+ti*	'Knossos (is) part of your sworn kingship in the Lasithi,'
23-25	*á-tu*$_6$ *ku* UTNA *ti*$_5$*-sa*$_6$ *ku mi*$_4$*-sa*$_6$ ***anulus****-sa*$_1$ *ra-sú-tu*$_6$	'in (the territory) what your district (is) what part (is) of my realm the Lasithi.'
26-28	*á-tu*$_6$ *mi*$_1$-SARU *ti*$_1$*-sa*$_1$ *ta+ti* *sa*$_3$*-ḫár-wa*$_{10}$	'In the Mesara there (is) Skheria yours,'
29-31	*á-tu*$_6$ *ku-ku-ta* ^{DU}***jugum+aratrum*** ' *mi*$_1$-SARU *sa*$_3$*-ḫár-wa*$_{10}$	in (the territory) wherever a team of oxen ploughs for Skheria (in) the Mesara.'

bridgeheads in Crete, like *e-ra-po ri-me-ne* /Elaphōn limenei/ 'at Deer Harbor' in PY An 657, which refers to the harbor of Malia (= Cretan hieroglyphic *Ayalu* < Semitic *ajalu-* 'deer'), and *o-pi-ke-ri-jo-de* 'to the area near Skheria' in PY An 724, which refers to the neighbourhood of Skheria (= Hagia Triada) in the coastal region of the Mesara, up till the end of the Bronze Age *c.* 1200 BC, see Best 1996-7 (= Best 2011): 120-127.

Side B

1-2	*á-tu*$_{6}$ *i-ya*$_{1}$*-sa*$_{2}$ *ku ná-sa*$_{2}$*-ta*	'In (the territory) of the following persons, what Nestor (has).'
3-4	*á-du -ti*$_{1}$ *TIWA+ti i-na-ku*	'To you Haddu brings 'life'.'
5-7	*wa*$_{8}$ *pa*$_{5}$*-yá-tu*$_{6}$ ^{LI}*ti*$_{1}$*-sa*$_{6}$ *as+ti mi*$_{1}$*-SARU -ḫà-wa*$_{8}$	'Phaistos is (part of) your sworn (district) and the Mesara,'
8-9	*TUZI sa*$_{2}$ *mi*$_{1}$*-SARU sa*$_{6}$*[+ti] i-du-ma*$_{2}$*-na*	'great intendant of the Mesara is Idomeneus,'
10-12	*sa*$_{2}$ *pa*$_{5}$*-ya*$_{1}$*-ta á-sú-wi-ya*$_{1}$ *ku-na-wa*$_{10}$ *SARU*	'of the Assuwian Phaistos (is) Gouneus king.'
13-15	*ú-pa*$_{5}$ *pa*$_{5}$*-yá-ta* ^{LI}*UTNA-sa*$_{6}$ *ú-wa*$_{8}$ *SARU*	'Behind Phaistos (is) part of (your) sworn district, Uwas (is) king,'
16-17	*mi*$_{4}$ *ta-ti*$_{5}$ *-ḫà-wa*$_{8}$ *á-ḫar*$_{1}$*-ku SARU*	'and for my father (was) Aḫarkus king.'
18-20	*ú-wi-sa*$_{2}$ *KATA+ti ú KATA-mi*$_{1}$ *ú ná-sa*$_{2}$*+ti*	'Yours <pl.> under you: under me: for Nestor.'
21-23	*i ú-wi-sa*$_{2}$ *KATA+ti ku ri-ti*$_{1}$*-na sa*$_{2}$ *sa*$_{6}$*-ta*	'This of You <pl.> under you to which Rhytion belonged,'
24-25	*sa*$_{2}$ *ná-sa*$_{2}$*+ti sa*$_{2}$ *ti*$_{1}$*-sa*$_{6}$ *-pa*$_{5}$	'concerning (the territory) for Nestor, i.e. concerning your (territory),'
26-28	*i ú-wi-sa*$_{2}$ *KATA+ti ḫar*$_{1}$*-ma-ḫà-sa*$_{6}$ *sa*$_{2}$ *á-mi*$_{4}$ *ta-ti*$_{1}$ *sa*$_{2}$	'this of You <pl.> under you (belonged) to the man with respect to (the territory) for my father with respect to (the territory):'
29-30	*ú ri-ti*$_{1}$*-na ná-sa*$_{2}$*+ti*	'(so) Rhytion (is) for Nestor.'

7.4 The Madduwattas-text

In the period of *c.* 1400-1370 BC between the aforegoing episodes about which we are informed by the so-called Indictment of Madduwattas (Beckman e.a. 2011: 69-100), the relationship of the king of Arzawa at the time, Kupantakuruntas I, and the 'man of Aḫḫiya', *Attarissiyas*, who went over to western Anatolia with a force of 100 chariots and troops numbering at least in the thousands at first instance in order to fight against Madduwattas, unfortunately remains unclear. As the predecessor of Kupantakuruntas I, Piyamakuruntas of Assuwa, had been deported by Tudḫaliyas II to Ḫatti-land together with 600 teams of horses for chariots and 10,000 foot-soldiers (Bryce 2010: 125), Attarissiyas may well have been invited by Kupantakuruntas to provide him with an auxiliary force against his foe, Madduwattas, but this remains speculative. Moreover, his base for actions in Asia Minor no doubt was *Millawanda* or Miletos, which the Mycenaean Greeks took over from the Minoans sometime after the for Crete disastrous Santorini-eruption of *c.* 1450 BC.[18] However this may be, the main point for our purposes is that the name *Attarissiyas* is the Hittite form of Greek *Atreus*, a king of Mycenae according to Homeros, so that we are confronted here with a direct involvement of the capital of the Mycenaean or Akhaian kingdom.

A question which remains to be answered is: what was the realm of Madduwattas? The Hittite text is unfortunately rather biased. This appears from the fact that Madduwattas orchestrated an ambush for the Hittite general Kisnapilis in Lycia and subsequently received the Siyanta river land or the Xanthos valley in Lycia as his fief from the Hittite great king Arnuwandas I (1400-1370 BC). Similarly, after the marriage of his daughter to Kupantakuruntas I of Arzawa it is claimed that Madduwattas took control of Arzawa in its entirety as if its king, Kupantakuruntas I, had evaporated in thin air. Apparently he did not, as he is mentioned once more later on in the text.

Something can be deduced, however, from the place-names mentioned in the text which can be located. In the first place, as just noted, Madduwattas campaigned against *Dalawa* and *Ḫinduwa*, which for their correspondence to Classical *Tlōs* and *Kandyba* are definitely situated in Lycia. Next, after the marriage of his daughter to the Arzawan king Kupantakuruntas I, he received the *Siyanta* river land in loan from the Hittite great king, which, as we have just reaffirmed, corresponds to the *Xanthos* valley in Lycia. Then it is claimed that Madduwattas took Arzawa in its entirety, which in reality can only mean that he had concluded a treaty with Kupantakuruntas I on the occasion of the marriage of his daughter to the latter and received the rule of some part of Arzawa in return. Presumably this part of Arzawa was situated in the east. At any rate, Madduwattas' next move was the annexation of *Ḫapalla*, the river land of the confluence of the Classical Sangarios river with that of the Porsuk. One of the informants of the Hittite king about this feat was Mazlauwas, the ruler of *Kuwaliya*, the region in between that of Beycesultan-Mira in the east of Arzawa and Ḫapalla. After this, Madduwattas is stated to have conquered various places in southwest Anatolia like *Wallarimma*, *Iyalanti*,

[18] Niemeier (1998a: 33) reports Late Helladic IIIA2 to Late Helladic IIIB ware for the second building period, which means from *c.* 1350 BC to 1318 BC in terms of absolute chronology.

Mutamutassa, and *Ḫursanassa*, corresponding to Classical *Hyllarima*, *Alinda*, *Mylasa*, and *Halikarnassos* in Caria. Then the Hittite great king decided to intervene and went to Sallapa in the neighbourhood of mount Salbakos, which caused Madduwattas to incite the people of *Pitassa* to the east of Beycesultan-Mira against their Hittite overlord, no doubt in an attempt to cut off the latter's route back to the capital Boğazköy-Ḫattusa. Finally, Madduwattas seized *Karkisa*, situated on the *Cyclades*, and together with his former foe Attarissiyas or Atreus raided *Alasiya* or *Cyprus*.

All in all, then, it seems likely that Madduwattas was a dignitary of the town of Mira, perhaps with a claim on the Arzawan throne, who carved out his realm either from using Mira as his base or after he had been driven out of Mira by Kupantakuruntas of Arzawa but managed to keep his forces in tact and to raid the environments of Mira from a base in the mountainous region to the south or the east. How this relates to his taking refuge at *Zipasla* or mount *Sipylos* at the outset of the Madduwattas-text is still to be determined.

7.5 Conclusion

From the archaeological evidence in the form of 12 objects with the names of Amenhotep III and his wife, queen Tiyi, it is clear that a central role in the Egyptian diplomatic policy was attributed to Mycenae, where as much as 6 of the total of 12 objects were found. It is entirely clear from the reference by the Hittite king in the Tawagalawas-letter, most likely Muwatallis II (1295-1271 BC), to his Akhaian colleague with the title LUGAL.GAL 'great king' (KUB 14.3 ii 13; iii 44) that Myceneaen Greece was a unified kingdom at the time and that the king of the capital Mycenae was the feudal overlord of the kings Kadmos and Eteokles of Thebes and Nestor of Pylos, in other words a great king, indeed (Kelder 2010). However, it is thanks to the tablets from El Amarna that we know that the main role in Amenhotep III's containment policy was attributed to the Arzawan king Tarḫundaradus, who is addressed in these letters as an equal and therefore recognized as a great king and with whom an alliance is solidified by the intended marriage of Amenhotep III to a daughter of Tarḫundaradus.[19] In the text of the Phaistos disc, Tarḫundaradus bolsters his claim on Phaistos by the use of the adjective 'Assuwian' (B10-11), so he definitely saw himself as the legitimate successor of the kings of Assuwa, one of whom, Piyamakuruntas, bears a name which is hereditary within the Arzawan royal family. As a matter of fact, the claim to the title great king may also go back to his predecessors of the Assuwian League (as evidenced by the Baltimore seal and the Thebes seal, see chapter 4), who headed a coalition of forces running from Lycia in the south to Troy in the north (cf. Bryce 2010: 124-125). In both our examples, the Mycenaean Greek kings, first Kadmos of Thebes and later Nestor of Pylos, were as far as the insular extension of their rule is concerned vassals of a Luwian overlord who controlled western Anatolia in its entirety, including Lycia. Accordingly, then, the

[19] In line with this observation, it deserves our attention in this connection that Amenhotep III's almost obsessive interest in western Anatolia emanates from its mention as *ʾI-s-y-w* 'Assuwa', *ʾI-r-ṯ-w* 'Arzawa', and *R-ỉ-wꜣ-ꜣ-n-ꜣ* 'Luwiya' in the texts on the statue bases from Kom el-Hetan, cf. Gander 2015: 445; 473 and note that, as most recently pointed out by Hawkins 2013: 32-35, Arzawa functions as a substitute for Luwiya in the Old Hittite law codes.

diplomatic intervention by the Egyptian pharaoh Amenhotep III in the period of *c.* 1370-1350 BC aimed at solidifying a coalition between the Luwians of western Anatolia on the one hand and the Mycenaean Greeks or Akhaians on the other hand bears testimony of his acute perception of the political realities of the wider Aegean region.

8. The Arzwan Language

8.1 Cuneiform Luwian

In the Hittite cuneiform texts there are found rituals by Arzawan practitioners, but these are conducted in the Hittite language (Melchert 2013). Similarly, the letter by the Arzawan great king Tarḫundaradus from the Amarna archive is also written in Hittite (Bryce 2010: 147-148 with note 98). Direct evidence of the Arzawan language—apart from mainly the recently discovered Luwian hieroglyphic inscriptions from western Anatolia from the final stage of the Bronze Age (see section 8.2)—is traceable, though, in the Luwian cuneiform texts. Among these texts, there can be found so-called 'Songs from Istanuwa', of which the date according to Frank Starke (1985: 301-304) goes back to the Old Hittite period or 16th century BC. Now, Istanuwa is associated with the *Saḫiriya* or Classical *Sangarios* (Yakubovich 2010: 22), and therefore likely to be situated in Ḫapalla, one of the four Arzawa lands as mentioned in the Alaksandus-treaty (Woudhuizen 2015b: 8-9). If so, the songs from Istanuwa may reasonably be assumed to be conducted in the language of Ḫapalla or in other words: in an Arzawan tongue. In any case, with a view to its date, this evidence of the Arzawan language precedes the infiltration of Thracian and Phrygian population groups into Ḫapalla from the 15th century BC onwards as referred to in chapter 1.

In the following I present a selection of the texts catalogued as songs from Istanuwa with phrases that are reasonably understandable and can be translated word for word with the help of the lexicon by Craig Melchert of 1993.

KBo 4.11 Rs. (Starke 1985: 341 [song from Istanuwa])

46. *aḫ-ḫa -ta -ta a-la-ti a-ú-i-en-ta Ú-i-lu-ša-ti*	'When they came to steep Wilusa.'

This text, to which attention has been drawn by Calvert Watkins in 1986, has been considered as the first phrase of a Wilusiad, the Luwian counterpart of Homeros' *Iliad*. In any case, it clearly indicates contacts between the inhabitants of Ḫapalla with *Wilusa* or *(W)ilion* in the northwest corner of Anatolia. The phrase starts with the adverb *aḫ-ḫa* 'when', which is followed by the nominative plural of the enclitic pronoun *-ta* 'they'. The verb is expressed by *a-ú-i-en-ta*, the 3rd person plural of the past tense in *-nta* of the verbal root *aúi-* 'to come, approach'. The combination surrounding the verb, *a-la-ti Ú-i-lu-ša-ti* 'to steep Wilusa', is characterised by the ablative singular ending in *-ti*. The function of the remaining particle *-ta* is unclear.

KUB 32.13 Vs. i (Starke 1985: 301; 353 [song from Istanuwa])

6. *[li]-la-i-lu li-la-i-lu [*	'I must purify from sin, I must purify from sin (...)!'

7. *li-la-an-du -an* DINGI[R^{MEŠ}*-in-zi*	'They should purify him from
8. *ku-um-ma-i-in-zi a[-*	sin, the gods, the pure (ones),
	(...)!'

The repetitive *li-la-i-lu* renders the 1st person singular of the imperative in *-lu* of the verb *lila(i)-* 'to purify from sin'. In the next phrase, *li-la-an-du* confronts us with the 3rd person plural of the imperative in *-ndu* of the same verbal root. The enclitic *-an* renders the accusative singular of the gender of the enclitic pronoun of the 3rd person. The subject is formed by DINGI[R^{MEŠ}*-in-zi* and *ku-um-ma-i-in-zi*, which are both characterised by the nominative plural ending of the gender in *-nzi*.

KBo 4.11 Rs. (Starke 1985: 341 [song from Istanuwa])

43. *za-an-ni -in* KASKAL*-an ku-i-in*	'This (is) it, the (divine) offering
a-at-ti	pit, which he makes.'
ku-i-iš ni-mi-ya-an-ni	'He, who (is) one of a kind,'
44. *an-na-a-an i-li*	'you (pl.) should always listen to
du-du-um-ma-ni-ta-an	that (person)!'

The form *za-an-ni* renders the accusative singular in *-ni* of the common gender of the demonstrative pronoun *za-* 'this'. It is followed by the accusative singular of the common gender of the enclitic pronoun of the 3rd person *-in*. The vowel of this form deviates from regular [a] as in *-an* of the preceding text and determines the redundant vowel [i] in the preceding *zanni*. KASKAL*-an* is the accusative singular of the common gender in *-n* of the root KASKAL- '(divine) earth-road' or '(divine) offering pit' as per Hawkins 1995: 44-45 (cf. esp. *ma-aš-ša-na-al-li-in* KASKAL*-an* [A(m/f) sg.] in 35.45 Vs. ii 24). The following *ku-i-in* is the accusative singular of the common gender in *-n* of the relative pronoun *kui-* 'who, what'. The final *a-at-ti* of the first phrase consists of the 3rd person of the present/future in *-ti* of the verb *a-* 'to make'.

The first word of the next phrase, *ku-i-iš*, renders the nominative singular of the common gender in *-š* of the relative pronoun *kui-* 'who, what'. In my opinion the endingless *ni-mi-ya-an-ni* is composed of the elements *ni-* 'not, un-' and *miya-* 'great, many' < PIE **méĝh*$_2$- (Mallory & Adams 2007: 317) in like manner as *maya-* 'adult'. For similar formations, cf. *ni-wala/i-* 'powerless, innocent' and *ni-warala/i-* 'alien, hostile (= not one's own)'.

The third phrase starts with the preposition *an-na-a-an* 'under'. Its function in the phrase is weak. The following *i-li* is the dative singular in *-i* of a demonstrative pronoun *il-* comparable to Latin *ille* 'that person or thing'. For a comparable root among the pronouns, cf. Hittite *-ila* 'self' (Friedrich 1960: 62, § 99) and Luwian hieroglyphic *ila* 'personally' (Woudhuizen 2015a: 272). The last form *du-du-um-ma-ni-ta-an*, finally, I take as the 2nd person plural of the imperative in *-tan* of the reduplicated (= intensified) verbal root *dummani-* corresponding to *tummanti-* 'to hear, listen'.

54. *du-uš-ša-ni-ya-al-la-aš -mi*	'A mediator (?) will be installed

a-ya-tar pa-a-i-ú	by me, he should sacrifice!'
55. *ḫal-[d]a -me -it-ta du-wa-an-ta*	'They placed for me the *ḫalda-*
wa-šu pád-du	here, it should *pad-* good!'

KBo 30.167 (Starke 1985: 331 [song from Istanuwa)

8. *du-uš-ša-ni-ya-la-aš -m[i]*	'A mediator (?) will be installed
9. *a-ya-at-tar pa-a-i-ú*	by me, he should sacrifice!'
ḫal-ti -mi -[i]t-ta [du-wa-an-ta]	'They placed for me the *ḫalti-*
10. *wa-a-šu pa-ad-du*	here, it should *pad-* good!'

These nearly identical sections can be treated together. The first word, *du-uš-ša-ni-ya-al-la-aš*, renders the nominative singular of the common gender in *-š* of the noun *duššaniyalla-* to which I attribute the meaning 'mediator' on the basis of the context. The element *-mi* attached to it is the dative of the enclitic pronoun of the 1st person singular. The following *a-ya-tar* is the 3rd person singular of the middle-passive in *-tar* of the verb *aya-* 'to make'. Cf. also 35.135 Rs. iv 22 (Starke 1985: 322) for the repetition of the first phrase with the defective variant writing *a-a-ya-at-ra*. The final *pa-a-i-ú* is also a verbal form, this time the 3rd person singular of the imperative in *-u* of the verb *pai-* 'to give, sacrifice'.

The second and last phrase is characterised by two verbal forms, *du-wa-an-ta*, the 3rd person plural of the past tense of the verb *duwa-* 'to place' and *pád-du* or *pa-ad-du*, the 3rd person singular of the imperative in *-du* of a verb *pad-* of unknown meaning. Of the remaining elements, *wa-šu* or *wa-a-šu* is an adverb expressing the meaning 'good' and *-me* or *-mi* is the dative of the enclitic pronoun of the 1st person singular, again. Finally, *-it-ta* bears testimony of the locative particle *-ta* 'here' with connecting vowel [i] determined by the preceding *-me* or *-mi*.

KUB 25.39 Rs. i (Starke 1985: 329-330 [song from Istanuwa])

26. *li-lu-u-wa ta-a-in mi-mi-en*	'You should pour oil, you
tu-u-wa-a [ ]	should place *mimie-*!' (...)
27. *li-lu-u-wa li-lu-u-wa i-ya-a*	'You should pour, you should
na-an-na-a l[i-	pour these *nana-*'s, (...)!'

The initial *li-lu-u-wa* renders the endingless 2nd person singular of the imperative of the verb *liluwa-* 'to pour'. The following *ta-a-in* is the endingless nominative-accusative singular of the neuter of the noun *tāin-* 'oil'. Next, *mi-mi-en* confronts us with the accusative singular of the common gender in *-n* of the noun *mimie-* of unknown meaning. The verbal form in final position, *tu-u-wa-a*, is the endingless 2nd person singular of the imperative of the verb *tuwa-* (also *duwa-* as in the preceding section) 'to place'.

The form *i-ya-a* renders the nominative-accusative of the neuter plural in *-a* of the demonstrative pronoun *i-* 'this' and corresponds to Luwian hieroglyphic *īā* of the same function (Woudhuizen 2015a: 232-233). Obviously, therefore, the Arzawan language is characterised, alongside *za-* as encountered in KBo 4.11 Rs. 43 in the above, by *i-* for the expression of the demonstrative pronoun. The following *na-an-na-a* corresponds to the preceding *i-ya-a* and likewise renders the nominative-accusative plural in *-a*, but unfortunately the meaning of the noun *nanna-* is unclear.

Rs. iv

11. *ku-wa-la-na-al-li-in -tar*	'He (who from haste) engaged
12. *la-al-ḫi-ya-an ḫa-ad-da-ya*	violently (= in violation of
ú-wi-ši-da KI.MIN	regular procedures) in a
	campaign of the army:
	likewise.'

The verbal form of this phrase is expressed by *ú-wi-ši-da*, the 3rd person singular of the past tense in *-da* of *úwisi-* 'to engage'. The combination *ku-wa-la-na-al-li-in la-al-ḫi-ya-an* renders the accusative singular of the common gender in *-n* of the noun *lalḫiya-* 'campaign' and corresponding adjective *kuwalanalli-* 'of the army'. The following *ḫa-ad-da-ya* is an adverb expressing the meaning 'violently'. Of the remaining elements, *-tar* is a sentence introductory particle and KI.MIN means 'likewise'.

The following observations deserve attention with respect to the conjugation of the verb (cf. Meriggi 1980: 350, § 229):

(1) The 1st person singular of the imperative in *-lu* goes unattested in Luwian hieroglyphic, but this may merely be due to chance. Within the IE Anatolian languages, it corresponds to Hittite *-allu*.

(2) The 2nd person plural of the imperative in *-tan* likely corresponds to Luwian hieroglyphic *-tana*. In my sketch of Luwian hieroglyphic grammar I have taken this ending for the 2nd person plural of the present/future (Woudhuizen 2015a: 248). However, in the two cases of its use an imperative functioning as subjunctive seems preferable.

(3) The use of the ending *-u* alongside *-du* for the expression of the 3rd person singular of the imperative is a feature the Arzawan language shares with Hittite and Lycian.

Finally, a typical feature of the Arzawan language unparalleled for the other cuneiform Luwian texts is the use of the demonstrative pronoun *i(ya)-* 'this' alongside *za-* 'this'. As we have noted, in this respect the Arzawan language shows the closest affinity with Luwian hieroglyphic.

(PRO)NOUN

	sg.	pl.
N	*-š*	*-nzi*
A	*-n*	
N-A(n)	—	*-a*
D	*-i*	
Abl.	*-ti*	

VERB

	sg.	pl.
3rd pers. pres./fut.	*-ti*	
3rd pers. past tense	*-da*	*-nta*
1st pers. imp.	*-lu*	
2nd pers. imp.	—	*-tan*
3rd pers. imp.	*-du*, *-u*	*-ndu*
3rd pers. mid.-pas.	*-tar*	

Table X. Grammatical sketch of the cuneiform Luwian evidence on the Arzawan language.

8.2 Luwian Hieroglyphic

The Luwian hieroglyphic texts from western Anatolia inform us about the Arzawan language. It deserves our attention therefore that in these texts we come across the following evidence for (pro)nominal declension and verbal conjugation (see Table XI).

From the use of Akkadisms like the genitive particle *SA* 'of', and the prepositions *A-NA* 'in' and *I-NA* 'in', however, it may safely be deduced that the Arzawan scribes, writing in Luwian hieroglyphic, were also acquainted with the cuneiform script.

The latter inference coincides neatly with the fact that another source on the Arzawan language is formed by the Istanuwan songs in cuneiform Luwian (see section 8.1). Note, however, that the distinction between the two scripts did involve a certain amount of code-switching, as, for example, the N and A(m/f) pl. are both expressed by *-i* in Luwian hieroglyphic, but by *-nzi* and *-nza* in cuneiform Luwian.

It further deserves our attention in this connection that, on account of the correspondence of the D sg. of the enclitic pronoun of the 3rd person *-la* to Lydian *-λ*, the Arzawan language can be shown to be a direct forerunner of the later Lydian.

(PRO)NOUN

	sg.	pl.
N	—, *-sa*	
A	—, *-na*	*-i*
N-A(n)	—, *-sa*	*-a*
D		*-āi*
G	*-sa*	
Abl.	*-ti*	
Loc.	*-ti*, *+r(i)*	

VERB

	sg.	pl.
1st pers. pres./fut.	*-wa*	
3rd pers. pres./fut.	*-ti*	
1st pers. past tense	*-ḫa*	
3rd pres. past tense	*-ta*	*-^{n}ta*
2nd pers. imp.	—	
3rd pers. imp.	*-tu*	
participle act.	*-^{n}t-*	
participle mid.-pas.	*-mi-*	

Table XI. Grammatical sketch of the Luwian hieroglyphic evidence on the Arzawan language.

The evidence from cuneiform Luwian and Luwian hieroglyphic on the Arzawan language shows that it is straightforwardly Luwian. It is true that in one instance, *árwana-* 'to send; mission' (Beyköy 2, §§ 46, 48) < *ḫarwan-* 'to send', the initial laryngeal [ḫ] is lost, but this is not unparalleled for Luwian hieroglyphic in general (Woudhuizen 2011: 412-413; cf. in particular in this connection the Arzawan royal name *Uḫḫazitis* < *ḫuḫḫa-* 'grandfather'). Furthermore, the Arzawan language distinguishes itself by the use of *ánama-* instead of regular *átìma-* for 'name' (Beyköy 2, § 33)—a form closer to the PIE root *$h_1$nómn̥* (Mallory & Adams 2007, 356). Finally, there are place-names mentioned in the Luwian hieroglyphic texts from western Anatolia which are of non-Luwian type for the fact that PIE *[h_2] is not represented by laryngeal [ḫ] and the voiced velars are not lost. But these types of place-names can plausibly be attributed to an Indo-European substrate language most likely to be identified as Pelasgian (see chapter 10). Accordingly, the concept of 'Luwic' as developed by Craig Melchert and further worked out by Ilya Yakubovich (2010: 6) for the language of western Anatolia during the Late Bronze Age may safely be dismissed.

9. The Language of the Trojans[1]

9.1 Introduction

Of the language spoken by the Trojans during the Late Bronze Age we have (apart from the recently rediscovered Luwian hieroglyphic inscription from Edremit, on which see below) no direct evidence in the form of texts conducted in the Trojan language. Therefore, we have to rely solely on indirect evidence in the form of toponyms, ethnonyms, and onomastics. It should be acknowledged from the start that this category of evidence need not be representative of the language spoken by the Trojans, it just might give us merely an indication of the general nature of this language. Furthermore, given the fact that the date of the relevant Homeric evidence is still subject to considerable debate—does it reflect Late Bronze Age realities or have a bearing only on the Early Iron Age—I will first treat the relevant Late Bronze Age data from Hittite, Luwian, and Egyptian sources (section 9.2) and then only secondarily the relevant Homeric evidence (section 9.3).

Before we set out on this endeavor, which takes up the thread where Calvert Watkins has left it in 1986, it is necessary to address the question of the location of the Hittite place-name *Wilusa*. With this place-name, namely, most of our Late Bronze Age evidence from the Hittite sources is linked up. At first, the majority of the scholars in the field took it for granted that Hittite *Wilusa* is a reflex of the same root as Homeric *Ilion* and that the place in question is to be situated in the Troad, i.e. in the northwest corner of Anatolia. Doubts about this location, however, were raised by, amongst others, Jacques Freu, in the latter case from as early as from 1980 onwards. Later on, in 2009, an alternative location of *Wilusa* in the neighbourhood of present-day Beycesultan was proposed by Vangelis Pantazis, who drew attention to the similarly sounding *Ilouza* as recorded for a polis and a bishopric in this region in Christian texts from the 5th century AD onwards. In this alternative positioning of *Wilusa* he was subsequently followed by Frank Kolb in 2010 and by Susanne Heinhold-Krahmer in 2013. This alternative, however, is definitely ruled out by the fact that the ancient name of Beycesultan can positively be identified as *Mira* on the basis of the reading of the legend of the stamp seal discovered at this site[2] as arrived at independently by Fabrizio Giovanetti (e-mail October 18, 2012) and myself (see chapter 2).

In his most recent contribution on the topic of 2014, Freu on p. 83 does not embrace the alternative by Pantazis, but persists in his rejection of the identification of *Wilusa* with present-day Hisarlık or Classical Troy.[3] His reservations in the matter are based on the observation that no tablets have been found at this site whereas according to the Hittite evidence *Wilusa* clearly was ruled by a literate administration and that in one case, the so-called *Alaksandus*-treaty, it was even stipulated that the tablet on which

[1] This chapter is a reworked version of Woudhuizen 2017c.
[2] Mora 1987, XIIb 3.3.
[3] So already Freu 1998: 109.

is was written should be read to the local king thrice a year (§ 19).[4] Therefore, Freu suggests an alternative location somewhere in the north of the western coastal region of Anatolia, without going into specifics. In reaction to this argument, it needs to be stressed that the same lack of tablets characterises all the other main settlements in the west, like *Millawanda* or Miletos, *Apasa* or Ephesos, and *Mira* or Beycesultan—even though we know from the Hittite sources that messages written on clay tablets were exchanged with the ruling administrations of these cities.

As it seems, then, doubts raised about the identification of *Wilusa* with present-day Hisarlık or Classical Troy are without proper foundation and may therefore safely be dismissed. At any rate, in the following we will argue from the point of view that this identification is valid.

9.2 The Relevant Late Bronze Age Data

1. The relevant data from the Hittite sources on the language of the Trojans, most of which have already been presented by Hans Gustav Güterbock in his paper on the topic of 1986, are the following:

(1) the place-names *Wilusa* or *Wilusiya* and *Tarwisa*;

(2) the personal names *Kukunnis*, *Alaksandus*, and *Walmus* of subsequent rulers of *Wilusa*;

(3) the divine name *Appaliunas*, an oath deity of the *Wilusian* side in the *Alaksandus*-treaty (§ 20).[5]

(1) From a linguistic point of view, the place-name *Wilusa* or *Wilusiya*, which occurs most frequently in the Hittite texts and which generally has been analyzed as a reflex of the same root as Greek *Ilion*, may reasonably be argued to be a derivative in *-sa* or *-sa-* and *-iya* of a root related to Hittite *wēllu-* 'meadow'[6] and therefore likewise be traced back to the PIE root **wel-* 'grass'.[7] Similarly, the place-name *Tarwisa*, which, like the variant form *Wilusiya* of *Wilusa*, only occurs in the annals of the Hittite great king Tudḫaliyas II (1425-1390 BC) and which according to the present *communis opinio* confronts us with a reflex of the same root as Greek *Troia* (cf. Linear B *to-ro* and *to-ro-ja* [f]),[8] also likely consists of a derivative in *-sa* or *-isa* of a root *tarw-* related to Hittite *tāru-* 'wood, tree'[9] and, if so, bears the testimony of the PIE root **dóru-* 'wood, tree'.[10] If our analysis of the two place-names applies, it allows us to conclude that the northwest corner of Asia Minor is most likely inhabited by speakers of an Indo-European tongue during the Late Bronze Age.

4 Latacz 2010: 166.
5 Latacz 2010: 166.
6 Neumann 1999: 21, note 20.
7 Mallory & Adams 2007: 163-164; 519.
8 Ventris & Chadwick 1973: 587.
9 Friedrich 1991, s.v.
10 Mallory & Adams 2007: 156.

(2) Of the rulers of *Wilusa*, according to the *Alaksandus*-treaty (§ 3) *Kukunnis* was a contemporary of the grandfather of the Hittite king who made the treaty in question, Muwatallis II (1295-1272 BC), i.e. Suppiluliumas I (1350-1322 BC).[11] As acknowledged by Craig Melchert, in lenited variant form *Xuχune* (D sg.) this name is attested for Lycian.[12] In addition, a reflex of the personal name *Kukunnis* can also be found in an Egyptian hieroglyphic text from Byblos, dating from the reign of Abishemu II in the late 18th century BC, where it occurs in form of *Kwkwn* and happens to be specified as that of a Lycian by the following sequence *sꜣ Rw-q-q* 'representative of the Lycian(s)'.[13] Apart from the evidence given so far, which appears to be indicating that we are in fact dealing with a typical Lycian name, a reflex of the personal name *Kukunnis* can also be found in Greek *Kuknos*, a ruler of Kolonai along the Propontis to the northeast of Troy, who in various versions of the Greek myth is slain by Akhilleus either at Tenedos or at the Trojan shore, but the explanation of his name in Greek terms as 'swan' clearly results from a secondary *interpretatio Graeca* of an indigenous Anatolian name.[14] As to the nature of this name, it deserves our attention that in its Greek form *Kuknos* it is exactly paralleled for a Ligurian king, whose realm according to Pausanias, *Guide to Greece* I, 30, 3 is situated along the river *Eridanos* or Rhône.[15] It may reasonably deduced from this observation, namely, that the personal name in question is of Old Indo-European type. A subsequent ruler of *Wilusa* is *Alaksandus*, who is a contemporary of the Hittite great king Muwatallis II and with whom the treaty named after him is conducted. His name, as all scholars in the field agree, corresponds to Greek *Aleksandros* and is therefore definitely Greek.[16] The last ruler of *Wilusa* known to us is *Walmus*, who according to the *Milawata*-letter had been deposed and taken refuge to *Millawanda* or Miletos, but the Hittite great king to whom the letter is attributed, Tudḫaliyas IV (1239-1209 BC), makes it absolutely clear that this vassal needs to be restored to his rightful throne.[17] Strangely enough, the name of this ruler has thus far not been subject to linguistic analysis, but there can be little doubt that it corresponds to *Halmos* or *Almos* from Greek literary sources in like manner as *Helena* originates from *Welena*, *Hermos* from *Warmala*, and *Holmoi* from *Walma*.[18] It deserves attention in this connection that *Halmos* or *Almos* is not considered a Greek, but a member of the non-Greek population groups of central and northern Greece still present there during the Late Bronze Age.[19] In my view, these population groups—if not Pelasgian—can be positively identified as Thracians (cf. Linear B *o-du-ru-wi-jo* 'Odrysian' on vases from Thebes destined for its hinterland) and Phrygians (cf. mythical *Pelops* after whom the Peloponnesos is named).[20] In sum, then, the evidence of the personal names seems to be puzzlingly diverse, running from Lycian, which is a Luwian dialect, to contemporary non-Greek of central and northern Greece, most likely

[11] Latacz 2010: 162.
[12] Melchert 2004: 110.
[13] Montet 1962: 96, Fig. 5; cf. Woudhuizen 2014b.
[14] Graves 1990: 292; 296.
[15] Schulten 1950: 117.
[16] Güterbock 1986: 34 (cf. Linear B *a-re-ka-sa-da-ra* [f]); 43; Watkins 1986: 48-49.
[17] Güterbock 1986: 38.
[18] For *Velena-*, see Jeffery 1990: 90 (= Pl. 7, 1).
[19] Esp. associated with Minyan Orkhomenos, see Pausanias, *Guide to Greece* IX, 34, 10; 36, 4.
[20] Woudhuizen 2013c.

to be identified as Thraco-Phrygian, to patently Greek. But on the bright side: all of this remains within the sphere of the Indo-European language group.

(3) The divine name *Appaliunas*, the reading of which was considered uncertain in the past[21] but now seems to be generally accepted,[22] corresponds, as already observed by Güterbock, most closely to Doric Greek *Apellōn*. But the question remains whether Apollon is of origin a Greek deity. Güterbock rightly stresses the fact that in Homeros Apollon is on the side of the Trojans. So he might be a local Trojan god after all. One can also find in the literature the suggestion that Apollon with his mother Leto and sister Artemis forms a Lycian divine triad.[23] In any case, our earliest mention of this divine name consists of Linear B *[a]-pe-ro$_2$-ne* as attested for a text from Knossos (KN E 842.3),[24] which is interesting against the backdrop that according to Greek myth the cult of Apollon at Delphi is introduced by Cretans from Knossos.[25] To this it might be added that the name itself, which, as shown by Paul Kretschmer, consists of a reflex of PIE **apelo-* 'strength', is definitely of an Indo-European nature.[26] By means of conclusion, we cannot be any more specific about the ethnic affiliation of *Appaliunas* or Apollon than stating that, apart from its Indo-European nature in general, it might be a local Trojan god or a Lycian one or even a Cretan one—whatever the implications of the latter observation might be (on which see below).

2. The Luwian evidence relevant to our topic, to which our attention has been first drawn by Watkins in his contribution of 1986, is provided by a phrase from what are generally referred to as songs of Istanuwa in the literature. This phrase runs as follows (KBo 4.11, 46): *aḫḫa -ta -ta alati awienta Wilušati* 'When they came from steep Wilusa', and in an ashtoning way seems to confront us with the first line of a lay which may aptly be called a *Wilusiad*.[27] Now, Ilya Yakubovich situates the Luwians responsible for the songs from Istanuwa, which date to the Hittite Old Kingdom period (1680-1500 BC), in the region of the bend of the Sangarios river for their association with the river *Saḫiriya*.[28] Even though this regions lacks the typical Luwian place-names in *-ss-* and *-nd-* (see chapter 1), it seems highly plausible that the Arzawan country *Ḫapalla*, which has a typical Luwian name based on *ḫapa-* 'river' with the adjectival suffix in *-(a)lla*, is rightly located by Frank Starke in the river-land formed by the bend of the *Saḫiriya* or Classical Sangarios (= present-day Sakariya) and its tributary the present-day Porsuk or Classical Tembris (see chapter 2).[29] Accordingly, the phrase from the song from Istanuwa under consideration may reasonably be argued to bear testimony to *contacts* between *Wilusa* or Ilion in the northwest corner of Asia Minor with a Luwian population group in its immediate hinterland *Ḫapalla* or the Sangarios basin. It does not follow from this

21 Güterbock 1986: 42.
22 Latacz 2010: 166.
23 Palmer 1965: 347; Beekes 2003: 14-17.
24 Ruijgh 1967: 274, § 237.
25 *Homeric Hymn to Pythian Apollo* 388 ff.
26 Pokorny 1994: 52; note the Luwian reflex of the same root in the Karkamisian royal name *Aplaḫandas*.
27 Watkins 1986: 58-59; cf. chapter 8.
28 Yakubovich 2010: 125; 22
29 Starke 1997: 449, Abb. 1.

particular piece of evidence, as Watkins frankly admits, that the language current in *Wilusa* at the time was Luwian.[30]

3. The relevant Egyptian evidence concerns the mention of two ethnonyms, *Drdny* and *Tjeker*, and possibly one place-name, *Wiriya*. The ethnonym *Drdny* occurs in the context of the battle of Kadesh, 1274 BC, between the Egyptians headed by Ramesses II and the Hittites under the leadership of Muwatallis II. It is grouped here with the allies of the Hittites, and reasonably explained as a reference to the people of the Troad who are also known in Greek as *Dardanoi*. This observation cannot be used as an argument against the identification of *Wilusa* with Greek Ilion as Freu seems to do, who apparently assumes that if the identification applies **Wilusians* would have been expected rather than *Dardanoi*.[31] In actual fact, namely, a people is usually known by various ethnonyms used simultaneously, like Deutscher-Germans-Allemans-Nemski, depending from the country of origin of the observer. In like manner, the Mycenaean Greeks are called *Aḫḫiyawa* or Akhaians by the Hittites but *Tanayu* or Danaoi by the Egyptians,[32] and the Minoans are simultaneously referred to by the Egyptians as *Kftȉw* (cf. cuneiform *Kaptara* and Biblical *Kaphtor*) and *Mnws* 'Minoans'.[33] Therefore, it should not surprise us that we come across *Trōes* together with *Dardanoi* in an enumeration of ethnonyms in an Homeric line.[34] In the period of the upheavals of the Sea Peoples at the end of the Bronze Age, on the other hand, the people from the Troad who took part in these resurrections are referred to as *Tjeker* which ethnonym is generally assumed to correspond to Greek *Teukroi*. What is most interesting about this latter ethnonym is that it likely corresponds to cuneiform *Tukri*, a variant form of address used by Hammurabi of Babylon (1792-1750 BC) for the earliest Indo-Europeans mentioned in Near Eastern texts, the *Guti*. Related forms of both these ethnonyms, *Tocri* and *Kuči*, namely, are used as references to the Tokharians, an Indo-European people recorded for the Tarim basin during Late Antiquity.[35] The third and last instance of Egyptian evidence with a bearing on the Troad is likely to be provided by the place-name *Wiriya* in the list of Aegean place-names on statue bases from the mortuary temple of Amenhotep III (1390-1352 BC) at Kom el-Hetan. Given the predilection of the Minoans and after them the Mycenaean Greeks with the north-Aegean, it may reasonably be suggested that the only remaining place-name without proper identification, *Wiriya*, is more likely to be explained as a reflex of **Wilios* or Ilion than Greek Elis—even though it cannot be denied that both these place-names can ultimately be traced back to one and the same PIE root. What we gain from this overview of the relevant Egyptian data, then, is that the Trojans were addressed by an ethnonym *Tjeker* (= Greek *Teukroi*) which is likely of very ancient Indo-European antecedents. This piece of evidence coincides with the Indo-European nature of the toponyms and deity name from the Hittite sources and the fact that the parallels for the personal names from the Hittite sources, however puzzlingly diverse, remain within the sphere of the Indo-European language group.

30 Watkins 1986: 62.
31 Freu 2014: 88-89.
32 Kelder 2010: 21-39.
33 Vercoutter 1956: 162-163, docs. 57 and 58.
34 Watkins 1986: 52 (Τρῶες καὶ Λύκιοι καὶ Δάρδανοι).
35 I am indebted to Krzysztof T. Witczak for suggesting to me this relationship.

Also worth mentioning in this section are the inscriptions as discovered in the Bronze Age layers of Hisarlık or Troy. In the first place, this entails a biconvex seal inscribed on both sides with Luwian hieroglyphic legends, the front side presumably bearing testimony of a *Tarḫunt*-name. The seal came to light in a Troy VIIB2-early layer, dated to the late 12th century BC, but should probably be considered as having been found out of its proper context because there can be little doubt that it originally belonged to a Hittite official stationed at Hisarlık or Troy in the period that the Hittite empire still functioned, i.e. before *c.* 1190 BC.[36] As such, it cannot be used, as some scholars have done, as evidence of the local Trojan language. The same verdict might well apply to the recently rediscovered Luwian hieroglyphic text from Edremit. It is true that this inscription has been dedicated by the Trojan ruler Muksas, but, with a view to the fact that his name is of Phrygian type and that place-names like Pityeia, Arisbe, and Perkote near his seat Apaisos are of Thracian type, it seems more likely that the dominant language in the Troad was of Thraco-Phrygian than Luwian nature. It seems no coincidence, therefore, that the inscription has been erected in the region of the Indo-European Anatolian or Luwian Leleges, the literate members of which tribe could read it. Furthermore, as shown by Louis Godart and Paul Faure, there have been found at Hisarlık or Troy four Linear A inscriptions, two of which are assigned to early in Troy VI whereas the other two are reported to belong to Troy IV.[37] The validity of this evidence, however, has been questioned by Jean-Pierre Olivier as well as the Linear B specialists John Bennet and Thomas Palaima.[38] With the proviso that these Linear A inscriptions cannot possibly be dated earlier than the end of the 18th century BC, when this particular script was devised in the island of Crete, I personally see no reason why this evidence should be dismissed, as it generally is by Anatolian specialists, or not be used, in like manner as the Luwian hieroglyphic seal, as an argument that the local Trojan language was 'Minoan'. The latter inference, I would maintain, is by no means as ridiculous as it might seem at first sight if we realize that inscriptions in Linear A, although in the majority of the cases conducted in a northwest Semitic vernacular, also bear the testimony of a local Cretan variant of Luwian most closely related to Lycian and, in three instances in sum, of Pelasgian, a language of Old Indo-European type.[39] Instead of getting overexcited, however, in reality we are of course dealing here with either Cretan imports or the radiation of Cretan culture to the Troad.

9.3 The Relevant Homeric Data

In connection with the relevant Homeric data it will be assumed that the Greek poet, or epic tradition epitomized by Homeros, has been subject to a tendency to change Trojan names into the for his public more familiar Greek ones. If we are right in this assumption, the onomastic evidence significant to our purposes is formed by the non-Greek names. Accordingly, we will focus our efforts in the following discussion on this particular category. Another problem posed by the Homeric evidence is formed by the

---

36 Latacz 2010: 97 ff.

37 Godart 1994a; Godart 1994b: esp. pp. 714-722; Faure 1996; cf. Latacz 2010: 170, note 159.

38 Olivier 1999: 431; cf. Latacz 2010: 170, note 159.

39 Sakellarakis & Olivier 1994: KY Za 2 (*da-ma-te*); Godart & Olivier 1982: 142-143: AR zf 1-2 (*i-da-ma-te*). See now Woudhuizen 2016: 303-312.

question to which period it dates, the Late Bronze Age in which the story is situated or the Early Iron Age when Homeros or the representatives of the epic tradition epitomized by him was/were actually performing. Now, as to the dating of the Homeric onomastic evidence it deserves our attention that the Kaska as recorded in the Hittite sources, which caused the Hittites so much troubles along the northern border of their realm subsequent to the Old Kingdom period (note that in this period the town of Zalpa along the coast of the Black Sea is still an integrated part of the Hittite kingdom), are characterised by place-names and personal names of a Thraco-Phrygian background.[40] Therefore, the poet is probably right in his statement that Phrygian troops headed by Otreus and Mygdon were mustered along the banks of the Sangarios already when Priamos was still able to fight himself, which, as *Aleksandros-Paris* is the latter's son, in Hittite terms means more then a generation before the reign of *Alaksandus* in the early 13th century BC (see above).[41] Apparently, these Phrygians ousted the local Luwians which, as we have noted in the above, were responsible for the songs of Istanuwa, to the extent that, apart from the country name *Ḫapalla* and the personal names of its rulers *Tarkasnallis* (a contemporary of the Hittite great king Mursilis II [1321-1295 BC]) and *Uraḫattusas* (a contemporary of the Hittite great king Muwatallis II [1295-1272 BC]),[42] no trace of them is left—like, for example, in the form of the typically Luwian place-names in *-ss-* and *-nd-*, which are absent here (see chapter 1). From this observation, then, it may reasonably be deduced that the Homeric onomastic evidence, with the proviso of the aforementioned tendency to progressive Hellenization, could well be chronologically adequate as well.

Now, the first Homeric name which comes to mind is that of the Trojan king *Priamos*. This has been analyzed by Emmanuel Laroche and Vladimir Georgiev as a reflex of Luwian *Pariyamuwas*,[43] of which the first element may well be traced back to the PIE root **priyó-* 'dear, (be)love(d)' so that the name in its entirety means 'strongly beloved'.[44] Following this Luwian trail, Watkins further points out the case of 'Asios, son of Hurtakos' in Homeros, *Iliad* 13, 759, as both these names can be meaningfully explained as reflexes of a Luwian or Hittite (so IE Anatolian) root. In the case of *Asios* the root in question is **Asw-* as represented by the Luwian geographic name *Assuwa*, which is related to the Linear B ethnic adjective *a-si-wi-jo* and Classical *Asia* (< **Aswia*), whereas in the case of *Hurtakos* the closest parallel is provided by Hittite *ḫartakas* < PIE **h_2ŕ̥tk̂os* 'bear'.[45] Note that the lenition of Anatolian [ḫ] into [h] as evidenced by the latter example, or even

[40] Cf. the personal names *Pittagatallis*, *Pittaparas*, *Pendumlis* and the place-names *Pittalaḫsa*, *Zagapura*, *Ḫuḫazalma* among which we can determine the Thracian onomastic or toponymic elements *Pitta-*, *Bend-*, *-para*, *-poris*, *-zelmis* (cf. Detchew 1976) sometimes in combination with IE Anatolian elements, like the formation of agent nouns in *-talli-* and *ḫuḫa-* 'grandfather'. Cf. further the personal names *Asḫapalas*, *Kurijallis*, *Taskuwalis* and the place-names *Midduwa*, *Duma* or *Tumma*, *Kurtalisa*, *Pargalla*, *Zidaparḫa*, *Taskulija*, bearing testimony of the Phrygian onomastic or toponymic elements *Aska-*, *Kurija-*, *Dasky-*, *Mida-*, *Gord-*, and *Briga-* sometimes in combination with IE Anatolian elements, again, like adjectival *-ali-* and *zida-* 'man', and the vocabulary word *duma-* for some sort of social organization. On the Kaska names, see von Schuler 1965 and cf. Woudhuizen 2012a: 265.

[41] Homeros, *Iliad* 3, 184-187.

[42] Bryce 2010: 196; 214; Latacz 2010: 165 (*Alaksandus*-treaty § 17).

[43] Watkins 1986: 57.

[44] Cf. Mallory & Adams 2007: 204-205; 208; 222; 343.

[45] Watkins 1986: 53-55; cf. Mallory & Adams 2007: 88; 135; 138.

its loss without a trace ([ḫ] > [h] > ø), may, at least within the IE Anatolian sphere of influence, reasonably be attributed to the influence of an Old Indo-European substrate on IE Anatolian (see further chapter 10).[46]

However, as soon as we turn to the second name of *Aleksandros-Paris*, one of the sons of Priamos whose first name, as we have seen in the above, is a patent loan from Greek and corresponds to Hittite *Alaksandus*, it has to be admitted that the closest comparable evidence is provided by Thracian *Paris*.[47] If for the sake of argument we follow this particular trail, we soon stumble upon the pathbreaking results of Leonid Gindin in his work on the relations between Troy and Thrace of 1999. In this work, then, he presents numerous comparisons of Trojan onomastics to Thraco-Phrygian counterparts. Worth mentioning in this connection are the correspondence of the root of the *Skaiai* gates to that of the Thracian ethnonym *Skaioi*,[48] of the *Kebrionēs* to that of the Thracian ethnonym *Kebrēnioi*,[49] *Laomedōn ho Phruks*, i.e. the Phrygian, and his wife *Strumō*, whose name corresponds to that of the Thracian river *Strumōn*,[50] and we may add to this series the Phrygian descent of Priamos' wife *Hekabē* as reported by Homeros, *Iliad* 16, 718-719.[51]

On the basis of the foregoing evidence the conclusion seems justified that, as far as their names are concerned, the overwhelming majority of the Trojans were of Thraco-Phrygian descent. This inference is in conformity with our analysis of the name of the ruler of *Wilusa* during the reign of Tudḫaliyas IV, *Walmus*, which on the basis of its relationship to *Halmos* or *Almos* from Greek literary tradition we have been able to determine as being of non-Greek and, more in specific, Thraco-Phrygian nature as well. Working from this observation, the Luwian or IE Anatolian type of names may safely be ascribed to Trojan interactions with their neighbours in Anatolia resulting from diplomacy, trade, and intermarriage. The latter explanation no doubt also holds good for the Greek nature of the name of *Walmus'* predecessor, *Alaksandus*.

At first glance, our conclusion that the Trojan language is of Thraco-Phrygian nature seems to be at odds with the evidence from the *Homeric Hymn to Aphrodite*, lines 107-116, according to which the language of the daughter of the Phrygian king Otreus is distinct from the Trojan one.[52] It should be realized in this context, however, that Aphrodite in the guise of the daughter of Otreus speaks to Ankhises, the father of Aineas, who represents a Trojan royal line distinct from that of Priamos, presumably of Luwian antecedents as it appears to be linked up with the region south of mount Ida, characterized by typically Luwian place-names in *-ss-* and *-nth-* (= Greek variant of Anatolian

[46] Cf. Yakubovich 2010: 91-95 (on the first element of the Arzawan royal name *Uḫḫazitis* < Luwian *ḫuḫḫa-* 'grandfather'). Cf. Woudhuizen 2011: 412-414.
[47] Detschew 1976: 358.
[48] Detschew 1976: 453-454.
[49] Detschew 1976: 236-237.
[50] Detschew 1976: 483-485.
[51] Gindin 1999: 57-58; 62-64; 263.
[52] *Hesiod, The Homeric Hymns and Homerica*, Loeb edition, pp. 412-415.

-nd-).[53] In other words: the language of the Trojan Ankhises need not be representative of that of the Trojans more in general!

As long as texts in the Trojan language are lacking, we will never be sure about its actual nature before the colonization of Troy by Aiolian Greeks. Against the backdrop of the relevant onomastic data, it seems permissible to suggest that the Trojans spoke a vernacular closely related to Thracian and/or Phrygian. If we add to this category of evidence that of the toponyms and the deity name discussed, one thing appears to be clear, namely that the region of northwest Asia Minor was inhabited by speakers of an Indo-European tongue already during the Late Bronze Age. It should further be realized that the latter dating serves as a *terminus ante quem*. There are indications, namely, that the aforesaid Thracian and/or Phrygian linguistic layer was preceded by a substrate of Old Indo-European type. One such an indication is formed by the name of the most formidable mountain in the region, *Ida*, which originates from the PIE root **wid^{h}u-* 'tree, forest' and is paralleled for Crete. What is even more, in one of the indigenous Cretan scripts, Linear A, this name occurs as a constituent element of a divine name, *i-da-ma-te* 'Mother Ida', which is attested twice and by means of deduction can positively be attributed to the language of the Pelasgians inhabiting Crete according to Homeros, *Odyssey* 19, 177 since of the remaining Indo-European languages spoken in Minoan Crete Luwian lacks an equivalent of Proto-Indo-European **méh$_2$tēr-* and the Greek reflex of **wid^{h}u-* is *wi-da-* (as in Knossian Linear B *wi-da-jo*, *wi-da-ka-so*, *wi-da-ma-ro*, and *wi-da-ma-ta$_2$*).[54] Yet another indication for an Old Indo-European substrate in the Troad is formed, as we have noted in the above, by the lenition of IE Anatolian [ḫ] into [h] as observed in connection with the personal name *Hurtakos*. Furthermore, we might add in this connection that the citadel of Troy is called *Pergamos* in various passages of Homeros' *Iliad*,[55] which confronts us with a reflex of PIE **b^{h}r̥ĝ^h(i)-* 'high' in which the voiced velar, contrary to the procedures in Luwian, is maintained. Finally, it may be attributed to this same Old Indo-European substrate that in the Trojan river names showing a reflex the PIE root **h$_2$ep-/h$_2$eb$^{(h)}$-* 'water, rivulet', i.e. *Apidanos*[56] and *Aisēpos* (Homeros, *Iliad* 4, 91), the within the IE Anatolian sphere of influence expected IE Anatolian [ḫ] (as in *ḫapa-* 'river') is lost without a trace.

[53] *Der Neue Pauly*, s.v. *Dardanidae*; cf. TNs *Lyrnēssos* and *Smynthē*. Cf. chapter 1.

[54] Ventris & Chadwick 1973: 591. See now Woudhuizen 2016: 303-312.

[55] Homeros, *Iliad* 4, 508; 5, 446; 460; 6, 512.

[56] Rosenkranz 1966: 136. Note that the second element consists of a reflex of PIE **dānu-* 'river', which is also typical of Old Indo-European river names.

10. Evidence for an Old Indo-European Substrate in Western Anatolia

10.1 Late Bronze Age Hydronyms and Toponyms of Indo-European nature in Western Anatolia[1]

For various reasons, the study of hydronyms and toponyms of western Anatolia has not received much attention within the circle of Indo-Europeanists. As far as I know, no single article is attributed to this topic. Only Emmanuel Laroche, in the late 50s and early 60s of the former century, showed convincingly that the place-names in *-ss-* and *-nd-*, which are so common in western and southwestern Asia Minor, are definitely of an Indo-European nature, if not actually of an IE Anatolian one (Laroche 1957; Laroche 1961; see Fig. 1 above).[2]

In order to meet this *desideratum*, I have assembled from the Late Bronze Age sources at our disposal, which means in the main Hittite cuneiform texts supplemented by some relevant Luwian hieroglyphic ones, a number of toponyms and hydronyms which in my view are of patent Indo-European background. I focus on the Late Bronze Age material, because it provides us with the earliest data on the topic, which are most likely not yet 'contaminated' by secondary influences from other IE languages, like Greek and Latin, and therefore presumably most reliable to work with.

A handy tool in the course of this undertaking is provided by previous studies on the localization of hydronyms and toponyms with a bearing to western Anatolia as mentioned in the Hittite cuneiform texts and, to a lesser degree, the Luwian hieroglyphic ones. Most recently, this question received extensive treatment by Max Gander in 2010. In my view Gander is much too pessimistic about the possibilities to reconstruct the geography of southwest Asia Minor during the period of Hittite dominance over this region and many place-names can actually be put on the map (cf. Woudhuizen 2010-1b). What is even more, with the help of suggestions made in the literature on the topic by scholars like Jacques Freu (2008b: 110) and John David Hawkins (2002: 95-98) and the recently rediscovered Luwian hieroglyphic texts (see chapter 6), even the geography of western Anatolia, including the regions to the north of its southwestern area, can also be reconstructed in its bare outlines (cf. Woudhuizen 2014a; see Fig. 5).

For the present exercise, then, I have selected a total of 16 western Anatolian hydronyms and toponyms as rendered in our Table XII below in the order of their location on the map when going from the north to the south. In this table, furthermore, the geographic names, making up column 1, are lined with *comparanda* from the Hittite and Luwian languages, or, if these are so far unavailable, from other IE languages (placed between square brackets), in column 2 and the Proto-Indo-European (= PIE) roots in column 3.

---

1 This is a reworked version of Woudhuizen 2012c.

2 Note that in our set of selected geographic names features one example of each of these types, viz. *Ḫursanassa* and *Arinnanda*, respectively.

Geogr. name		Hit./Luw. cognate	PIE root
1.	*Taruisa*	*tāru-* 'wood, tree'	**dóru-* 'wood, tree'
2.	*Wilus(iy)a*	*wēllu-* 'meadow'	**wel-* 'grass'
3.	*Seḫa*	*[Sequana]*	*$seik^{w}$- 'to seep, soak'
4.	*Páraḫáma*	*parku-* 'high'	*$b^{h}\hat{r̥}g^{h}(i)$- 'high'
5.	*Appawiya*	*ḫapa-* 'river'	*h_2ep-/$h_2eb^{(h)}$- 'water, rivulet'
6.	*Arzawa*	*ars-* 'to flow, stream'	*h_1er-/h_3er- 'to move, stir, raise'
7.	*Kurupiya*	*Kurunt-* (GN/MN)	*$\hat{k}erh_1$- 'head, horn'
8.	*Dura*	*[Doúrios, Durias]*	*?
9.	*Apasa*	*ḫapa-* 'river'	*h_2ep-/$h_2eb^{(h)}$- 'water, rivulet'
10.	*Arinnanda*	*arinna-* 'source'	*h_1er-/h_3er- 'to move, stir, raise'
11.	*Sallapa*	*[Salapia]*	**sal-* + *h_2ep-/$h_2eb^{(h)}$- 'water, rivulet'
12.	*Astarpa*	*ḫastēr-* 'star'	*$h_2st\acute{\bar{e}}r$- 'star' + *h_2ep-/$h_2eb^{(h)}$- 'water, rivulet'
13.	*Ḫursanassa*	*gurta-* 'fortress'	*$g^{h}ord^{h}$- 'city, town'
14.	*Lukka*	[Λοῦγοι, *Lugii*]	*$l(e)ug^{h}$- 'to bind'
15.	*Awarna*	*arinna-* 'source'	*h_1er-/h_3er- 'to move, stir, raise'
16.	*Parḫa*	*parku-* 'high'	*$b^{h}\hat{r̥}g^{h}(i)$- 'high'

Table XII. Overview of western Anatolian hydronyms and toponyms of Indo-European nature.

Notes to Table XII:

1. PIE **dóru-* 'wood, tree' > Hit. *tāru-*, see Mallory & Adams 2007: 156; for the connection with *Tarwisa*, see the preceding chapter.

2. PIE **wel-* 'grass' > Hit. *wēllu-* 'meadow', see Mallory & Adams 2007: 163-164; for the connection with *Wilus(iy)a* as suggested by Neumann 1999: 21, note 20, see the preceding chapter.

3. The root of the river name *Seḫa*, which is to be identified with the Classical Kaikos according to the evidence from the recently rediscovered Luwian hieroglyphic

inscriptions from Yazılıtaş and Dağardı (see chapter 6), is likely to be compared to that of Gaulish *Sequana*; this latter hydronym is derived from PIE **seik*^{w}- 'to seep, soak' by Whatmough 1963: 68 (note thet the actual form †*sek̑*^{w}- here results from a printing error).

4. The place-name *Párahǽma* 'Pergamon', the capital of Teuthrania during the Classical period. This town is located in the realm of the Seḫa river land according to the evidence from the recently rediscovered Luwian hieroglyphic inscription from Dağardı (see chapter 6). Just like its relatives like *Pergamon* (Πέργαμος), the name of the citadel of Troy in Classical literary tradition, and *Parḫa*, corresponding to Classical *Pergē* (Πέργη), it shows a reflex of the PIE root **b*^{h}*r̥ĝ*^{h}*(i)*- 'high'. Also derived from this root is Hit. *parku*- 'high', see Mallory & Adams 2007: 289, 292. But, as this toponym is situated in territory inhabited by speakers of a Luwian tongue, one would have expected the voiced velar [ĝ^{h}] to have been dropped, as, in line with our observation sub 13 and 14, is regular for the latter language. Obviously, we are confronted here with a form foreign to the Luwian language and likely to be attributable to the influences of an Old Indo-European substrate. Note in this connection that *Pariyana* (= Classical *Priēnē*) shows the regular Luwian reflex of PIE **b*^{h}*r̥ĝ*^{h}*(i)*-.

5. *Appawiya* is a geographic name based, just like the place-name *Apasa*, on the root *apa*- originating from PIE **h*$_{2}$*ep*-/*h*$_{2}$*eb*$^{(h)}$- 'water, rivulet', but this time characterised not by the suffix *-sa* but the suffix *-wiya*. A reflex of this name for the eastern province of Seḫa, situated along the upper course of the river known in the Classical period as the *Makestos* (Μέκεστος), can be traced in Classical *Abbaitis*. As PIE **h*$_{2}$*ep*-/*h*$_{2}$*eb*$^{(h)}$- is represented in Hittite and Luwian by *ḫapa*- 'river', in which the PIE laryngeal *[h$_{2}$] is regularly represented by IE Anatolian [ḫ], the consequence of the given analysis is that *Appawiya* represents speakers of an Indo-European tongue other than IE Anatolian. Presumably we are dealing here with an Old Indo-European substrate which was already present before of the settlement of the Luwians in this particular region.

6. Hit. *ars*- 'to flow, stream' > *Arzawa*, see Carruba 2011: 321; for the basic PIE root **h*$_{1}$*er*-/*h*$_{3}$*er*- 'to move, stir, raise', see Krahe 1964: 45 and Rosenkranz 1966: 135.

7. For the identification of *Kurupiya* with Greek *Koruphē* (Κορυφή), see Freu 2008b: 110; working from this identification, the toponym is related to the Luwian GN or MN *Kurunt*- and may likewise be traced back to PIE **k̑erh*$_{1}$- 'head, horn'. Note that this toponym underlines the *centum* nature of the Luwian language as established in Woudhuizen 2011: 407-409.

8. For the identification of *Dura* with Classical *Tyrrha* (Τύρρα) and modern *Tire(h)* along the southern bank of the river later called Kaystros, see Freu 2008b: 110; even though the PIE root remains enigmatic, the pertinent parallels are provided by the Iberian or Lusitanian river name *Doúrios* or *Durius* and its Ligurian equivalent *Durias* (cf. also in this connection the *Duranius*, a branch of the Garumna or Garonne in

southwestern Gaul, see Map to Ceasar's *de Bello Gallico* in the edition by Sigmund Herzog of 1895), both of which are associated with Old Indo-European population groups, namely Lusitanians and Ligurians. Further of relevance in this context, especially for the interchange between the voiced dental [d] and unvoiced [t], is the Kimmerian name for the river Dniestr, Τύρης, see Herodotos, *Histories* IV, 11; 47; 51.

9. The identification of *Apasa* with Classical *Éphesos* (Ἔφεσος) and modern *Efes* is of long standing and can already be found in the map of Garstang & Gurney 1959. For its analysis as being based on the root *apa-* (for the suffix *-sa*, cf. *Wilusa* being based on a root related to Hit. *wēllu-*) < PIE *h_2ep-/$h_2eb^{(h)}$- 'water, rivulet', see Woudhuizen 2018: 66, note 64. As the reflex of the latter PIE root in Hittite and Luwian consists of *ḫapa-* 'river', in which the PIE laryngeal *[h_2] is regularly represented by IE Anatolian [ḫ], the consequence of the given analysis is that *Apasa* represents speakers of an Indo-European tongue other than IE Anatolian. Presumably we are dealing here with an Old Indo-European substrate which was already present before of the settlement of the Luwians in this particular region.

10. The name of mount *Arinnanda*, identified by Hawkins 2002: 97-98 with Classical mount *Mycalē* or present-day Samsun Dağ, is based on the root *arinna-*, which occurs here with the well-known suffix *-nd-*. Now, Hit. *arinna-* is identified by Rosenkranz 1966: 127 as the word for 'source' in like manner as this is the case with the related Greek Ἄρνη (so also Tischler 1983: 57-58, who situates the given Greek parallel in Arkadia, whereas according to Homeros, *Iliad* II, 507, Strabo, *Geography* 1, 3, 8; 9, 2, 34-35, Pausanias, *Guide to Greece* IX, 40, 5, and Stephanos of Byzantion, *Etnica*, s.v. Χαιρώνεια, the same toponym is attested for Boiotia, too). In its turn, this word for source is, like the related river name *Arnos* attested for Tuscany, a derivative of the basic PIE root *h_1er-/h_3er- 'to move, stir, raise', see Krahe 1964: 45.

11. he place-name *Sallapa*, situated along the southern bank of the upper course of the Maiandros river is, in my opinion, not based on Hit. *salli-* 'great', but, on the analogy of Illyrian *Salapia*, referred to by Gamkrelidze & Ivanov 1995: 581, note 11, on PIE **sal-* 'salt' (cf. also in this connection *Salapia* in the region of Taras or Tarentum in southern Italy as referred to by Huss 2004: 253). Whatever the extent of this suggestion, it is absolutely clear that its second element consists of *-apa*, a reflex of PIE *h_2ep-/$h_2eb^{(h)}$- 'water, rivulet' which we already came across in connection with *Appawiya* and *Apasa* (see sub 5 and 9 above).

12. For the analysis of the river name *Astarpa* as a compound of a reflex of PIE *$h_2st\acute{\bar{e}}r$- 'star', see Gamkrelidze & Ivanov 1995: 39, 591, 772, and the element *-(a)pa*, also present, as we have just noted, in *Sallapa*, which likewise originates from PIE *h_2ep-/$h_2eb^{(h)}$- 'water, rivulet', see Woudhuizen 2018: 66. As in Hit. *ḫastēr-* 'star', just like in the case of Hittite and Luwian *ḫapa-* 'river' < PIE *h_2ep-/$h_2eb^{(h)}$- 'water, rivulet', the PIE laryngeal *[h_2] is regularly represented by IE Anatolian [ḫ], we are once more confronted with a hydronym rooted in the Old Indo-European substrate inferred already sub 5 and 9 above.

13. The toponym *Ḫursanassa*, which in my opinion is to be identified as a Late Bronze Age reference to what is known in Classical times as *Halikarnassos* (Ἁλικαρνασ(σ)ός), confronts us with a lenited variant of *Gurtanassa* as attested for the province of Tarḫuntassa. The root of this place-name corresponds to Hit. *gurta-* 'fortress', see Gamkrelidze & Ivanov 1995: 647, which in turn originates from PIE *g^hord^h-* 'city, town'. If we realize that voiced velars are regularly lost in Luwian already since the time of one set of its earliest records, the Kültepe-Kanesh texts, see Yakubovich 2010: 211-212 with reference to the Luwian onomastic element *wawa-* < PIE *g^wow-* 'ox', the representation of the voiced velar *[g^h] by the velars [g] or [ḫ] is remarkable.[3] Against the backdrop of our explanation of the loss of laryngeal *[h_2] in *apa-* < *$h_2$ep-/$h_2$eb$^{(h)}$-* 'water, rivulet' and *astar-* < *$h_2$stḗr-* 'star' as indicative of an Old Indo-European substrate, one might legitimately assume that the same verdict applies in this particular case as well.

14. According to a commonly held view, the ethnonym and country-name *Lukka* 'Lycia' is based on the PIE root **l(e)uk-* 'light' in like manner as the name of the Greek island *Lefkas*, related to Greek λευκός 'white'. In IE Anatolian this root is further represented by Hittite *lukke-* 'to kindle', see Mallory & Adams 2007: 328, and related forms like *luk-* 'become bright, becoming day' and *lukatta* 'in the morning, at daybreak', see Friedrich 1991, s.v. However, this view disregards the fact that in its function as an ethnonym *Lukka* corresponds most closely to Celtic Λοῦγοι as reported by Ptolemaios in his *Geographia* II, 3, 12 for Scotland and Germanic Λοῦγοι or *Lugii* as referred to by Ptolemaios in his *Geographia* II, 11, 10 as a designation of people living in the region north of Bohemia (according to Sergent 1995: 211 = Sergent 2005: 224 the latter were, notwithstanding their habitat in Germania, a 'peuple sans doute celtique'). Along the latter line of approach, then, *Lukka* originates, notwithstanding the fortition of the velar in Greek Λυκία, from PIE **l(e)ug^h-* 'to bind' (Pokorny 1994, s.v. no. 2 [p. 687]). In like manner as in the case of *Ḫursanassa* < PIE *g^hord^h-* 'city, town' (see sub 13 above), we would have expected the voiced velar *[g^h] to have been dropped, as actually happens to be the case with the related country-name *Luwiya* presumably referring to population groups to the north and east of Lukka. Again, the preservation of the voiced velar, foreign to Luwian proper, is likely to be attributed to the influence of an Old Indo-European substrate.

15. Yet another place-name attested only for Luwian hieroglyphic sources, *i.c.* the texts from Yalburt and Emirgazi, is *Awarna*. From the context it is clear that it lies in *Lukka* 'Lycia' and that, as first realized by Massimo Poetto (1993: 76-78), it corresponds to the later indigenous Lycian name of Xanthos, *Arñna*, which appears in Greek as Ἄρνα. With a view to these later forms, it lies at hand to assume that we are dealing here with the same root *arinna-* 'source' (Rosenkranz 1966: 127; cf. Tischler 1983: 57-58) as we came across in the discussion of *Arinnanda* sub 10 above, which in turn is a derivative of the basic PIE root *$h_1$er-/$h_3$er-* 'to move, stir, raise', cf. Krahe 1964: 45.

[3] The same verdict applies to the TNs *Kurtisa* (Beyköy 2, § 8) and *Kurtasa* (Dağardı 2, (F)), located in the Troad and Seḫa, respectively. Note that the related MN *Kurti(a)s* has to be set apart as a loan from Phrygian *Gordias*.

16. The place-name *Parḫa* along the *Kastaraya* has been cogently argued by Heinrich Otten (1988: 37) to correspond to Classical *Pergē* (Πέργη) along the *Kestros* (Κεστρος). There can be no doubt that this toponym, just like its relatives like *Pergamon* (Πέργαμος), the name of the citadel of Troy in Classical literary tradition, etc., shows a reflex of the PIE root **bʰr̥ĝʰ(i)-* 'high'. Also derived from this root is Hit. *parku-* 'high', see Mallory & Adams 2007: 289, 292. But, as this toponym is situated in territory inhabited by speakers of a Luwian tongue, one would have expected the voiced velar to have been dropped, as, in line with our observation sub 4, 13, and 14, is regular for the latter language. Once more, then, we are confronted with a form foreign to the Luwian language and likely to be attributable to the influences of an Old Indo-European substrate. Note in this connection that *Pariyana* (= Classical *Priēnē*) shows the regular Luwian reflex of PIE **bʰr̥ĝʰ(i)-*.

Summarizing the salient points of our preceding notes to Table XII, the following remarks may be of relevance:

(1) On account of the Indo-European nature of all 16 geographic names selected and discussed, which cover the region of western Anatolia from the Troad in the north to Lukka in the southwest, it may safely be deduced that this region was inhabited by speakers of an Indo-European tongue during the period from which our sources date, *i.e.* the Late Bronze Age.

(2) In 6 instances, namely *Tarwisa*, *Wilus(iy)a*, *Arzawa*, *Kurupiya*, *Arinnanda*, and *Awarna*, the geographic name is based on a root with a crystal clear comparison in the IE Anatolian languages, Hittite and Luwian. Note, however, that this does not necessarily mean that the language of the inhabitants of western Anatolia must be speakers of an IE Anatolian tongue as well, because the PIE roots in question are a common feature of Indo-European languages more in general. Nevertheless, it may plausibly be argued on the basis of the evidence at our disposal that the kingdoms of Arzawa and Seḫa and the country of Lukka were inhabited by speakers of a Luwian tongue. If Homeric evidence may be called into play, the dominant language in the Troad was, as cogently argued by Leonid Gindin (1999), presumably of Thraco-Phrygian nature.

(3) In 7 other instances, viz. *Apasa*, *Astarpa*, *Appawiya*, *Párahâma*, *Ḫursanassa*, *Lukka*, and *Parḫa*, the relationship of the root with a comparison in the IE Anatolian languages, in particular the expected Luwian, is not so straightforward but hampered by foreign linguistic features. In the first place, we are confronted here in the first 3 of the given cases with the absence of the reflex of PIE laryngeal *[h_2] as [ḫ], whereas this particular reflex is a distinguishing feature of the IE Anatolian language group. Secondly, in the last 4 of the given cases we encounter the preservation of the voiced velars *[g^h] and *[$\hat{g}^h$], which are regularly lost in the Luwian language. As the roots on which these geographic names are based are of patent IE nature, it lies at hand to attribute these features to influences from an IE substrate other than IE Anatolian.

(4) The latter inference is further underlined by the fact that in 3 instances, *Dura*, *Sallapa*, and *Seḫa*, the closest comparative data are provided by, in Krahe's terms Old European

but for clarity's sake rather referred to here as Old Indo-European, hydronymy, namely Lusitanian or Ligurian *Dourios* or *Durias*, Illyrian *Salapia*, and Gaulish *Sequana*. If these comparisons hold water, as I maintain, the IE substrate other than IE Anatolian as inferred sub 3 above may be identified as speakers of the earliest form of Indo-European as reconstructed on the basis of hydronyms and toponyms and referred to here as Old Indo-European.

(5) Whatever the extent of the latter inference, on the basis of the examples of *Kurupiya* < *$\hat{k}erh_1$- 'head, horn' and *Páraháma* and *Parḫa* < *$b^h\d{r}\hat{g}^h(i)$- 'high', the language of the inhabitants of western Anatolia, irrespective of the question whether this concerns Luwian or Old Indo-European, may safely be grouped with the *centum* group among the Indo-European family.

Owing to the fact that the Luwian hieroglyphic legend of the stamp seal from Beycesultan, discovered in a dividing line between levels VI and V and hence likely dating to *c.* 2000 BC, starts with the place-name *Mira*, we appear to be facilitated with yet another fixed point in our reconstruction of the geography of western Anatolia, namely: present-day *Beycesultan* = Bronze Age *Mira* (see chapter 2).[4]

In connection with our understanding of the meaning of the place-name *Mira*, it might be of relevance to note that, as Gregory Nagy (2010: 235-236) points out, the federal sanctuary of the Aiolians was called *Messon* (= present-day *Mesa*) and, in line with its meaning 'middleground', situated in the center of the island of Lesbos. This observation reminded me of the following remark by Wolfgang Meid in connection with Celtic *Mide* in Ireland (Meid 2010: 68): 'The "middle" province, *Mide* (anglicized *Meath*), with *Tara* as the sacral centre of Ireland, was preponderantly of symbolic significance.' Against this backdrop, the Peloponnesian place-name *Midea* (Μιδέα), also originating from PIE *med^hiyo- (cf. Mallory & Adams 2007: 290), may also be suggested to have once functioned as a federal sanctuary situated in a central location of its surrounding members.

The relevance of this information as to our understanding of the place-name *Mira* becomes clear if we realize that medial [r] may well originate from medial [d] by means of the phonetic development called *rhotacism*. In my opinion, this particular phonetic development is already attested for yet another Middle Bronze Age Luwian hiero-glyphic inscription known as the Erlenmeyers' seal, in the legend of which the MN *Tarkundimuwas* (= Classical Ταρκονδίμοτος) appears in form of *Tarkunaramuwas* (see chapter 3).

[4] It is interesting to note that Fabrizio Giovanetti independently achieved the reading of the place-name *Mira* at the start of the legend of this stamp seal, but on the basis of archaeological evidence downdates the transition from level VI to level V at Beycesultan to that of level II to level Ib at Kültepe-Kanesh, which means to *c.* 1830 BC, see Giovanetti 2012 (my thanks are due to the author for sending me a pdf-version of his paper, and to Willemijn Waal for drawing my attention to the former's treatment of the Luwian hieroglyphic legend of the stamp seal from Beycesultan).

If we are right, then, in our analysis of the place-name *Mira* as originating from an earlier **Mida* (< PIE **med^{h}iyo-*), we may, in the light of the given parallels, well be dealing here with an of origin federal sanctuary of the Luwians situated in the center of the members involved, which, by and large, would coincide with a land called *Luwiya* running all the way from the region of *Apasa* 'Ephesos', the capital of the later kingdom of Arzawa, in the west up to that of Konya, an important site in the later Hittite Lower Land, in the east. In any case, it is no coincidence that this particular region in the given period of time can be positively identified as the cradle of the Luwian hieroglyphic script (see chapter 3).

10.2 On the Identity of the Indo-European Substrate in Western Anatolia[5]

In the previous section I observed that a number of the names discussed shows features foreign to the Luwian language, which might be attributed to an Indo-European substrate. The relevant data in this respect are provided by *Apasa*, *Astarpa*, and *Appawiya*, in which instances the PIE laryngeal *[h$_2$] is not represented by [ḫ] as in the related IE Anatolian *ḫapa-* 'river' and *ḫastēr-* 'star', and *Ḫursanassa*, *Lukka*, *Párahâma*, and *Parḫa*, in which instances the voiced velars *[g^h] and *[$\hat{g}^h$] are, contrary to their regular loss in Luwian, preserved and variously expressed by laryngeal [ḫ] and/or velar [k]. Of this Indo-European substrate it could further be established that, for example, the root of the river name *Seḫa* may be attributed to it as it, in like manner as its Old Indo-European equivalent *Sequana*, can be traced back to PIE **seik^w-* 'to seep, soak' (Pokorny 1994: 893). It finally deserves attention in this connection that, on account of the reflex of PIE *[$\hat{g}^h$] by laryngeal [ḫ]—which against the backdrop of the related Hittite *parku-* 'high' in turn originates from velar [k] by lenition—in *Parḫa* < PIE **b^{h}r̥$\hat{g}^h$(i)-* 'high', the Old Indo-European substrate of western Anatolia clearly belongs to the *centum*-group among the Indo-European family.

The question which arises after this exercise is: can the representatives of the Indo-European substrate in question be identified with a population group known from the historical sources? With this question in mind I reread I think for the fourth time the study by Fritz Lochner-Hüttenbach about the Pelasgians of 1960, and, much to my surprise, I came across references by Classical Greek authors to Pelasgians along the entire coastal region of western Anatolia, from Lycia in the south to the southern part of the Troad in the north. In fact, these sources even provide evidence for Pelasgians outside the borders of the geographic entity under discussion, viz. western Anatolia, by extending into the region to the east of Troy, namely the Propontis, Paphlagonia, up to and including the coastal area of Armenia (see Table XIII).

Now, it is well known that the Pelasgians belong to the pre-Greek population groups in Greece. Sometimes their heros eponym Pelasgos is expressly stated to be the first inhabitant, as in case of the Peloponnesos (Pausanias, *Guide to Greece* VIII, 1, 4). More in general, the Pelasgians are addressed as being ἀρχαιότατοι 'most old' (Strabo, *Geography* 7, 7, 10; 8, 8, 3), which in effect boils down to autochthonous in a relative sense, *i.e.* in

[5] This is a reworked version of Woudhuizen 2013d.

region		source	page
1.	Lycia	Diodoros of Sicily, *The Library of History* 5, 81	p. 33
2.	Caria	Strabo, *Geography* 14, 2, 27	p. 41
		Kallimachos, *Hymnos of Ceres* VI, 25	p. 23
3.	Ionia	Menekrates van Elaia	p. 28
		Scholia Graeca in Homeri Iliadem 10, 429	p. 76
		Dionysos Periegetes 533	p. 57
4.	Lydia	Homeros, *Iliad* 2, 840-843	p. 1
		Strabo, *Geography* 13, 3, 2	p. 39-40
5.	Teuthrania	Hellanikos F 93	p. 5
		Strabo, *Geography* 5, 2, 4	p. 34-35
		Strabo, *Geography* 13, 3, 2	p. 39
6.	N Aegean	Strabo, *Geography* 13, 3, 3	p. 40
		Diodoros of Sicily, *The Library of History* 5, 81	p. 33
		Strabo, *Geography* 5, 2, 4	p. 34
		Herodotos, *Histories* IV, 145, 2	p. 8
		Herodotos, *Histories* VI, 137-138	p. 8-9
		Herodotos, *Histories* V, 26	p. 8
		Herodotos, *Histories* II, 51	p. 6-7
		Herodotos, *Histories* I, 57	p. 5-6
		Thucydides, *Peloponnesian War* IV, 109, 2	p. 11-12
7.	S Troad	Herodotos, *Histories* VII, 42	p. 10
		Scholia Graeca in Homeri Iliadem 6, 397	p. 76
8.	Propontis	Herodotos, *Histories* I, 57	p. 5-6
		Deilochos of Kyzikos (= Scholia ad Apollonios Rhodios, *Argonautica* I, 987a)	p. 20-21
		Agathokles of Kyzikos (= Stephanos of Byzantion, *Ethnica*, s.v. Besbikos)	p. 27-28
		Konon F1	p. 55
		Ephoros F 61	p. 18
		Apollonios Rhodios, *Argonautica* 1, 1024	p. 24
		Apollodoros, *Bibliotheke* 1, 9, 18	p. 29
9.	Paphlagonia	Strabo, *Geography* 8, 3, 17	p. 37
		Homeros, *Iliad* 2, 851 (Πυλαιμένης)	p. 154-155
10.	Armenia	Apollonios Rhodios, *Argonautica* 1, 1024	p. 24

Table XIII: Overview of literary evidence for Pelasgians in western Anatolia according to Lochner-Hüttenbach's *Die Pelasger* of 1960.

comparison to other population groups distinguished. The Pelasgians are in fact the earliest settlers in the Greek mainland speaking an Indo-European tongue, arriving in this region from *c.* 3100 BC onwards and in the main traceable only on the basis of some specific river- and place-names. Furthermore, Pelasgians are mentioned as early as from the times of Homeros onwards as one of the population groups inhabiting the island of Crete (Homeros, *Odyssey* 19, 175-177). As a matter of fact, the memory to the migration of the Pelasgians from Thessaly to Crete under the leadership of Teutamos as best preserved in Diodoros of Sicily, *The Library of History* 4, 60, 2 may be an ancient one, going back at least to Middle Minoan times (*c.* 2000-1600 BC) as a *terminus ante quem*. During the period of the upheavals of the Sea Peoples at the end of the Bronze Age, finally, we come across Pelasgians from Lydia in western Asia Minor and the island of Crete, who in the Egyptian hieroglyphic and Biblical sources feature as, respectively, *Peleset* (*Pwrs̱t*) and *Philistines* (van Binsbergen & Woudhuizen 2011: 273-277), and can even be traced in Luwian hieroglyphic in form of, first, the related country name *Pulasàti* 'Philistine' (Beyköy 2, § 25) and, later, the ethnonym *Patìsàtiná-* or *Wata$_4$sàtinà-* or *Watísàtinà-* (Woudhuizen 2015c). Most relevant in the present context, however, is the fact that the Pelasgians in the passage by Diodoros of Sicily, *The Library of History* 5, 81 are not merely addressed as autochthonous in a relative sense but more in specific as *the earliest inhabitants* in Lycia and the island of Lesbos!

Now, if we take the Greek literary sources serious, the Pelasgians are positively identifiable as speakers of an Indo-European tongue. In any case, they are related in the aforesaid sources with names ultimately based on an Indo-European root (see Table XIV).

In this overview, the case of the GN *Dēmētēr* is placed between brackets, because it is related by Herodotos in his *Histories* II, 52 that the Pelasgians of Dodona had no names for their gods and in the given passage of the same book that Pelasgian women

PIE root		Pelasgian name	source
1.	**teutā-* 'people, tribe'	Τεύταμος	Diod. Sic. 4, 60, 2
		Τευταμίας	Apollod. *Bibl.* 2, 4, 4
2.	**h$_2$erĝ-* 'white, bright'	Ἄργος	Aisch. *Suppl.* 250 ff.
3.	**h$_2$eb$^{(h)}$-* 'water, river'	Ἀπία	Schol. Aisch. *Or.* 990
4.	**g^{h}ord^h-* 'town'	Γυρτώνη	Strab. 9, 5, 22
5.	**h$_1$epero-* 'boar'	Ἐφύρα	Steph. Byz., s.v.
6.	**dānu-* 'river'	Ἀπιδανός	Apoll. Rhod. 2, 265
7.	**aƙr-* 'sharp, high'	Ἀκρίσιος	Kall. *Epigr.* 39, 2
8.	**méĝh$_2$-* 'great, many'	Μαγνῆτις	Strab. 9, 5, 22
9.	**b^{h}r̥ĝ^h(i)-* 'high'	Πύργοι	Strab. 5, 2, 8
10.	**l(e)ug^h-* 'to bind'	Λυκία	Diod. Sic. 5, 81
11.	(**méh$_2$tēr-* 'mother'	Δημήτηρ	Herod. II, 171-172)
12.	**h$_1$er-/h$_3$er-* 'to move'	Ἄρνη	—

Table XIV. Names based on a Proto-Indo-European root associated in the Greek sources with Pelasgians.

learned the cult of Demeter from the daughters of Danaos. So the relationship of the Pelasgians with the GN Demeter appears to be not original, but of a secondary nature.[6] Furthermore, the toponym *Arne* is attested for various regions of Greece in which we come across Pelasgians, namely Phthiotis, Boiotia (Homeros, Strabo, Pausanias, and Stephanos of Byzantion), and Arkadia (Rosenkranz 1966: 127), but in actual fact not directly associated with them. Notwithstanding so, it is highly attractive to consider the place-name *Arne* a Pelasgian name against the backdrop of the fact that cape Mycale, which according to Menekrates of Elaia (Lochner-Hüttenbach 1960: 28) and *Scholia Graeca in Homeri Iliadem* 10, 429 (Lochner-Hüttenbach 1960: 76) was once inhabited by Pelasgians, in the Hittite sources is addressed to as *Arinnanda*, a derivative in *-nd-* of the related Hittite vocabulary word *arinna-* 'source' (Starke 1997: 451; Hawkins 2002: 97-98), not to mention the fact that one of the main towns in Lycia, which according to Diodoros of Sicily, *The Library of History* 5, 81, is first inhabited by Pelasgians, is called *Arñna* in the epichoric Lycian texts.

Whatever one may be apt to think of these latter two suggestions, it cannot be denied that a significant number of PIE roots which, as we have seen in the above, are involved in our attribution of western Anatolian river- and place-names to an Indo-European substrate also feature in our list of Table XIV. This observation has a bearing on *$h_2eb^{(h)}$- 'water, river' from which *Apasa* and *Appawiya* are derived, *g^hord^h- 'town' to which the first element of *Ḫursanassa* can be traced back, *b^hr̥ĝ^h(i)- 'high' which stands at the basis of *Páraháma* and *Parḫa*, and *l(e)ug^h- 'to bind' which provides us with the most plausible root for *Lukka*. It also deserves our attention in this connection that in three cases an offshoot of the given roots is also traceable in Crete, namely in the case of *Gortyns* < *g^hord^h- 'town', *Pyrgiotissa* < *b^hr̥ĝ^h(i)- 'high', and *ru-ki-to* 'Lyktos', related to western Anatolian *Lukka* and therefore likewise originating from *l(e)ug^h-. It might be added to this that in Crete we further find the presumably Pelasgian GN *da-ma-te* 'Demeter' in a Linear A inscription, not to mention the related form of the Old Indo-European river-name *Seḫa* < *seik^w- in the form of the TN *Saḫarwa* 'Skheria (= presumably Hagia Triada)' (Woudhuizen 2016: 303-312). Finally, the examples provided by *ak̂r- 'sharp, high', *$h_2$erĝ- 'white, bright', *méĝh_2- 'great, many', and *b^hr̥ĝ^h(i)- 'high' as represented by the MN *Akrisios* and the TNs *Argos*, *Magnetis*, and *Pyrgoi* definitely point out that the language of the Pelasgians, just like the Indo-European substrate in western Anatolia, belongs to the *centum*-group among the Indo-European family.

In line with the foregoing observations, then, it seems highly likely that the Indo-European substrate in western Anatolia as deducible from hydronyms and toponyms is to be identified with the Pelasgians recorded by the Greek sources for the region in

[6] Note however that Pausanias, *Guide to Greece* I, 14, 2 informs us that Pelasgos receives Demeter in his house and that the latter deity is even straightforwardly called 'Pelasgian' in Pausanias, *Guide to Greece* II, 22, 1 (cf. Lochner-Hüttenbach 1960: 61-62). Furthermore, against the backdrop of the association of Zeus with Pelasgian Dodona in Homeros, *Iliad* 16, 233 (cf. Lochner-Hüttenbach 1960; 1), it stands to reason that the incorporation of Zeus and Demeter in the Lydian pantheon in form of *Levś* or *Lefś* and *Lametru-*, respectively, both cases of which are characterised by *d/l*-change with respect to the initial dental [d], results from influence exercized by the Pelasgians living in the region of Larissa Phryconis on the Lydians. If this argument holds water, it may reasonably be inferred that the Pelasgians venerated a male deity whose name originates from **deus* 'god' and bears testimony of the widely attested PIE root **Dyēws* for the sky-god.

question. This population group settled along the coastal areas and did not penetrate into the inner parts of Asia Minor, in contrast to the Luwians whose distribution by and large can be traced on the basis of that of the in this respect diagnostic place-names in *-ss-* and *-nd-* (see Fig. 1 above). Of course, seen within the framework of the evidence for an Indo-European deep-layer in, amongst other regions, Anatolia which may reasonably be dated as early as from *c.* 3100 BC onwards (Woudhuizen 2018: 61 ff.) and therefore precedes the IE Anatolian one introduced in this particular region from *c.* 2300 BC onwards (Woudhuizen 2018: 47 ff.), the Pelasgians were to all likelihood only *one* of the population groups which all together formed an Old Indo-European substrate layer in Anatolia as a whole.

At any rate, what counts in the long run is that the scenario we thus arrive at is particularly devastating for the theory propagated by scholars like Colin Renfrew (1987) and Robert Drews (2001) which maintains that Anatolia is the Indo-European homeland. In actual fact, the IE Anatolian languages, which are generally considered to represent the oldest stage of the Indo-European language family, were latecomers in the Anatolian subcontinent and preceded by speakers of related languages which lack the preservation of PIE laryngeal *[h_2] in form of [ḫ]—i.e. precisely the feature which is considered diagnostic for the earliest stage of Indo-European!

Bibliography

Atlasses

Droysen, G.
1886 Professor G. Droysens Allgemeiner Historischer Handatlas.
P. 13 (Coloë, Tyrrha).
Bielefeld und Leipzig: Verlag von Velhagen & Klasing.

Calder, William Moire, & Bean, George E.
1958 A Classical Map of Asia Minor. Being a partial revision, by kind permission of Messrs. John Murray, of J.G.C.Anderson's Map of Asia Minor. Supplement to *Anatolian Studies* 7 [1957] (Coruphe M., Salbace M., but aberrant opinion on the location of Coloë, the uncertainty of which is also stressed by Zgusta 1984, 277-278 [s.v. Κολόη], whereas for Tyrrha no location is suggested).
London: The British Institute of Archaeology at Ankara.

Barrington (Richard J.A. Talbert, ed.)
2000 Atlas of the Greek and Roman World. (Alternative location of Salbake Mons, near Herakleia and Apollonia, to the southeast of Kadmos Mons).
Princeton and Oxford: Princeton University Press.

Times Atlas
1994 The Times Atlas of the World, Comprehensive Edition. Plate 36. (Emir = Lykos, Honaz = Kolossai).
London: Times Books, Harper Collins*Publishers*.

Books and articles

Achterberg, Winfried, Best, Jan, Enzler, Kees, Rietveld, Lia, & Woudhuizen, Fred
2004 The Phaistos Disc: A Luwian Letter to Nestor. Publications of the Henri Frankfort Foundation 13.
Amsterdam: Dutch Archaeological and Historical Society.

Alexander, Robert L.
1973-6 The Tyszkiewicz Group of stamp-cylinders. *Anatolica* 5. Pp. 141-215; Plates I-V.

Alp, Sedat
1968 Zylinder- und Stempelsiegel aus Karahöyük bei Konya.
Ankara: Türk Tarih Kurumu Basımevi.
1988 Einige weitere Bemerkungen zum Hirschrhyton der Norbert Schimmel-Sammlung. In: Imparati, Fiorella, (ed.), Studi di Storia e di Filologia Anatolica dedicati a Giovanni Pugliese Carratelli. Eothen 1. Pp. 17-23.
Firenze: Elite.

Alparslan, Metin
2005 Einige Überlegungen zur Ahhiyawa-Frage. In: Süel, Aygül, (ed.), Acts of thVth International Congress of Hittitology, Çorum, September 02-08, 2002. Pp. 33-41.
Ankara.

Aravantinos, V.L., Godart, Louis, & Sacconi, Anna
2001 Thèbes, Fouilles de la Cadmée I, Les Tablettes en linéaire B de le odos Pelopidou, Édition et commentaire.
Pisa-Roma.
Archi, Alfonso
2015 A Royal Seal from Ebla (17th cent. B.C.) with Hittite Hieroglyphic Symbols. *Orientalia* 84, 1. Pp. 18-28; Tab. I.
Aro, Sanna
2003 Art and Architecture. In: Melchert, H. Craig, (ed.), The Luwians. Handbook of Oriental Studies, Section One: The Near and Middle East 68. Pp. 281-337.
Leiden-Boston: Brill.
Azize, Joseph
2005 The Phoenician Solar Theology, An Investigation into the Phoenician Opinion of the Sun Found in Julian's *Hymn to King Helios*. Gorgias Dissertations 15, Near Eastern Studies Volume 6.
New Jersey: Gorgias Press.
Bányai, Michael
forthc. Westanatolische Geographie und Geschichte.
(retrieved from his academia.edu site).
Baudet, Guillaume, Joannès, Francis, Lafont, Bertrand, Soubeyran, Denis, & Villard, Pierre
1984 Archives Royales de Mari (= ARM) XXIII. Archives administratives de Mari 1.
Paris: Editions Recherche sur les Civilisations.
Beckman, Gary M., Bryce, Trevor R., & Cline, Eric H.
2011 The Ahhiyawa Texts. Writings from the Ancient World 28.
Atlanta: Society of Biblical Literature.
Beekes, Robert S.P.
2003 The Origin of Apollo. *Journal of Ancient Near Eastern Religions* 3. Pp. 1-21.
Beran, Thomas
1967 Die hethitische Glyptik von Boğazköy. I. Teil: Die Siegel und Siegelabdrücke der vor- und althethitischen Perioden und die Siegel der hethitischen Grosskönige.
Berlin: Verlag Gebr. Mann.
Best, Jan
1996-7 The Ancient Toponyms of Mallia: A Post-Eurocentric reading of Egyptianising Bronze Age documents. In: Binsbergen, Wim M.J. van, (ed.), *Black Athena*: Ten Years After (= *Talanta, Proceedings of the Dutch Archaeological and Historical Society* 28-29). Pp. 99-129.
2011 The Ancient Toponyms of Mallia: A Post-Eurocentric reading of Egyptianising Bronze Age documents. In: Binsbergen, Wim van, (ed.), Black Athena comes of age, Towards a constructive re-assessment. Pp. 99-129.
Münster: Lit Verlag.
Best, Jan, & Woudhuizen, Fred
1989 Lost Languages from the Mediterranean.
Leiden-New York-København-Köln: E.J. Brill.

Betancourt, Philip P.
2008 Minoan Trade. In: Shelmerdine, Cynthia W., (ed.), The Cambridge Companion to the Aegean Bronze Age. Pp. 209-229.
New York, etc.: Cambridge University Press.
Binsbergen, Wim M.J. van, & Woudhuizen, Fred C.
2011 Ethnicity in Mediterranean Protohistory. British Archaeological Reports, International Series 2256.
Oxford: Archaeopress.
Blegen, Carl, & Haley, J.B.
1928 The Coming of the Greeks. *American Journal of Archaeology* 32. Pp. 141-154.
Boardman, John
1966 Hittite and Related Hieroglyphic Seals from Greece. *Kadmos* 5. Pp. 47-48, Figs. 1-4.
Boehmer, Rainer Michael, & Güterbock, Hans Gustav
1987 Glyptik aus dem Stadtgebiet von Boğazköy.
Grabungskampagnen 1931-1939, 1952-1978.
Berlin: Verlag Gebr. Mann.
Börker-Klähn, Jutta
1995 Archäologische Anmerkungen zum Alter Bild-Luwischen.
In: Carruba, Onofrio, Giorgieri, Mauro, & Mora, Clelia, (eds.), Atti del II Congresso Internazionale di Hittitologia, Pavia, 28 giugno - 2 luglio 1993. Studia Mediterranea 9. Pp. 39-54.
Pavia: Gianni Iuculano Editore.
Bossert, Helmuth Th.
1942 Altanatolien, Kunst und Handwerk in Kleinasien von den Anfängen bis zum völligen Aufgehen in der griechischen Kultur.
Berlin: Verlag Ernst Wasmuth G.M.B.H. Berlin.
Boysan, N., Marazzi, M., & Nowicki, H.
1983 Sammlung hieroglyphischer Siegel, Bd. 1: Vorarbeiten.
Wurzburg: Verlag Dr. Johannes Königshausen + Dr. Thomas Neumann.
Brosnahan, Tom
1990 Turkey, A Travel Survival Kit.
Hawthorn/Berkeley: Lonely Planet Publications (3rd ed.).
Bryce, Trevor R.
2010 The Kingdom of the Hittites.
Oxford: Oxford University Press (reprint of new edition of 2005).
2011 The Late Bronze Age in the West and the Aegean. In: Steadman, Sharon R., & McMahon, Gregory, (eds.), The Oxford Handbook of Ancient Anatolia. Pp. 363-375.
Oxford: Oxford University Press.
Canby, Jeanny Vorys
1975 The Walters Art Gallery Cappadocian Tablet and Sphinx in Anatolia in the Second Millennium B.C. *Journal of Near Eastern Studies* 34. Pp. 225-248.
Carruba, Onofrio
1996 Neues zur Frühgeschichte Lykiens. In: Blakolmer, Fritz, e.a., (Hrsg.), Fremde Zeiten, Festschrift für Jürgen Borchhardt zum sechzigsten Geburtstag. Pp. 25-39.
Wien: Phoibos Verlag.

2011 Die Gliederung des Anatolischen und der erste indoeuropäische Name der Anatolier. In: Strobel, Karl, (Hrsg.), Empires after the Empire: Anatolia, Syria and Assyria after Suppiluliuma II (ca. 1200-800/700 BC), Eothen, Collana di studi sulle aviltà dell'Oriente antico 17. Pp. 309-329.
Firenze: LeGisma editore.

Chapouthier, Fernand
1930 Les écritures minoennes au palais de Mallia d'après le dépôt d'archives exhumé, sous la direction de Charles Picard, par Louis Renaudin et Jean Charbonneaux.
Paris: Librairie Orientaliste Paul Geuthner.

Cline, Eric H.
1987 Amenhotep III and the Aegean: A Reassessment of the Egypto-Aegean Relations in the 14th Century B.C. *Orientalia* 56. Pp. 1-36.
1994 Sailing the Wine-Dark Sea, International trade and the Late Bronze Age Aegean. BAR International Series 591.
Oxford: Tempus Reparatum.

Collon, Dominique
1975 The Seal Impressions from Tell Atchana/Alalakh.
Kevelaer: Verlag Butzon & Bercker.
Neukirchen: Neukirchner Verlag.

Cornelius, Friedrich
1973 Geschichte der Hethiter, mit besonderer Berücksichtigung der geographischen Verhältnisse und der Rechtsgeschichte.
Darmstadt: Wissenschaftliche Buchgesellschaft.

Detournay, Béatrice, Poursat, Jean-Claude, & Vandenabeele, Frieda
1980 Fouilles exécutées à Mallia, Le Quartier Mu II: Vases de pierre et de métal, vannerie, figurines et reliefs d'applique, éléments de parure et de décoration, armes, sceaux et empreintes. Études Crétoises XXVI.
Paris: Librairie Orientaliste Paul Geuthner.

Detschew, Dimiter
1976 Die Thrakische Sprachreste, 2. Auflage mit Bibliographie 1955-1974 von Živka Velkova.
Wien: Verlag der Österreichischen Akademie der Wissenschaften.

Doblhofer, Ernst
2008 Die Entzifferung alter Schriften und Sprachen.
Stuttgart: Philipp Reclam jun.

Doğan-Alparslan, Meltem
2015 Ein Hieroglyphensiegel aus Şarhöyük. *Istanbuler Mitteilungen* 65. Pp. 273-279.

Dossin, Georges.
1970 La Route d'étain en Mésopotamie au temps de Zimri-Lim. *Revue d'Assyriologie et d'Archeologie Orientale* 64. Pp. 97-106.

Drews, Robert
2001 Greater Anatolia, Proto-Anatolian, Proto-Indo-Hittite, and Beyond. In: Drews, Robert, (ed.), Greater Anatolia and the Indo-Hittite Language Family, Papers Presented at a Colloquium Hosted by the University of Richmond, March

18-19, 2000. Journal of Indo-European Studies Monograph Series, Number 38: 248-283.
Washington D.C.: The Institute for the Study of Man.

Ehringhaus, Horst
2005 Götter Herrscher Inschriften, Die Felsreliefs der hethitischen Großreichszeit in der Türkei.
Mainz am Rhein: Philipp von Zabern.

Erdem, Sargon
1969 Einige Neue Funde im Museum von Kayseri I, Hieroglyphisch-hethitische Inschriften. *Athenaeum* 47, Studi in Onore di Piero Meriggi. Pp. 106-115; Tav. I-V.

Erlenmeyer, Marie-Louise, & Hans
1965 Zu den kretischen Siegeln mit Hieroglypheninschrift. *Kadmos* 4. Pp. 1-4; Abb. 1-11.

Faure, Paul
1996 Deux inscriptions en écriture Linéaire A découvertes à Troie par Schliemann. *Cretan Studies* 5. Pp. 137-146.

Fimmen, Diedrich
1924 Die Kretisch-Mykenische Kultur.
Leipzig und Berlin: B.G. Teubner (zweite Auflage).

Flinders Petrie, William Matthew
1933 Ancient Gaza III.
London: British School of Archaeology.

Freu, Jacques
1980 Luwiya — Géographie historique des provinces méridionales de l'empire hittite: Kizzuwatna, Arzawa, Lukka, Milawatta. Centre de Recherches Comparatives sur les Langues de la Méditerranée Ancienne, Document N° 6, Tome 2. Pp. 177-352.
Nice: Université de Nice, Faculte des Lettres.
1998 Les relations entre Troie et le monde hittite, Une problème de géographie historique. In: Isebaert, L., & Lebrun, R., (éds.), *Qaestiones Homericae*, Acta Colloquii Namurcensis habiti diebus 7-9 mensis Septembris anni 1995. Pp. 95-118.
Louvain-Namur, Édition Peeters-Société des Études Classiques.
2007 L'Affirmation du nouvel empire Hittite (c.1465-1319 av. J.C.). In: Freu, Jacques, & Mazoyer, Michel, (éds.), Les débuts du nouvel empire Hittite, Les Hittites et leur histoire [II]. Collection Kubaba, Série Antiquité XII. Pp. 9-311.
Paris: L'Harmattan.
2008a Quatre-vingts ans d'histoire Hittite (c. 1320-1240 av. J.C.).
In: Freu, Jacques, & Mazoyer, Michel, (éds.), L'apogée du nouvel empire Hittite, Les Hittites et leur histoire [III]. Collection Kubaba, Série Antiquité XIV. Pp. 9-286.
Paris: L'Harmattan.
2008b Homère, La Guerre de Troie et le Pays de Wiluša. In: Mazoyer, Michel, (éd.), Homère et L'Anatolie. Collection Kubaba, Série Antiquité. Pp. 107-147.
Paris: L'Harmattan.

2010 Les derniers Grand Rois de Ḫatti (c. 1240-1185 av. J.C.). In: Freu, Jacques, & Mazoyer, Michel, (éds.), Le déclin et la chute du nouvel empire Hittite, Les Hittites et leur histoire IV.
Paris: L'Harmattan.
2014 Les Pays de Wilusa et d'Aḫḫiyawa et la Geographie de l'Anatolie Occidentale à l'Age du Bronze. In: Faranton, Valérie, & Mazoyer, Michel, (éds.), Homère et l'Anatolie 2. Pp. 71-118.
Paris: L'Harmattan.

Friedrich, Johannes
1930 Staatsverträge des Ḫatti-Reiches in hethitischer Sprache. Mitteilungen der Vorderasiatisch-Aegyptischen Gesellschaft 34. Band, 1. Heft.
Leipzig: J.C. Hinrichs'sche Buchhandlung.
1960 Hethitisches Elementarbuch I. Kurzgefaßte Grammatik.
Heidelberg: Carl Winter Universitätsverlag.
1991 Kurzgefaßtes Hethitisches Wörterbuch.
Heidelberg: Carl Winter Universitätsverlag (Unveränderter Nachdruck der Ausgabe 1952-1966).

Gamkrelidze, Thomas V., & Ivanov, Vjačeslav V.
1995 Indo-European and the Indo-Europeans, A Reconstruction and Historical Analysis of a Proto-Language and a Proto-Culture, Part I: The Text, Part II: Bibliography, Indexes.
Berlin-New York: Mouton de Gruyter.

Gander, Max
2010 Die geographischen Beziehungen der Lukka-Länder. Texte der Hethiter 27.
Heidelberg: Universitätsverlag Winter GmbH.
2015 Asia, Ionia, Maeonia und Luwiya? Bemerkungen zu den neuen Toponymen aus Kom el-Hettan (Theben-West) mit Exkursen zu Westkleinasien in der Spätbronzezeit. *Klio* 97(2). Pp. 443-502.

Gardiner, Sir Alan
1994 Egyptian Grammar, Being an Introduction to the Study of Hieroglyphs.
Oxford: Griffith Institute, Ashmolean Museum (Third edition).

Garelli, Pierre, & Collon, Dominique
1975 Cuneiform Texts from Cappadocian Tablets in the British Museum VI.
London: The Trustees of the British Museum.

Garstang, John, & Gurney, Oliver R.
1959 The Geography of the Hittite Empire.
London: The British Institute of Archaeology at Ankara.

Gindin, Leonid
1999 Troja, Thrakien und die Völker Altkleinasiens, Versuch einer historisch-philologischen Untersuchung. Innsbrucker Beiträge zur Kulturwissenschaft, Sonderheft 104.
Innsbruck: Innsbrucker Beiträge zur Kulturwissenschaft.

Giovanetti, Fabrizio
2012 A Revaluation of the Chronology of the Burnt Palace of Level V at Beycesultan. In: Matthews, R., & Curtis, J., (eds.), Proceedings of the 7th International Congress on the Archaeology of the Ancient Near East, 12 April -

16 April 2010. The British Museum and UCL, London, Volume 3: Fieldwork & Recent Research, Posters: 517-526.
Wiesbaden: Harrassowitz Verlag.

Godart, Louis
1994a La scrittura di Troia. *Atti della Accademia Nazionale dei Lincei*, serie 9, vol. 5. Pp. 457-460.
1994b Les écritures Crétoises el le basin Méditerranéen. *Comptes Rendus de l'Académie des Inscriptions & Belles Lettres 1994*. Pp. 709-731.

Godart, Louis, & Olivier, Jean-Pierre
1982 Recueil des inscriptions en linéaire A, Volume 4: Autres documents.
Paris: Librairie Orientaliste Paul Geuthner.

Graves, Robert
1990 The Greek Myths 2.
London: Penguin Books.

Gurney, Oliver R.
1990 The Hittites.
London: Penguin Books.
2002 The Authorship of the Tawagalawas Letter. In: Taracha, Piotr, (ed.), *Silva Anatolica*, Anatolian Studies Presented to Maciej Popko on the Occasion of His 65th Birthday. Pp. 133-141.
Warsaw: Agade.

Gusmani, Roberto
1964 Lydisches Wörterbuch.
Heidelberg: Carl Winter Universitätsverlag.

Güterbock, Hans Gustav
1940 Siegel aus Boğazköy I.
Berlin: Im Selbstverlage des Herausgebers.
1956 Review of Margarete Riemschneider, Die Welt der Hethiter, Stuttgart, 1954. *Orientalistische Literaturzeitung* 51, Nr. 11/12. Pp. 512-522.
1967 The Hittite Conquest of Cyprus Reconsidered. *Journal of Near Eastern Studies* 26, 2. Pp. 73-81.
1975 Hieroglyphensiegel aus dem Tempelbezirk. Boğazköy V, Funde aus den Grabungen 1970 und 1971. Pp. 47-75.
Berlin: Verlag Gebr. Mann.
1977 The Hittite Seals in the Walters Art Gallery. *Journal of the Walters Art Gallery* 36 (= Essays in Honor of Dorothy Kent Hill). Pp. 7-16.
1981-2 The Hieroglyphic Inscriptions on the Hittite Cylinder, No. 25. In: Porada, Edith, (ed.), The Cylinder Seals found at Thebes in Boeotia. *Archiv für Orientforschung* 28. Pp. 71-72.
1986 Troy in Hittite Texts? Wilusa, Ahhiyawa, and Hittite History. In: Mellink, Machteld J., (ed.), Troy and the Trojan War, A Symposium Held at Bryn Mawr College, October 1984. Pp. 33-44.
Bryn Mawr, PA: Bryn Mawr College.
1989a A Note on the Frieze of the Stag Rhyton in the Schimmel Collection. In: Bayburtluoğlu, C., (ed.), Festschrift Akurgal, *Anadolu* 22, 1981/1983. Pp. 1-5.
Ankara.

1989b Hittite *Kursa* 'Hunting Bag'. In: Leonard Jr., A., & Williams, B.B., (eds.), Essays in Ancient Civilization Presented to Helene J. Kantor. Studies in Ancient Oriental Civilization 47. Pp. 113-123.
Chicago, Illinois: Oriental Institute of the University of Chicago.

1992 A new look at one Ahhiyawa text. In: Otten, Heinrich, Ertem, Hayri, Akurgal, Ekrem, & Süel, Aygül, (eds.), Hittite and Other Anatolian and Near Eastern Studies in Honour of Sedat Alp.
Ankara: Türk Tarih Kurumu Basımevi.

Haas, Volkert

1994 Das Pferd in der hethitischen religiösen Überlieferung. In: Hänsel, Bernhard, & Zimmer, Stefan, (Hrsg.), *Die Indogermanen und das Pferd, Festschrift für Bernfried Schlerath*, 77-90.
Budapest: Archaeolingua Alapítvány.

Hagenbuchner, Albertine

1989, 1 Die Korrespondenz der Hethiter, 1. Teil: Die Briefen unter ihren kulturellen, sprachlichen und thematischen Gesichtspunkten.
Heidelberg: Carl Winter Universitätsverlag.

1989, 2 Die Korrespondenz der Hethiter, 2. Teil: Die Briefe mit Transkription, Übersetzung und Kommentar.
Heidelberg: Carl Winter Universitätsverlag.

Haider, Peter W.

2006 Der Himmel über Tarsos, Tradition und Metamorphose in der Vorstellung von Götterhimmel in Tarsos vom Ende der Spätbronzezeit bis ins 4. Jahrhundert v.Chr. In: Hutter, Manfred, & Hutter-Braunsar, Sylvia, (Hrsg.), Pluralismus und Wandel in den Religionen im vorhellenistischen Anatolien, Akten des religiongeschichtlichen Symposiums in Bonn (19.-20. Mai 2005). Alter Orient und Altes Testament, Veröffentlichungen zur Kultur und Geschichte des Alten Orients und des Alten Testaments, Band 337: 41-54.
Münster: Ugarit-Verlag.

Hawkins, John David

1995 The Hieroglyphic Inscription of the Sacred Pool Complex at Hattusa (SÜDBURG), With an Archaeological Introduction by Peter Neve. Studien zu den Boğazköy-Texten, Beiheft 3.
Wiesbaden: Harrassowitz Verlag.

1998a The Land of Išuwa: The Hieroglyphic Evidence. In: Alp, Sedat, & Süel, Aygül, (eds.), Acts of the IIIrd International Congress of Hittitology, Çorum, September 16-22, 1996. Pp. 281-295.
Ankara.

1998b Tarkasnawa King of Mira, 'Tarkondemos', Boğazköy sealings and Karabel. *Anatolian Studies* 48. Pp. 1-31.

2000 Corpus of Hieroglyphic Luwian Inscriptions, Vol. I: Inscriptions of the Iron Age, Parts 1-3.
Berlin-New York: Walter de Gruyter.

2002 The historical geography of western Anatolia in Hittite texts.
In: Easton, D.F., Hawkins, J.D., Sherratt, A.G., & Sherratt, E.S., Troy in recent perspective. *Anatolian Studies* 52. Pp. 75-109 (pp. 94-101).

2004 The Stag-God of the Countryside and Related Problems.
Penney, J.H.W., (ed.), Indo-European Perspectives, Studies in Honour of Anna Morpurgo Davies. Pp. 355-369.
Oxford: Oxford University Press.
2006 Tudḫaliya the Hunter. In: Hout, Theo P.J. van den, (ed.), The Life and Times of Ḫattušili III and Tudḫaliya IV, Proceedings of a Symposium held in honour of J. de Roos, 12-13 december 2003, Leiden. Pp. 49-76.
Leiden: Nederlands Instituut voor het Nabije Oosten.
2011 Early Recognisable Hieroglyphic Signs (?) in Anatolia. In: Kulakoğlu, Fikri, & Kangal, Selmin, (eds.), Anatolia's Prologue, Kültepe Kanesh Karum, Assyrians in Istanbul. Kayseri Metropolitan Municipality Cultural Publication No. 78. Pp. 96-97.
Istanbul: Kayseri Buyuksehir Belediyesi.
2013 Luwians versus Hittites. In: Mouton, Alice, Rutherford, Ian, & Yakubovich, Ilya, (eds.), Luwian Identities, Culture, Language and Religion Between Anatolia and the Aegean. Culture and History of the Ancient Near East 64. Pp. 25-40.
Leiden-Boston: Brill.

Heinhold-Krahmer, Susanne
1977 Arzawa, Untersuchungen zu seiner Geschichte nach den hethitischen Quellen. Texte der Hethiter 8.
Heidelberg: Carl Winter Universitätsverlag.
2003 Zur Gleichsetzung der Namen Ilios-Wiluša und Troia-Taruiša. In: Ulf, Christoph, (Hrsg.), Der neue Streit um Troia, Eine Bilanz. Pp. 146-168.
München: Verlag C.H. Beck oHG.
2013 Zur Lage des hethitischen Vasallenstaat Wiluša im südwesten Kleinasiens. In: Mazoyer, Michel, & Hervé, Sydney, (éds.), De Hattuša à Memphis, Jacques Freu *in honorem*. Pp. 59-74.
Paris: L'Harmattan.

Herbordt, Suzanne
2005 Die Prinzen- und Beamtensiegel der hethitischen Grossreichszeit auf Tonbullen aus dem Nişantepe-Archiv in Hattusa, mit Kommentaren zu den Siegelinschriften und Hieroglyphen von J. David Hawkins. Boğazköy-Ḫattuša, Ergebnisse der Ausgrabungen XIX, Hrsg. Peter Neve.
Mainz am Rhein: Verlag Philipp von Zabern.

Herda, Alexander
2013 Greek (and our) views on the Karians. In: Mouton, Alice, Rutherford, Ian, & Yakubovich, Ilya, (eds.), Luwian Identities, Culture, Language and Religion, Between Anatolia and the Aegean. Pp. 421-506.
Leiden-Boston: Brill.

Herzog, S.
1895 *C. Iulii Caesaris commentarii de Bello Gallico.*
Stuttgart: Paul Neff Verlag.

Hirsch, Hans
1961 Untersuchungen zur altassyrischen Religion. *Archiv für Orientforschung*, Beiheft 13/14.

Hoffner, Harry A.
1982 The Milawata Letter Augmented and Reinterpreted. 28. Rencontre Assyriologique Internationale in Wien, 6.-10. Juli 1981. Archiv für Orientforschung, Beiheft 19. Pp. 130-137.
Hogarth, David George
1920 Hittite Seals, with particular reference to the Ashmolean Collection. Oxford: At the Clarendon Press.
Houwink ten Cate, Philo H.J.
1961 The Luwian Population Groups of Lycia and Cilicia Aspera during the Hellenistic Period.
Leiden: E.J. Brill (dissertation).
Huss, W.
2004 Die Karthager.
München: C.H. Beck oHG (Dritte, überarbeitete Auflage; first edition 1990).
Işık, Fahri, Atıcı, Mahir, & Tekoğlu, Recai
2011 Die nachhethitische Königsstele von Karakuyu beim Karabel-Pass, Zur kulturellen Kontinuität vom bronzezeitlichen Mira zum eisenzeitlichen Ionia. In: Schwertheim, Elmar, (Hrsg.), Studien zum antiken Kleinasien VII , Asia Minor Studien 66. Pp. 1-33; Taf. 1-11.
Jakovidis, Spyros
1964 An inscribed Mycenaean Amulet. *Kadmos* 3. Pp. 149-155.
Jaeger, Bertrand, & Krauss, Rolf
1990 Zwei Skarabäen aus der mykenischen Fundstelle Panaztepe.
Mitteilungen der Deutschen Orient-Gesellschaft zu Berlin 122. Pp. 153-156.
Jeffery, Lilian H.
1990 The Local Scripts of Archaic Greece.
Oxford: At the Clarendon Press.
Katz, Joshua T.
2005 Review of Joachim Latacz's *Troy and Homer, Towards a Solution of an Old Mystery.* Oxford: Oxford University Press, 2004. *Journal of the American Oriental Society* 125, nr. 3, July-September 2005. Pp. 422-425.
Kelder, Jorrit Martin
2007 Review of Latacz, J.—Troy and Homer, Towards a Solution of an Old Mystery, Oxford University Press, Oxford, 2004.
Bibliotheca Orientalis 59, N° 5-6, september-december 2007. Pp. 743-745.
[2009] The Kingdom of Mycenae: A Great Kingdom in the Late Bronze Age Aegean. *Sine loco* (dissertation).
2010 The Kingdom of Mycenae, A Great Kingdom in the Late Bronze Age Aegean. Bethesda, Maryland: CDL Press.
Kenna, Victor E.G.
1972 Glyptic. In: Åström, Lena, & Paul, (eds.), The Swedish Cyprus Expedition, Vol. IV, Part 1D. Pp. 623-674.
Lund: The Swedish Cyprus Expedition.
Klock-Fontanille, Isabella
2007 The Invention of [the] Luwian Hieroglyphic Script.
<http://www.caeno.org/origins/papers/KlockFontanille_LuvianHieroglyphs.pdf>.

Knapp, A. Bernard
2008 Prehistoric & Protohistoric Cyprus, Identity, Insularity and Connectivity. Oxford: Oxford University Press.
Kolb, Frank
2010 Tatort »Troia«, Geschichte, Mythen, Politik. Paderborn: Verlag Ferdinand Schöningh.
Krahe, Hans
1964 Unsere ältesten Flussnamen. Wiesbaden: Otto Harrassowitz.
Kretschmer, Paul
1970 Einleitung in die Geschichte der griechischen Sprache. Göttingen: Vandenhoeck & Ruprecht (2., unveränderte Auflage).
Lambrou-Phillipson, C.
1990 Hellenorientalia, The Near Eastern Presence in the Bronze Age Aegean, ca. 3000-1100 B.C., Interconnections based on the material record and the written evidence, Plus: Orientalia, A Catalogue of Egyptian, Mesopotamian, Mitannian, Syro-Palestinian, Cypriot and Asia Minor Objects from the Bronze Age Aegean. Göteborg: Paul Åstrøms Förlag.
Laroche, Emmanuel
1957 Notes de toponymie anatolienne. In: Kronasser, H., (Hrsg.), MNHMHX ΣARIN, Gedenkschrift Paul Kretschmer, 2 Mai 1866 – 9 März 1956, Band II: 1-7. [Wiesbaden]: Otto Harrassowitz; Wien: Brüder Hollinek.
1960 Les hiéroglyphes hittites, Première partie: L'écriture. Paris: Éditions du Centre National de la Recherche Scientifique.
1961 Études de toponymie anatolienne. Revue Hittite et Asianique 69. Pp. 57-98.
1966 Les Noms des Hittites. Paris: Librairie C. Klincksieck.
Latacz, Joachim
2003 Troia und Homer, Der Weg zur Lösung eines alten Rätsels. München-Zürich: Piper.
2004 Troy and Homer, Towards a Solution of an Old Mystery. Oxford: Oxford University Press.
2010 Troia und Homer, Der Weg zur Lösung eines alten Rätsels. Leipzig: Koehler & Amelang GmbH (6., aktualisierte und erweiterte Auflage).
Liebhart, R.F. & Brixhe, Claude
2009 The Recently Discovered Inscriptions from Tumulus MM at Gordion, A preliminary Report. *Kadmos* 48. Pp. 141-156.
Littauer, Mary A. & Crouwel, Joost H.
1979 Wheeled Vehicles and Ridden Animals in the Ancient Near East. Leiden-Köln: E.J. Brill.
Lloyd, Seton, & Mellaart, James
1962 Beycesultan I. London: The British Institute of Archaeology at Ankara.
Lochner-Hüttenbach, Fritz
1960 Die Pelasger. Arbeiten aus dem Institut für vergleichende Sprachwissenschaft.

Wien: Gerold & Co.
Loon, Maurits N. van
1985 Anatolia in the Second Millennium B.C.
Leiden: E.J. Brill.
Makkay, J.
1998 Greek ἀξίνε and πέλεκυς as Semitic Loan-Words in Greek and the Corresponding Axe Type. In: Mikasa, H.I.H. Prince Takahito, (ed.), Essays on Ancient Anatolia in the Second Millennium B.C. Pp. 183-197.
Wiesbaden: Harrassowitz Verlag.
Mallory, J.P., & Adams, D.Q.
2007 The Oxford Introduction to Proto-Indo-European and the Proto-Indo-European World.
Oxford: University Press (Reprint of 2006 edition).
Masson, Emilia
1980 Les inscriptions louvites hiéroglyphiques de Köylütolu et Beyköy. *Kadmos* 19. Pp. 106-122.
Matouš, Lubor, & Matoušová-Rajmová, Marie
1984 Kappadokische Keilschrifttafeln mit Siegel aus den Sammlungen der Karlsuniversität in Prag.
Praha: Univerzita Karlova.
Meid, Wolfgang
2010 The Celts. Innsbrucker Beiträge zur Kulturwissenschaft, Neue Folge, Band 2.
Innsbruck: Innsbrucker Beiträge zur Kulturwissenschaft.
Melchert, Harold Craig
1993 Cuneiform Luvian Lexicon. Lexica Anatolica 2.
Chapel Hill N.C. (On line version: 2001).
2003 The Luwians. Handbook of Oriental Studies, Section One: The Near and Middle East 68.
Leiden-Boston: Brill.
2004 A Dictionary of the Lycian Language.
Ann Arbor-New York: Beech Stave Press.
2013 Luvian Language in "Luvian" Rituals in Hattuša. In: Collins, Billie Jean, & Michalowski, Piotr, (eds.), Beyond Hatti, A tribute to Gary Beckman. Pp. 159-172.
Atlanta: Lockwood Press.
Mellaart, James
1954 Preliminary Report on a Survey of Pre-Classical Remains in Southern Turkey. *Anatolian Studies* 4. Pp. 175-240.
1959 Summary of Archaeological Research in Turkey in 1958. *Anatolian Studies* 9. Pp. 15-33.
Mellaart, James, & Murray, Ann
1995 Beycesultan Vol. III, Part II.
The British Institute at Ankara.
Meriç, Recep
2003 Excavations at Bademgediği Tepe (Puranda) 1999-2002: a Priliminary Report. *Istanbuler Mitteilungen* 53. Pp. 79-98.

Meriggi, Piero
1975 Manuale di eteo geroglifico, Parte II: Tavole - 2ª e 3ª serie. Incunabula Graeca Vol. XV. Roma: Edizioni dell'Ateneo.
1980 Schizzo grammaticale dell'anatolico. Atti della Accademia Nazionale dei Lincei 1980, Memorie, Classe di Scienze morali, storiche e filologiche, serie VIII, Volume XXIV, Fascicolo 3. Roma: Accademia Nazionale dei Lincei.
Miller, Jared L.
2006 Ein König von Ḫatti an einen König von Aḫḫijawa (der sogenannten Tawagalawa-Brief). In: Janowsky, Bernd, & Wilhelm, Gernot, (Hg.), Briefe. Texte aus der Umwelt des Alten Testaments. Pp. 240-247. Gütersloh: Gütersloher Verlagshaus.
2010 Some disputed passages in the Tawagalawas Letter. In: Singer, Itamar, (ed.), *ipamati kistamati pari tumatimis*, Luwian and Hittite Studies presented to J. David Hawkins on the occasion of his 70th Birthday. Tel Aviv University, Sonia and Marco Nadler Institute of Archaeology, Emery and Clair Yass Publications in Archaeology, Monograph Series 28. Pp. 159-169. Tel Aviv: Institute of Archaeology, Tel Aviv University.
Monte, Giuseppe F. del
1992 Die Orts- und Gewässernamen der hethitischen Texte, Supplement. Répertoire Géographique des Textes Cunéiformes 6/2, Beihefte zum Tübinger Atlas des Vorderen Orients, Reihe B (Geisteswissenschaften) Nr. 7/6. Wiesbaden: Dr. Ludwig Reichert.
Monte, Giuseppe F. del, & Tischler, Johann
1978 Die Orts- und Gewässernamen der hethitischen Texte. Répertoire Géographique des Textes Cuneiformes 6. Beihefte zum Tübinger Atlas des Vorderen Orients, Reihe B (Geisteswissenschaften) Nr. 7/6. Wiesbaden: Dr. Ludwig Reichert.
Montet, Pierre
1962 Notes et documents pour servir à l'histoire des relations entre l'Égypte et la Syrie. *Kêmi* 16. Pp. 76-96.
Mora, Clelia
1987 La glittica anatolica del II millennio A.C.: Classificazione tipologica. Studia Mediterranea 6. Pavia: Gianni Iuculano Editore.
1990 La glittica anatolica del II millennio A.C.: Classificazione tipologica, I. I sigilli a iscrizione geroglifica, Primo supplemento. Studia Mediterranea 6. *Sine loco*: Gianni Iuculano Editore.
1991 Sull'origine della scrittura geroglifica anatolica. *Kadmos* 30. Pp. 1-28.
Morris, Ian
2005 Review of Joachim Latacz's Troy and Homer: Toward a Solution of an Old Mystery. <http://www.princeton.edu/~pswpc/pdfs/morris/120506.pdf>.
Mouton, Alice, Rutherford, Ian, & Yakubovich, Ilya (eds.)
2013 Luwian Identities, Culture, Language and Religion Between Anatolia and the Aegean. Culture and History of the Ancient Near East 64.

Leiden-Boston: Brill.
Murray, A.S., Smith, A.H., & Walters, H.B.
1900 Excavations in Cyprus.
London: Trustees of the British Museum.
Muscarella, Oscar W.
1974 Ancient Art, The Norbert Schimmel Collection.
Mainz: Philipp von Zabern.
Nagy, Gregory
2010 Homer the Preclassic. Sather Classical Lectures, Volume Sixty-Seven.
Berkeley-Los Angeles-London: University of California Press.
Neumann, Günter
1999 Wie haben die Troer im 13. Jahrhundert gesprochen? *Würzburger Jahrbücher für die Altertumswissenschaft*, Neue Folge 23. Pp. 15-23.
Newberry, Percy E.
1906 Egyptian Antiquities Scarabs, An Introduction to the Study of Egyptian Seals and Signet Rings.
London: Archibald Constable and Co Ltd.
Niemeier, Wolf-Dietrich
1998a The Mycenaeans in Western Anatolia and the Problem of the Origins of the Sea Peoples. In: Gitin, Seymor, Mazar, Amihai, & Stern, Ephraim, (eds.), Mediterranean Peoples in Transition, Thirteenth to Early Tenth Centuries BCE, in honor of Professor Trude Dothan. Pp. 17-65.
Jerusalem: Israel Exploration Society.
1998b Mycenaeans and Hittites in War in Western Asia Minor. In: Laffineur, Robert, (éd.), Polemos, Le contexte guerrier en Égée à l'âge du Bronze, Actes de la 7e Rencontre égéenne internationale, Université de Liège, 14-17 avril 1998. Pp. 141-156.
Eupen: Université de Liège-Program in Aegean Scripts and Prehistory, The University of Texas Austin.
2007a Milet von den Anfangen menschlicher Besiedlung bis zu Ionischen Wanderung. In: Cobet, Justus, Graeve, Volkmar von, Niemeier, Wolf-Dietrich, & Zimmermann, Konrad, (Hrsg.), Frühes Ionien, Eine Bestandsaufnahme, Panionion-Symposion Güzelçamlı, 26. September — 1. Oktober 1999. Milesische Forschungen 5. Pp. 5-20.
Mainz am Rhein: Philipp von Zabern.
2007b Westkleinasien und die Ägäis von den Anfängen bis zur ionischen Wanderung: Topographie, Geschichte und Beziehungen nach dem archäologischen Befund und den hethitischen Quellen. In: Cobet, Justus, Graeve, Volkmar von, Niemeier, Wolf-Dietrich, & Zimmermann, Konrad, (Hrsg.), Frühes Ionien, Eine Bestandsaufnahme, Panionion-Symposion Güzelçamlı, 26. September — 1. Oktober 1999.
Milesische Forschungen 5. Pp. 37-96.
Mainz am Rhein: Philipp von Zabern.
2008 Ḫattusas Beziehungen zu West-Kleinasien und dem mykenischen Griechenland (Aḫḫijawa). In: Wilhelm, Gernot, (Hrsg.), Ḫattuša—Boğazköy, Das Hethiterreich im Spannungsfeld des Alten Orients, 6. Internationales

Colloquium der Deutschen Orient-Gesellschaft, 22.-24. März 2006, Würzburg. Pp. 291-349.
Wiesbaden: Harrassowitz Verlag.

Nilsson, Martin Persson
1972 Homer and Mycenae.
Philadelphia (2nd impression).

O'Connor, David, & Cline, Eric H.
2004 Amenhotep III, Perspectives on His Reign.
Ann Arbor: The University of Michigan Press.

Olivier, Jean-Pierre
1999 Rapport 1991-1995 sur les textes en écriture hiéroglyphique crétoise, en Linéaire A et en Linéaire B. In: Deger-Jalkotzy, Sigrid, Hiller, Stefan, & Panagl, Oswald, (Hrsg.), *Floreant Studia Mycenaea*, Akten des X. Internationalen Mykenologischen Colloquiums in Salzburg vom 1.-5. Mai 1995, Band II. Pp. 419-435.
Wien: Verlag der Österreichischen Akademie der Wissenschaften.

Oreshko, Rostislav
2013 Hieroglyphic Inscriptions of Western Anatolia: Long Arm of the Empire or Vernacular Tradition(s)? In: Mouton, Alice, Rutherford, Ian, & Yakubovich, Ilya, (eds.), Luwian Identities, Culture, Language and Religion Between Anatolia and the Aegean. Culture and History of the Ancient Near East 64. Pp. 345-420.
Leiden-Boston: Brill.

Otten, Heinrich
1988 Die Bronzetafel aus Boğazköy, Ein Staatsvertrag Tudḫalijas IV. Studien zu den Boğazköy-Texte, Beiheft 1.
Wiesbaden: Otto Harrassowitz.

Özgüç, Nimet
1980 Seal Impressions from the Palaces at Acemhöyük. In: Porada, Edith, (ed.), Ancient Art in Seals. Pp. 61-99.
Princeton, New Jersey: Princeton University Press.

Palmer, Leonard R.
1965 Mycenaeans and Minoans, Aegean Prehistory in the Light of the Linear B Tablets.
London: Faber and Faber Ltd (second revised edition).

Pantazis, Vangelis D.
2009 Wilusa: Reconsidering the Evidence. *Klio* 91. Pp. 291-310.

Parrot, André
1951 Cylindre hittite nouvellement acquis (AO 20138). *Syria* 28. Pp. 180-190, Pls. XIII-XVI.

Peschlow-Bindokat, Anneliese, & Herbordt, Suzanne
2001 Eine hethitische Großprinzeninschrift aus dem Latmos.
Archäologischer Anzeiger 2001, Heft 3. Pp. 363-378.

Phillips, Jacke
2007 The Amenhotep III 'Plaques' from Mycenae: Comparison, Contrast and a Question of Chronology. In: Bietak, Manfred, & Czerny, Ernst, (eds.), The Synchronisation of Civilisations in the Eastern Mediterranean in the Second

Millennium B.C. III. Contributions to the Chronology of the Eastern Mediterranean IX. Österreichische Akademie der Wissenschaften, Denkschriften der Gesamtakademie XXXVII. Pp. 479-493. Wien: Verlag der Österreichischen Akademie der Wissenschaften.

Poetto, Massimo

1993 L'iscrizione luvio-geroglifica di Yalburt, Nuove acquisizioni relative alla geografia dell'anatolia sud-occidentale. Studia Mediterranea 8. Pavia: Gianni Iuculano Editore.

Poetto, Massimo, & Bolatti Guzzo, Natalia

1994 La legenda in luvio geroglifico sulla cretula 81/402 del Museo Archeologico di Kayseri: una revisione. *Studi Epigrafici e Linguistici sul Vicino Oriente antico* 11. Pp. 11-15.

Pokorny, Julius

1994 Indogermanisches Etymologisches Wörterbuch. Tübingen-Basel: Francke Verlag (3. Aufl.).

Pope, Maurice

1999 The Story of Decipherment, From Egyptian hieroglyphs to Maya Script. London: Thames and Hudson Ltd (Revised Edition).

Porada, Edith

1981-2 The Cylinder Seals found at Thebes in Boeotia. *Archiv für Orientforschung* 28. Pp. 1-72.

Reeves, Nicholas

2002 Achnaton, Valse Profeet en Geweldadig Farao. Baarn: Tirion Uitgevers bv.

Renfrew, Colin

1987 Archaeology and Language, The Puzzle of Indo-European Origins. London: Jonathan Cape.

Rosenkranz, Bernhard

1966 Flusz- und Gewässernamen in Anatolia. *Beiträge zur Namenforschung*, N.F. 1. Pp. 124-144.

Ruijgh, Cornelis J.

1967 Études sur la grammaire et le vocabulaire du grec mycénien. Amsterdam: Adolf M. Hakkert, Éditeur.

Rüster, Christel, & Neu, Erich

1989 Hethitisches Zeichenlexicon: Inventar und Interpretation der Keilschriftzeichen aus den Boğazköy-Texten. Studien zu den Boğazköy-Texten, Beiheft 2. Wiesbaden: Otto Harrassowitz.

Şahin, Seracettin, & Tekoğlu, Recai

2003 A Hieroglyphic Stele from Afyon Archaeological Museum. *Athenaeum* 91. Pp. 540-545.

Sakellarakis, Iannis, & Olivier, Jean-Pierre

1994 Un vase de Pierre avec inscription en linéaire A de Cythère. *Bulletin de Correspondence Hellénique* 118. Pp. 343-351.

Schachermeyr, Fritz

1983 Die griechische Rückerinnerung im Lichte neuer Forschungen.

Wien: Verlag der Österreichischen Akademie der Wissenschaften.

Schuler, Einar von

1965 Die Kaškäer, Ein Beitrag zur Ethnographie des Alten Kleinasien.
Berlin: Walter de Gruyter & Co.

Schulten, Adolf

1950 Tartessos, Eine Beitrag zur ältesten Geschichte des Westens.
Universität Hamburg, Abhandlungen aus dem Gebiet der Auslandkunde, Band 54, Reihe B: Völkerkunde, Kulturgeschichte und Sprachen, Band 30.
Hamburg: Cram, de Gruyter & Co.

Sergent, Bernard

1995 Les Indo-Européens, Histoire, langues, mythes.
Paris: Éditions Payot & Rivages.

2005 Les Indo-Européens, Histoire, langues, mythes.
Paris: Éditions Payot & Rivages (Nouvelle édition revue et augmentée).

Sethe, Kurt

1907 Urkunden der 18. Dynastie. Historisch-Biographische Urkunden.
Leipzig: Hinrichs.

Singer, Itamar

2011 *The Calm before the Storm*, Selected Writings of Itamar Singer on the End of the Late Bronze Age in Anatolia and the Levant. Society of Biblical Literature, Writings from the Ancient World Supplements 1.
Atlanta: Society of Biblical Literature.

Smit, Daniel W.

1990-1 KUB XIV 3 and Hittite History, A Historical Approach to the Tawagalawa-letter. *Talanta, Proceedings of the Dutch Archaeological and Historical Society* 22-23. Pp. 79-111.

Sommer, Ferdinand

1932 Die Aḫḫijawā-Urkunden.
München: Verlag der Bayerischen Akademie der Wissenschaften.

Starke, Frank

1981 Die Keilschrift-luwischen Wörter für Insel und Lampe.
Zeitschrift für Vergleichende Sprachwissenschaft 95. Pp. 142-152.

1985 Die keilschrift-luwischen Texte in Umschrift. Studien zu den Boğazköy-Texten 30.
Wiesbaden: Harrassowitz.

1997 Troia im Kontext des Historisch-Politischen und Sprachlichen Umfeldes Kleinasiens im 2. Jahrtausend. *Studia Troica* 7. Pp. 447-487.

Stavi, Boaz

2015 The Reign of Tudhaliya II and Šuppiluliuma I, The Contribution of the Hittite Documentation to a Reconstruction of the Amarna Age. Texte der Hethiter 31.
Heidelberg: Universitätsverlag Winter.

Teffeteller, Anette

2013 Singers of Lazpa: Reconstructing Identities on Bronze Age Lesbos. In: Mouton, Alice, Rutherford, Ian, & Yakubovich, Ilya, (eds.), Luwian Identities, Culture, Language and Religion Between Anatolia and the Aegean. Culture and History of the Ancient Near East 64. Pp. 567-589.

Leiden-Boston: Brill.
Tischler, Johann
1983 Hethitisches Etymologisches Glossar, Teil I: a-k.
Innsbrucker Beiträge zur Sprachwissenschaft 20.
Innsbruck: Innsbrucker Beiträge zur Sprachwissenschaft.
Ventris, Michael, & Chadwick, John
1973 Documents in Mycenaean Greek.
Cambridge: At the University Press (2nd ed.).
Vercoutter, Jean
1956 L'Égypte et le monde Égéenne préhellénique, Étude critique des sources égyptiennes du début de la XVIIIe à la fin de la XIXe dynastie.
Le Caire: Institut Français d'Archéologie Orientale.
Watkins, Calvert
1986 The Language of the Trojans. In: Mellink, Machteld J., (ed.), Troy and the Trojan War, A Symposium Held at Bryn Mawr College, October 1984. Pp. 45-62.
Bryn Mawr, PA: Bryn Mawr College.
Whatmough, Joshua
1963 The Dialects of Ancient Gaul, Grammar Part I.
Ann Arbor-Michigan: Edwards Brothers.
Woudhuizen, Fred C.
1984-5 Origins of the Sidetic Script. *Talanta, Proceedings of the Dutch Archaeological and Historical Society* 16-17. Pp. 115-127.
1994 Tablet RS 20.25 from Ugarit: Evidence of Maritime Trade in the Final Years of the Bronze Age. *Ugarit-Forschungen* 26. Pp. 509-538.
1994-5 Luwian Hieroglyphic Monumental Rock and Stone Inscriptions from the Hittite Empire Period. *Talanta, Proceedings of the Dutch Archaeological and Historical Society* 26-27. Pp. 153-217.
1995 The Late Hittite Empire in the light of recently discovered Luwian hieroglyphic texts [= Paper to the Sixth Annual UCLA Indo-European Conference, Los Angeles 26-28 May, 1994]. *The Journal of Indo-European Studies* 23, 1&2. Pp. 53-81.
2004a Luwian Hieroglyphic Monumental Rock and Stone Inscriptions from the Hittite Empire Period. Innsbrucker Beiträge zur Kulturwissenschaft, Sonderheft 116.
Innsbruck: Innsbrucker Beiträge zur Kulturwissenschaft.
2004b Towards a Historical Frame for the Phaistos Disc. In: Achterberg, Winfried, Best, Jan, Enzler, Kees, Rietveld, Lia, & Woudhuizen, Fred, The Phaistos Disc: A Luwian Letter to Nestor. Publications of the Henri Frankfort Foundation 13. Pp. 115-118.
Amsterdam: Dutch Archaeological and Historical Society.
2004c Selected Luwian Hieroglyphic Texts [1]. Innsbrucker Beiträge zur Kulturwissenschaft, Sonderheft 120.
Innsbruck: Innsbrucker Beiträge zur Kulturwissenschaft.
2004-5a Some More on Cretan Hieroglyphic Seals. *Talanta, Proceedings of the Dutch Archaeological and Historical Society* 36-37. Pp. 171-186.

2004-5b Mira: Evidence for Continuity in Western Anatolia during the Transition from the Late Bronze to Early Iron Age. *Talanta, Proceedings of the Dutch Archaeological and Historical Society* 36-37. Pp. 165-169.

2005a Selected Luwian Hieroglyphic Texts 2. Innsbrucker Beiträge zur Kulturwissenschaft, Sonderheft 124.
Innsbruck: Innsbrucker Beiträge zur Kulturwissenschaft.

2005b Middle Bronze Age Luwian Hieroglyphic and its Ramifications to Crete. In: Süel, Aygül, (ed.), Acts of the Vth International Congress of Hittitology, Çorum September 02-08, 2002. Pp. 731-746.
Ankara.

2006-7 Two Assuwian Royal Seals. *Jaarbericht Ex Oriente Lux* 40. Pp. 125-129.

2007 On the Byblos Script. *Ugarit-Forschungen* 39. Pp. 689-756.

2009 The Earliest Cretan Scripts 2. Innsbrucker Beiträge zur Kulturwissenschaft, Sonderheft 129.
Innsbruck: Innsbrucker Beiträge zur Kulturwissenschaft.

2010a Towards a Chronological Framework for Significant Dialectal Tendencies in Indo-European. *Journal of Indo-European Studies* 38. Pp. 41-131.

2010b Reflections of a Trifunctional Religious Ideology among Indo-European Population Groups of the 3rd and 2nd Millennia BC. *Studia Indo-Europaea* 4. Pp. 207-230.

2010-1a Two Notes on Lydian. *Talanta, Proceedings of the Dutch Archaeological and Historical Society* 42-43. Pp. 207-213.

2010-1b The Geography of Southwest Anatolia, Notes to Gander 2010. *Talanta, Proceedings of the Dutch Archaeological and Historical Society* 42-43. Pp. 235-240.

2011 Selected Luwian Hieroglyphic Texts: The Extended Version. Innsbrucker Beiträge zur Sprachwissenschaft 141.
Innsbruck: Innsbrucker Beiträge zur Sprachwissenschaft.

2012a The Saga of the Argonauts: A Reflex of Thraco-Phrygian Maritime Encroachment on the Southern Pontic Littoral. In: Tsetskhladze, Gocha R., (ed.), The Black Sea, Paphlagonia, Pontus and Phrygia in Antiquity, Aspects of Archaeology and Ancient History. British Archaeological Reports, International Series 2432. Pp. 263-271.
Oxford: Archaeopress..

2012b Stamp Seal from Beycesultan. *Journal of Indo-European Studies* 40. Pp. 1-10.

2012c Late Bronze Age Hydronyms and Toponyms of Indo-European Nature in Western Anatolia. *Živa Antika* 62. Pp. 5-16.

2013a Three Luwian Hieroglyphic Late Bronze Age Inscriptions. *Ancient West & East* 12. Pp. 1-15.

2013b On the Reading of the Luwian Hieroglyphic Legends of the Schimmel Rhyton. *Colloquium Anatolicum* 12. Pp. 333-344.

2013c Traces of Ethnic Diversity in Mycenaean Greece. *Dacia* N.S. LVII. Pp. 5-21.

2013d On the Identity of the Indo-European Substrate in Western Anatolia. *Živa Antika* 63. Pp. 5-11.

2014a Geography of Western Anatolia. In: Faranton, Valérie, & Mazoyer, Michel, (éds.), Homère et L'Anatolie 2. Collection Kubaba, Série Antiquité. Pp. 119-136.
Paris: L'Harmattan.

2014b The Earliest Recorded Lycian. *Res Antiquae* 11. Pp. 207-212.

2015a Luwian Hieroglyphic: Texts, Grammar, Indices. Heiloo (On line: academia.edu).

2015b The Geography of the Hittite Empire and the Distribution of Luwian Hieroglyphic Seals. *Klio* 97(1). Pp. 7-31.

2015c Some suggestions as to the improvement of our understanding of the contents of the recently discovered Luwian hieroglyphic text Aleppo 6. *Ancient West & East* 14. Pp. 293-300.

2015d Kuruntas, A Recollection of the Relevant Data. *Historische Sprachforschung* 128. Pp. 299-315.

2016 Documents in Minoan Luwian, Semitic, and Pelasgian. Publications of the Henri Frankfort Foundation 14. Amsterdam: Dutch Archaeological and Historical Society.

2017a The Language of Linear C and Linear D from Cyprus. Publications of the Henri Frankfort Foundation 15. Amsterdam: Dutch Archaeological and Historical Society.

2017b The Ankara Silver Bowl. *Ancient West & East* 16. Pp. 271-290.

2017c The Language of the Trojans. In: Faranton, Valérie, & Mazoyer, Michel, (éds), Homère et L'Anatolie 3. Collection Kubaba, Série Antiquité. Pp. 127-140. Paris: L'Harmattan.

2018 Indo-Europeanization in the Mediterranean, With particular attention to the fragmentary languages. PIP-TraCS—Papers in Intercultural Philosophy and Transcontinental Comparative Studies No. 16. Haarlem: Shikanda Press.

Yakubovich, Ilya

2010 Sociolinguistics of the Luvian Language. Brill's Studies in Indo-European Languages & Linguistics 2. Leiden-Boston: Brill.

2013 Anatolian Names in *-wiya* and the Structure of Empire Luwian Onomastics. In: Mouton, Alice, Rutherford, Ian, & Yakubovich, Ilya, (eds.), Luwian Identities, Culture, Language and Religion Between Anatolia and the Aegean. Culture and History of the Ancient Near East 64. Pp. 87-123. Leiden-Boston: Brill.

Yasur-Landau, Assaf

2010 The Philistines and Aegean Migration at the End of the Late Bronze Age. Cambridge: Cambridge University Press.

Zangger, Eberhard

2016 The Luwian Civilization, The Missing Link in the Aegean Bronze Age. İstanbul, Türkye: zerobooksonline.com.

2017 Die Luwier und der trojanische Krieg, Eine Entdeckungsgeschichte. Zürich: Orell Füssli Verlag.

Zangger, Eberhard, & Woudhuizen, Fred

2018 Rediscovered Luwian Hieroglyphic Inscriptions from Western Asia Minor. *Talanta, Proceedings of the Dutch Archaeological and Historical Society* 48-50. Pp. 9-56.

Zgusta, Ladislav
1984 Kleinasiatische Ortsnamen.
Heidelberg: Carl Winter Universitätsverlag.

Index

A

Abishemu II, 125

Abbaitis, 24, 74, 90, 134

Abydos, 25, 28, 89, 99

Acemhöyük, 38, 41, 46, 57, 158

Adana, 66, 68, 94

Adramyttion, 26, 28, 89–90, 99–101

Adriatic, 16

Aegean, i, 1, 7–8, 10, 13–14, 20–21, 29, 31, 34, 45, 49, 64–65, 107–108, 110–111, 116, 127, 140, 146–147, 152–154, 156–158, 160, 163

Afyon, iii, 21, 23, 30, 47–48, 74, 83–85, 159

Aḫḫiyawa, 27, 30, 76–77, 108–111, 127, 149

Aḫḫiyawan, 29, 64–65, 76, 109, 111

Aḫḫiyawans, 74, 109

Aineas, 130

Aiolian, 131

Aiolians, 138

Aitolia, 107

Akamas, 18, 77

Akhaia, 76, 110–112

Akhaian, 49, 65, 114–115

Akhaians, 108, 116, 127

Akhenaten, 60, 107

Akhilleus, 125

Akkadian, 55, 80

Akkadian cuneiform, 55

Akkadisms, 121

Akpinar, 47

Akraiphia, 14

Alacahöyük, 35, 46, 50, 55, 111

Alaksandus, 5, 28–29, 74, 109, 117, 123–125, 129–130

Alaksandus-treaty, 5, 29, 74, 109, 117, 123–125, 129

Alantallis, 20, 47, 75, 82–83, 87, 91

Alasiya, 17–18, 65, 76–78, 97, 115

Aleppo, 24, 70, 163

Alexander, 47, 56–59, 144, 152

Alp, 38, 40, 66–67, 144, 151

Alparslan, 61, 110, 144, 147

Amarna, 63, 65, 69, 107–108, 115, 117, 160

Amathus, 17–18

Amenhotep II, 108

Amenhotep III, i, 59, 107–108, 111, 115, 127, 147, 158

Amenhotep IV, 60, 107

Amorion, 30

Anatolia, i–ii, , iii, 1–3, 5, 7–8, 10, 13–14, 19–22, 25–29, 31–32, 34, 37, 41–42, 46, 48–52, 55–56, 58, 65–66, 71–74, 76, 78, 88–89, 91, 107–108, 114–117, 121–124, 130, 132, 137–140, 142–143, 146–147, 151–152, 155–160, 162–163

Anatolian, 3, 5, 7–8, 10, 13, 16, 20, 29, 41, 45–46, 49, 58–61, 63, 65–66, 72, 76, 89, 120, 125, 128–139, 142–144, 147, 150–151, 155, 163

Andania, 14

Ankara silver bowl, 6, 163

Ankhises, 130–131

Apaisos, 25, 89, 92, 96, 128

Apasa, 19–21, 23, 27, 35, 50, 56, 71, 74, 77, 84, 124, 133–135, 137, 139, 142

Appawiya, i, 5, 24, 26, 29, 46, 74–75, 90, 133–135, 137, 139, 142

Aphrodite, 130

Aplaḫandas, 5, 57–58, 126

Apollon, 126

Archi, 51–52, 145

Argive, 110
Argolid, 13
Arisbe, 25, 28, 89, 99, 128
Arkadia, 135, 142
Armenia, 139–140
Arna, 75
Arne, 142
Arnuwandas I, 58, 86, 114
Arnuwandas III, 87–88
Artemis, 25, 126
Arzawa, i, iii, 3, 5–7, 19–21, 23, 28–31, 34–35, 37, 42, 44–46, 48–50, 55–56, 59, 63, 65, 71–72, 74, 79, 86–88, 94–96, 108, 111, 114–115, 117, 133–134, 137, 139, 148, 152
Arzawan, iii, 2–3, 14, 49–50, 55–56, 58, 69, 71, 73–74, 114–115, 117, 120–122, 126, 130
Asaḫ[ ]s, 90
Ashkelon, 89, 94
Asia Minor, 14, 29–31, 59, 114, 124, 126, 131–132, 141, 143–144, 154, 157, 163
Asiatic, 59
Assuwa, i, 22–23, 26, 28, 34–35, 46–47, 49–50, 55, 64–65, 68–69, 71–72, 86, 88, 92–93, 110–111, 114–115, 129
Assuwian, i, 26, 31, 34–35, 49–50, 55–56, 58–59, 63, 66, 69, 71–73, 113, 115, 162
Assuwian League, 26, 31, 34–35, 49–50, 55–56, 58, 63, 69, 71–72, 115
Assyria, 42, 60, 76–77, 147
Assyrian, 42, 60, 73
Assyrian cuneiform, 42
Atapali, 24, 89, 93, 97
Atarneus, 90, 100
Athenian, 14
Athens, 14, 45
Atinas, 44–45
Atpas, 27
Atreus, 114–115
Atriya, 23, 26, 30–31, 75
Attarima, 77
Attarissiyas, 114–115
Attic, 14
Attica, 11, 25, 45–46, 108
Awarna, 19, 22, 30, 75–76, 100, 133, 136–137
Aydin, 34, 39, 47, 50, 54, 56–58, 69
Ayios Elias, 107
Azize, 66, 145

B

Babylon, 17, 60, 127
Babylonian, 60
Bademgediği, 21, 23, 26, 155
Baltimore, ii, 68–70, 115
Bányai, 22, 26, 145
Bean, 25, 144
Beirut, 38, 43, 46
Belediye Garden, 88
Bennet, 128
Betancourt, 45, 146
Beycesultan, 20–21, 23, 28, 36–37, 46, 50–51, 74, 114–115, 123–124, 138, 149, 154–155, 162
Beycesultan-Mira, 114–115
Beyköy, 1–3, 24, 47–48, 80–83, 85, 88–89, 91, 93, 103, 106, 110, 122, 136, 141, 155
Biblical, 127, 141, 145, 160
Bittel, 67
Black Sea, 129, 162
Boehmer, 36, 39, 53, 56, 146
Boğazköy, 19–20, 36–37, 44, 48, 56, 58, 67, 80, 82, 115, 145–146, 150–152, 157–160
Boğazköy-Ḫattusa, 19–20, 36–37, 48, 56, 58, 80, 82, 115
Bohemia, 136

Boiotia, 11, 13–14, 135, 142
Börker-Klähn, 36, 146
British, 66–67, 79, 88, 144, 146, 148–150, 154–155, 157, 162
British Museum, 66–67, 149–150, 157
Bronze Age, i–iii, 1–3, 5–8, 10, 12–16, 18, 29–30, 34, 36–37, 39, 41–42, 44–46, 50–52, 54, 57–59, 65–69, 77, 82, 85, 88, 90, 108, 111, 117, 122–125, 127–129, 131–132, 136–138, 141, 145–147, 153-154, 160–163
Bryce, 21, 29–31, 34–35, 55, 74–75, 111, 114–115, 117, 129, 145–146
Buchholz, 17
Burna-Buriaš II, 60
Byblian, 16
Byblos, 16, 94, 125, 162
Byblos script, 16, 162

C

Calder, 25, 144
Canby, 38, 146
Caria, 9, 14, 23, 26, 114, 140
Carian, 13–14, 29
Carians, 13, 29
Carruba, 25, 134, 146
Celtic, 31, 136, 138
central Anatolia, 1, 41–42
Christian, 28, 123
Chronicle of Tudḫaliyas IV, 76–77
Cilicia, 10, 22, 39, 51, 153
Cilicians, 8

Ç

Çivril, 47

C

Classical, iii, 3, 6, 8, 10, 12–14, 16, 18–22, 26–31, 35, 55, 74, 78–79, 88, 90, 114, 117, 123–124, 126, 129, 133–139, 144, 155, 157
Classical period, iii, 8, 10, 12–13, 18, 29, 134
Cline, 59, 107, 145, 147, 158
Cornelius, 20–21, 147

Ç

Çorum, 36, 144, 151, 162

C

Cretan, 13, 15–17, 44–45, 52, 57, 111, 126, 128, 131, 148, 162
Cretan hieroglyphic, 15–16, 44–45, 52, 57, 111, 162
Cretan linear, 16–17
Cretans, 15, 126
Crete, 1, 7–8, 10, 13–14, 16, 18, 34, 42, 45, 49, 59, 65, 71–72, 107, 111, 114, 128, 131, 141–142, 162
cuneiform Hittite, iii, 1, 22, 25
cuneiform Luwian, i, iii, 3, 7–8, 70, 117, 120–122
Cyclades, 11, 13, 29, 115
Cyprian, 17–18, 60–61, 63
Cypro-Minoan, 61, 77
Cyprus, 1, 10, 13–14, 16–18, 42, 45, 60, 76, 78, 83, 107, 115, 150, 153–154, 157, 163

D

Dağardı, ii, 2, 24, 26, 48, 88, 90, 101, 106, 134, 136
Daḫara, 30
Danaoi, 127
Danaos, 142
Dardania, 29
Dark Age, 60, 90
Delos, 29
Delphi, 126
Demeter, 14, 142

discus of Phaistos, 16, 111
Dniestr, 135
Dodona, 141–142
Doric, 126
Dresden, 66
Drews, 143, 147
Droysen, 25, 144
Dumézilian, 66, 73

E

Ea, 54, 108
Early Bronze Age, 36, 50
Early Iron Age, 13, 36, 59, 68–69, 85, 123, 129, 162
Early Minoan III, 45
Ebla, 51–52, 145
Edremit, ii, 2, 24–25, 28–29, 48, 88–90, 99, 104, 110, 123, 128
Egypt, 2, 16, 29, 74, 89, 94
Egyptiaca, 65
Egyptian, 15–16, 34, 41, 46, 49, 57, 59, 65, 71–72, 79, 88, 107–108, 111, 115, 123, 125, 127, 141, 149, 154, 157, 159
Egyptian hieroglyphic, 15, 46, 59, 71, 88, 107, 125, 141
Egyptians, 127
El Amarna, 108, 115
Elis, 127
Emir, 20–21, 23, 144
Emirgazi, 68, 70, 75, 77, 136
English, 59, 64
Enkomi, 17–18, 78, 107
Ephesos, 19–21, 27, 34–35, 49, 56, 71–72, 74, 77, 84, 95, 124, 139
Erlenmeyer, iii, 38, 43, 148
Eskiyapar, 39
Eteo-Cyprian, 18
Eteokles, 64–65, 110, 115
Euboia, 7–8, 11
Euboian, 65
Euphrates, 5
European, i, iii, 3, 5, 7–8, 15–16, 20, 31, 45, 50, 52, 54, 66, 72–73, 75, 89, 122, 124–128, 130–143, 148–149, 152, 155, 159, 161–163

F

Faure, 128, 148
First Syrian Group, iii, 37, 43–44
Forrer, 21, 64, 109
Frankfort, iv, 37, 43–44, 144, 161, 163
French, 5, 21, 79
Freu, 1, 5, 21, 26–27, 31, 34, 56, 79, 87, 123–124, 127, 132, 134, 148–149, 152

G

Gander, 22, 25–26, 55, 75, 115, 132, 149, 162
Gargara, 25, 28, 89, 99
Garstang, 19–21, 24, 34, 135, 149
Garonne, 134
Garumna, 134
Gaul, 135, 138, 161
Gaulish, 134
Gaza, 38, 46, 148
Georgiev, 129
Germania, 136
Germanic, 136
Gindin, 130, 137, 149
Giovanetti, 123, 138, 149
Godart, 65, 128, 145, 150
Gordion, 89, 154
Gortyns, 111, 142
Greece, iii, 1, 7–8, 10–14, 27, 42, 44, 59, 65, 76, 107–108, 115, 125, 135, 139, 142, 146, 153, 162
Greek, 2, 7–8, 10, 13–15, 22–26, 28–29, 35, 44–45, 49, 52, 64–65, 70, 89, 108–109,

114–115, 124–128, 130–132, 134–136, 139–142, 144, 150, 152, 155, 161
Greek mainland, 7, 65, 108, 140
Greeks, 3, 13, 30, 35, 74, 108–109, 114, 116, 127, 131, 146
Gurney, 19–21, 24, 34, 64, 87, 109–110, 135, 149–150
Güterbock, 36–37, 39, 47, 51, 53, 56, 62–63, 66–68, 76, 82, 124–126, 146, 150
Gyges, 25

H

Hagia Triada, 107, 111, 142
Halys, 5, 35, 46, 55
Hammurabi, 17, 127

Ḫ

Ḫapalla, i, 3, 5, 7, 24, 29–30, 46–47, 74–75, 80, 88, 93, 95, 98, 114, 117, 126, 129
Ḫartapus, 69, 85
Ḫatti, 19, 28, 30, 35, 46, 50, 55, 74, 77, 86, 92–94, 98–99, 110–111, 114, 149, 156
Ḫatti-land, 30, 35, 46, 50, 55, 74, 111, 114
Ḫattusa, iii, 19–20, 36–37, 48, 55–56, 58, 75, 80, 82, 87, 108, 115
Ḫattusilis, 30, 36–37, 58, 63–64, 75–76, 82, 86–87, 109–110
Ḫattusilis I, 36–37, 86
Ḫattusilis II, 63
Ḫattusilis III, 30, 58, 64, 75–76, 87, 109–110

H

Hawkins, 2–3, 20–21, 26–27, 30, 36–37, 47, 66–72, 74, 76–77, 80, 82–85, 115, 118, 132, 135, 142, 151–152, 156
Heinhold-Krahmer, 19–20, 27–28, 123, 152
Hellenization, 129
Hellespont, 8, 12
Herbordt, 47, 57–58, 77–78, 80, 82, 152, 158
Herda, 22, 152
Hermos, 26, 49, 72, 125
Herodotos, 13–14, 29, 135, 140–141
Herzog, 135, 152
Hisarlık, 25, 27, 123–124, 128
Hittite, i, iii, 1–3, 5–6, 8, 17, 19–25, 27–31, 33–37, 41, 46, 48–50, 55–58, 60, 63–65, 67–72, 74–79, 82–85, 88, 90, 108–111, 114–115, 117–118, 120, 123–130, 132, 134–137, 139, 142, 145–151, 153–154, 156, 158, 160–161, 163
Hittite cuneiform, iii, 2–3, 5–6, 49, 57, 64, 77–78, 110–111, 117, 132
Hittite empire, ii, 5, 19–20, 27, 31, 33, 35, 48–50, 67–69, 77, 82, 85, 128, 149, 161, 163
Hittite-Luwian, 36–37, 48
Hittites, 1, 3, 5, 19, 30, 42, 48, 50, 74, 85, 88, 108, 127, 129, 146, 148–150, 152, 154, 157
Hittitology, 36, 144, 151, 162
Hogarth, iii, 38, 41, 43–47, 153
Homer, 59, 64, 153–154, 156–158
Homeric, i, 27, 35, 111, 123, 126–130, 137
Homeros, 7–8, 13, 15, 34, 71, 89, 114, 117, 126, 128–131, 135, 140–142
Honaz, 21, 23, 144
Hrozný, 19

Ḫ

Ḫulana, 30, 97
Ḫurritic, 58, 70

I

Ialysos, 10, 107
Iberian, 134
Ida, 100, 130–131
Idomeneus, 111, 113
Idyma, 23, 31

IE Anatolian, 5, 8, 120, 129–132, 134–139, 143
Ilgaz Dağları, 30
Ilion, 18, 24, 34, 71, 77, 117, 123–124, 126–127
Illyrian, 135, 138
Imbros, 8, 24, 28, 89, 99
Indictment of Madduwattas, 114
Indilima, 36, 39, 51–53
Indo-European, i, iii, 3, 5, 7–8, 15–16, 20, 31, 45, 50, 52, 54, 66, 72–73, 89, 122, 124–128, 130–143, 148–149, 152, 155, 159, 161–163
Indo-European Anatolian, 89, 128
Indo-Europeanists, 132
Indo-Europeans, 127, 149
Indus, 20, 22, 31
Ireland, 138
Iron Age, 8, 13, 36, 59, 68–69, 85, 123, 129, 162
Isputaḫsus, 36
Istanuwa, 3, 7, 117–119, 126, 129
Istanuwan songs, 121
Isuwa, 47, 68–69, 72–73
Italy, 16, 135

İ

İzmir, 21, 23, 49

K

Kadesh, 29, 74, 76, 127
Kadmos, 64–65, 109–111, 115, 144, 146, 148, 153–156
Kaikos, 26, 46, 49, 74, 90, 133
Kalavassos, 78
Karabel, 20–21, 44, 47, 74, 82–83, 151, 153
Karkamis, 5–6, 8, 24, 48, 58, 77–78, 89, 94, 97
Karkamisian, 57, 126
Karkisa, 29, 115
Karkiya, 29
Karum, 42, 152
Kaska, 74, 78, 97, 129
Kaskan, 5
Kassite, 60
Kassiya, 30
Kassu, 30, 109
Kassus, 28
Kastaraya, 19, 22, 75–76, 137
Katz, 59, 64, 111, 153
Kaunos, 20, 22, 31
Kayseri, 38, 148, 152, 159
Kaystros, 21, 27, 134
Kelder, 59, 64–65, 115, 127, 153
Kestros, 19, 75, 137
Kimmerian, 135
Kirmir, 30
Kisnapilis, 114
Kizzuwatna, 1, 5–7, 36, 52, 89, 95, 97, 148
Kizzuwatna Luwian, 7
Klavdia, ii, 16–17, 38, 41, 45
Klock-Fontanille, 36, 153
Knossian, 131
Knossos, 7–8, 10, 35, 72, 107, 111–112, 126
Kocaoğuz, 47–48
Kolb, 28, 123, 154
Kolonai, 125
Kom el-Hetan, 115, 127
Konya, 1–2, 38, 139, 144
Köylütolu, 31, 58, 71, 77, 110, 155
Kourion, 17
Krahe, 134–137, 154
Karatepe, 88
Kretschmer, iii, 12, 126, 154
Kubaba, 49, 59, 62, 66, 148, 163
Küçük Menderes, 21, 23

Kulanamuwas, 89, 96
Kültepe-Kanesh, 15, 36–38, 41, 46, 52, 57–59, 136, 138
Kupantakuruntas I, 58, 86, 114
Kupantakuruntas II, 74–75, 87
Kupantakuruntas III, 28, 48, 82, 85, 87–89
Kurunt, 39–40, 50, 54, 57–58, 69–71, 91, 94, 97, 100, 133–134
Kuruntas, 19–20, 35, 46, 49–50, 57, 62, 75–78, 80, 82, 110, 114, 163
Kuwaliya, i, 5, 20–21, 23, 29–30, 46–48, 74–75, 84–85, 88, 92, 114
Kydonia, 107

L

Labarnas I, 37, 86
Laconia, 11, 13
Lalandos, 9, 30
Lambrou-Phillipson, 59–60, 108, 154
Laodikeia, 25, 31
Larissa Phryconis, 142
Laroche, 5, 7, 15, 26, 36, 56, 58–59, 129, 132, 154
Lasithi, 111–112
Latacz, 5, 29, 59, 64–65, 74, 108–109, 124–126, 128–129, 153–154, 156
Late Antiquity, 127
Late Bronze Age, i, iii, 2, 5–8, 10, 12–14, 30, 37, 57, 59, 65–69, 77, 85, 88, 90, 122–125, 129, 131–132, 136–137, 146–147, 153, 160, 162–163
Late Helladic I, 64
Late Helladic IIB-IIIA2 [early], 107
Late Helladic III, 107
Late Helladic IIIA, 107
Late Helladic IIIA1, 65
Late Helladic IIIA2, 26, 114
Late Helladic IIIB, 60, 107, 114
Late Helladic IIIB1, 26, 60, 65
Late Helladic IIIB2, 107
Late Helladic IIIC, 60
Late Minoan IB, 34, 49
Late Minoan IIIA, 107
Late Minoan IIIA1, 107
Late Minoan IIIA 1/2, 16
Late Minoan IIIA-B, 107
Latin, 14, 118, 132
Latmos, 27, 47–48, 77, 158
Laurion, 45
Leleges, 8, 13, 24–26, 28, 89–90, 99–100, 128
Lemnos, 14, 24, 28, 89, 99
Lesbos, 6, 12, 24, 26–28, 49, 89–90, 99–100, 138, 141, 160
Leto, 126
Levant, 1, 16, 42, 44–46, 51, 89, 160
Levantine, 45, 108
Ligurian, 125, 134, 138
Ligurians, 135
Linear A, 16, 128, 131, 142
Linear B, iii, 7–8, 15, 65, 72, 124–126, 128–129, 131, 158
Linear C, 17–18, 78, 163
Linear D, 18, 163
Lochner-Hüttenbach, iv, 139–140, 142, 154
London, 66–68, 144, 148–150, 154, 157–159
Louvre, ii, 34, 37, 39, 41, 46–47, 50, 56–59, 66, 72
Lower Land, 5–6, 30, 50, 94, 139
Lukka, 5–6, 14–15, 22, 29–30, 34, 55, 71, 78–79, 85, 133, 136–137, 139, 142, 148–149
Lusitanian, 134, 138
Lusitanians, 135
Lusitanians, 135
Luwian, i, iii, 1–3, 5–8, 12–28, 31, 34–37, 39, 41–42, 44–46, 48–67, 70–73, 75, 77–78, 80, 82–84, 86, 88–91, 110–111,

115, 117–118, 120–123, 125–139, 141, 144, 151–153, 156, 158, 160–163
Luwian cuneiform, 117
Luwian homeland, 5, 7, 16
Luwian hieroglyphic, i, iii, 1–3, 5–6, 15–17, 19–22, 25–28, 35–37, 39, 41–42, 44–46, 48-67, 70–73, 75, 77–78, 80, 82–83, 88-91, 110–111, 117–118, 120–123, 128, 132–134, 136, 138–139, 141, 153, 161–163
Luwianizing, 15, 45, 83
Luwians, i, 1, 3, 5, 7, 13–14, 50, 66, 72–73, 108, 115, 126, 129, 134–135, 139, 143, 145, 152, 155
Luwian Studies, 1–3, 88, 90
Luwiya, 1, 26, 115, 136, 139, 148–149
Luwoid, 45
Lycia, 9, 14, 19, 22, 27, 29–30, 34, 56, 79, 114–115, 136, 139–142, 153
Lycian, 13, 16, 19–20, 22–23, 25, 31, 70, 75–77, 79, 120, 125–126, 128, 136, 142, 155, 163
Lycian(s), 125
Lycians, 14, 34, 71
Lydia, 9, 14, 23, 25, 29, 46–47, 59, 69, 140–141
Lydian, 8, 13–14, 23, 25, 31, 52, 61, 83, 121, 142, 162
Lydians, 142
Lykomidai, 14
Lykos, 14, 21, 25, 144

M

Madduwattas, i, 110, 113–115
Madduwattas-text, i, 110, 113, 115
Maiandros, 20–21, 26, 50, 135
Makestos, 24–25, 27, 29, 46, 74, 90, 134
Makkay, 52, 155
Malia, 15, 44–45, 52–53, 84–85, 111
Malos, 77
Manapatarḫundas, 27–29, 58, 74, 87, 109
Manapatarḫundas-letter, 27–28, 74, 109
Manapatarḫundas-treaty, 29
Marassantiya, 5
Mari, 45, 145
Marsyas, 31
Masa, 25, 27, 29, 78–79, 85, 89, 92, 97
Masanatarḫunas, 48, 90, 101
Maşat-höyük, 36
Masḫuiluwas, i, 47, 74, 79–80, 87
Masḫuittas, i, 2, 27, 47–48, 77, 82–83, 85, 87–88, 91
Masson, 18, 80–81, 155
Masturis, 74–76, 87, 90, 109
Masturiwantasa, 90, 100–101
Mazlauwas, 114
Megarid, 13
Meid, 138, 155
Melchert, 1, 25, 117, 122, 125, 145, 155
Mellaart, 2–3, 20, 37, 47, 79, 88, 90, 154–155
Menekrates of Elaia, 142
Mersin, 85
Mesara, 111–113
Mesopotamian, 60, 154
Messenia, 8, 11, 13–14
Middle Bronze Age, i, iii, 5, 15–16, 30, 34, 36–37, 39, 41–42, 44–46, 50–52, 54, 57–58, 138, 162
Middle Minoan, 16, 45, 141
Middle Minoan I, 45
Middle Minoan II, 16
Middle Minoan IIIA, 16
Milawata, 23, 27, 30, 75–77, 125, 153
Milawata-letter, 27, 30, 75–77, 125
Miletos, 13–14, 19, 21, 27–31, 48, 64–65, 75, 77, 114, 124–125

Millawanda, 6, 9, 19, 21, 23, 26–27, 29–31, 48, 64–65, 75, 77, 110, 114, 124–125
Miller, 110, 156
Minoan, 14, 16, 29–30, 34, 45, 49, 57, 61, 77, 107, 128, 131, 141, 146, 163
Minoan Luwian, 16, 163
Minoan Pelasgian, 16
Minoans, 59, 114, 127, 158
Minoan Semitic, 16
Minoan thalassocracy, 14, 29
Minos, 13–14, 29
Minyan, 125
Mira, i, 2, 5, 15, 20–21, 23, 26–30, 37, 44, 46–48, 50, 54, 60, 74–86, 88–89, 91–94, 98, 114–115, 123–124, 138–139, 151, 153, 162
Mira-Kuwaliya, i, 5, 29, 46, 48, 74–75, 88
Mitannian, 56, 60, 154
Monte Morrone, 16
Mopsus, 89
Mora, ii, 34–39, 46–47, 50–51, 56, 66–70, 72, 79, 85, 123, 146, 156
Muksas, 28, 48, 89, 99, 128
Muksus, 89, 94, 96–97
Mursilis, 82
Mursilis II, 20, 26, 29, 34, 48–50, 74, 76, 79, 87, 129
Mursilis III, 75–76, 87
Muscarella, 66–67, 157
Muwatallis II, 5, 27, 29–30, 58, 64, 74, 76, 80, 87, 90, 109–110, 115, 125, 127, 129
Muwawalwas, 37–38, 41–42, 46, 58
Muwawalwis, 41, 76, 87
Mycale, 13, 142
Mycenae, 35, 59–60, 65, 107, 110–111, 114–115, 153, 158
Mycenaean, 3, 8, 13, 27, 29–30, 49, 52, 59, 65, 72, 74, 76, 108–109, 114–116, 127, 153, 161–162
Mycenaean Greece, 27, 59, 76, 162
Mycenaean Greek, 8, 49, 52, 65, 115, 161
Mycenaean Greeks, 3, 13, 30, 74, 108–109, 114, 116, 127
Mycenaeans, 108, 157–158
Mygdon, 7, 129
Mysia, 9, 25, 29, 79

N

Nagy, 138, 157
Near East, 17, 37, 74, 149, 152, 154, 156, 158, 161, 163
Near Eastern, 42, 59, 127, 145–146, 150–151, 154
Nestor, 65, 111–113, 115, 144, 161
Neumann, 59, 124, 133, 146, 157
Nevşehir, 36, 38
New Kingdom, 56, 74
Niemeier, 25–26, 30, 76, 114, 157
Nişantaş, 78
Nişantepe-archive, 58, 80
non-Greek, 125, 128, 130
non-Luwian, 89, 122
north-Aegean, 8, 10, 14, 49, 127
North Syria, 45–46, 78, 89

O

Old Babylonian, 60
Old European, 137
Old Hittite, 57, 67, 115, 117
Old Indo-European, i, 3, 31, 45, 66, 125, 128, 130–132, 134–139, 142–143
Old Iranian, 52
Old Kingdom, 36–37, 86, 126, 129
Olivier, 128, 150, 158–159
Oreshko, 28, 47–48, 158
Orkhomenos, 125
Ortakaraviran, 47, 79–80
Ortakaraviran Höyük, 47, 79–80

Otreus, 7, 129–130
Otten, iii, 6, 19, 75, 137, 151, 158

P
Pala, 78, 85
Palaima, 128
Palmer, 13, 126, 158
Pamphylia, 9, 19
Pamphylian, 75
Panaztepe, 107, 153
Pandion, 14
Pantazis, 28, 123, 158
Paphlagonia, 139–140, 162
Parḫa, 16, 19, 22, 31, 75–76, 133–134, 137–139, 142
Parion, 25, 28, 89, 99
Pausanias, 13–14, 125, 135, 139, 142
Pelasgian, 16, 122, 125, 128, 141–142, 163
Pelasgians, 3, 13–14, 131, 139–143
Pelasgos, 139, 142
Peloponnesian, 14, 29, 138, 140
Peloponnesos, 107, 125, 139
Perati, 59–60, 108
Pergamon, 24, 26, 88, 90, 101, 134, 137
Perge, 22, 75
Perkote, 25, 28, 89, 99, 128
Perrot, 88
Phlya, 14
Phaistos, i, 16, 65, 111–113, 115, 144, 161
Phaistos disc, i, 65, 111, 115, 144, 161
Philistia, 89, 94
Phoenician, 73, 145
Phokis, 11, 13
Phrygian, 3, 7, 75, 83, 88–89, 117, 126, 128–131, 136–137, 162
Phrygians, 13, 125, 129
Phthiotis, 142
Pinara, 22, 30, 75
Pina(tí), 19, 22
Pisidia, 9, 14
Pitane, 24, 26, 90, 101
Pitassa, 6–7, 19, 85, 92, 97, 115
Pityeia, 25, 28, 89, 99, 128
Piyamakuruntas, 34–35, 46, 50–51, 55–56, 58, 63, 71, 86–87, 94, 111, 114–115
Piyamakuruntas (son of Uḫḫazitis), 74
Piyamaradus, 27, 29
Poetto, 19, 47, 136, 159
Pontic, 5, 162
Porada, ii, 47, 60–62, 150, 158–159
Porsuk, 7, 24, 30, 74, 114, 126
Poruciuc, 52
pre-Greek, 7, 13–14, 139
Priamos, 7, 129–130
Propontis, 125, 139–140
proto-Celtic, 31
Proto-Indo-European, iii, 8, 52, 54, 131–132, 141, 155
Ptolemaios, 136
Puhvel, 62
Pylian, 111
Pylos, 7, 35, 65, 72, 111, 115

Q
Quartier Mu, 45, 147

R
Ramesses II, 72, 108, 127
Ras Shamra-Ugarit, 77–78
Reeves, 108, 159
Renfrew, 143, 159
Rhodes, 10, 13, 107
Rhône, 125
Rhytion, 111, 113
Roman, 35, 144

Ş
Şahankaya, 48, 88, 101, 106

S
Saḫarwa, 111, 142

Ş
Şahin, 47–48, 83, 159

S
Saḫiriya, 3, 5, 24, 30, 117, 126
Sakariya, 126
Salbakos, 115
Sallapa, 23, 25, 30–31, 85, 92, 97, 115, 133, 135, 137
Samsun Dağ, 21, 23, 135
Sangarios, 3, 5, 7, 24, 30, 74, 114, 117, 126, 129
Santas, 59, 66
Santorini-eruption, 34, 49, 114

Ş
Şarhöyük-Dorylaion, 61

S
Sarpedon, 14
Sart, 21, 24
Sauska, 58, 70–71, 73
Sauska(ku)runtis, 77
Sauskamuwa-treaty, 60, 76–77
Schimmel, i, 47, 66–68, 72–73, 144, 150, 157, 162
Scotland, 136
Sea Peoples, 13, 29, 79, 82, 88, 127, 141, 157
Seḫa, i, iii, 2, 5, 22, 24, 26–29, 31, 41, 46, 48, 58, 74–77, 86–90, 93, 100–101, 109, 133–134, 136–137, 139, 142
Seḫa-Appawiya, i, 5, 29, 46, 74–75
Sekundogenitur, 85, 90
Semitic, 16, 45, 111, 128, 155, 163
Sidetic, 61, 83, 161
Siyanta, 22, 30, 114
Skheria, 53, 111–112, 142
Slavic, 52
Smyrna, 20, 95
southeast Anatolia, 89
southern Anatolia, 5, 7
southwest Anatolia, 13–14, 114, 162
southwest Anatolian, 16
southwest Asia Minor, 14, 29, 132
Starke, 26–27, 30, 64–65, 108–110, 117–119, 126, 142, 160
Stephanos of Byzantion, 135, 142
Strabo, 8, 13–14, 25, 135, 139–140, 142
Stratonikeia, 31
Südburg, ii, 70–71, 78, 83, 85, 151
Suppiluliumas I, 5, 30, 67, 74, 76, 87, 125
Suppiluliumas II, 17, 20, 27, 48, 76–79, 82–83, 85, 87–88
Syrian, iii, 37, 43–44, 58

T
Talmitesup, 77
Tapalazunawalis, 74, 87
Taras, 135
Tarentum, 135
Tarḫunaradus (of Seḫa), 75, 76
Tarḫundaradus (of Arzawa), 63, 65, 69, 108, 111
Tarḫunt, 7, 13, 40, 49, 58–59, 62–63, 66, 83–85, 93, 95–97, 112, 115, 117, 128
Tarḫuntassa, 1, 5–7, 19–20, 22, 30–31, 48, 75–79, 85, 97–98, 110, 136
Tarim basin, 127
Tarkasnallis, 29, 129
Tarkondemos, 15, 44, 47, 63, 80–82, 151
Tarku, i–ii, 15, 20–21, 38–40, 43–44, 46–47, 50, 53–54, 57, 59, 63, 66, 72, 80–82, 86–87, 93, 96, 98, 101

Tarkundimuwas, 39, 43–46, 82, 86, 138
Tarkuwas, 20–21, 27–28, 44, 82–83
Tarpamaliawatas, 47, 84–85
Tarsos, 36, 39, 51, 94, 151
Tarwisa, 28, 71, 124, 133, 137
Tawagalawas, i, 27, 29, 31, 64–65, 74, 80, 108–110, 115, 150, 156
Tawagalawas-letter, i, 27, 29, 31, 64–65, 74, 80, 108–110, 115
Teffeteller, 49, 160
Tekoğlu, 28, 47–48, 83, 153, 159
Telipinus, 36, 86
Tell Atchana-Alalaḫ, 36–37, 39, 41–42, 46, 51, 57, 63
Tembris, 30, 126
Tenedos, 24, 28, 89, 99, 125
Teutamos, 141
Teuthrania, 24, 26, 134, 140
Thebaid, 65
Theban, 64–65, 111
Thebans, 60
Thebes, i, 7, 42, 44, 47, 59–66, 72, 107, 109–111, 115, 125, 150, 159
Thersander, 110
Thessaly, 11, 141
Thrace, 130
Thracian, 3, 7, 75, 89, 117, 128–131
Thracians, 13, 125
Thraco-Phrygian, 89, 126, 128–130, 137, 162
Thyateira, 24, 26, 90, 101
Tire(h), 21
Tiyi, 107–108, 115
Thucydides, 14, 29, 140
Tokharians, 127
Torbalı, 28, 47, 49
Tralles, 14
Troad, 2–3, 8, 10, 13, 22, 27–29, 74, 77, 79, 88–90, 123, 127–128, 131, 136–137, 139–140
Trojan, 7, 13, 34, 77, 109, 123, 125–126, 128–131, 150, 161
Trojans, i, 34, 123–124, 126–127, 130–131, 161, 163
Trojan War, 7, 13, 34, 109, 150, 161
Troy, 5, 7, 29, 56, 59, 64, 71, 74, 89, 91, 109, 115, 123–125, 128, 130–131, 134, 137, 139, 150–151, 153–154, 156, 161
Tudḫaliyas I, 34, 55, 63, 86
Tudḫaliyas II, 28, 34–35, 46, 49, 55–56, 58, 63, 71, 86, 111, 114, 124
Tudḫaliyas III, 30, 36, 86, 108
Tudḫaliyas IV, 17, 19–20, 27, 30–31, 58, 60, 67, 75–77, 79, 82, 87, 125, 130
Tukulti-Ninurta I, 60
Tuscany, 135
Tuthmosis III, 34, 49, 55, 71, 108
Tyrrhenians, 13–14
Tyszkiewicz, 39, 56, 58, 144

U

Ugarit, 17, 45, 77–78, 94, 151, 161–162
Ugaritic, 16, 79
Uḫḫazitis, 34, 49, 56, 74, 87, 122, 130
Ulmitesup, 110
Uluburun, 52
Unaras, 38, 43–44
Ur III, 60
Uraḫattusas, 29, 74, 129
Uratarḫundas, 74, 87
Urḫitesup, i, 47, 76, 80–81
Utima, 23, 30–31, 75

W

Waal, 36–37, 51, 138
Walma, 19, 21, 26, 78, 85, 125

Walmus, 26–27, 75, 77, 91, 124–125, 130
Walwamuwas, 29, 48, 87, 89–90, 100
Walters Art Gallery, 38, 146, 150
Wastizitis, 63, 65, 73
Watkins, 117, 123, 125–127, 129, 161
western Anatolia, i–iii, 1, 3, 5, 19–22, 25–29, 31–32, 34, 41–42, 46, 48–51, 55–56, 58, 65–66, 72–74, 76, 78, 88, 91, 107–108, 114–115, 117, 121–122, 132, 137–140, 142, 151, 157–158, 162–163
western Anatolian, 16, 46, 66, 132–133, 142
west-Luwian, 13, 61
(W)ilion, 77
Wilusa, 5, 7, 26–29, 48, 71, 74–75, 77, 88–93, 109, 117, 123–127, 130, 135, 149–150, 158
Wilusiad, 117, 126
Wilusiya, 24, 28, 34, 55, 124
Witczak, 127
Wiyanawanda, 6–7, 9–10, 22, 30, 78, 85

X

Xanthos, 19–20, 22, 30–31, 75, 114, 136

Y

Yakubovich, 1, 7, 15, 36–37, 41, 48–49, 57, 117, 122, 126, 130, 136, 152, 156, 158, 160, 163
Yalburt, 6, 19–20, 30–31, 70, 75, 77–78, 136, 159
Yazılıtaş, ii, 2, 26, 28, 48, 88–90, 100, 105, 134

Z

Zakynthos, 7, 11
Zalpa, 129
Zangger, ii, 1–2, 33, 47–48, 88, 90, 103, 163
Zeus, 142
Zidas, 58
Zimrilim, 45
Zippalanda, 5